MYTHICAL
TRICKSTER
FIGURES

MYTHICAL TRICKSTER FIGURES

FIGURES

Contours, Contexts, and Criticisms

EDITED BY

WILLIAM J. HYNES & WILLIAM G. DOTY

The University of Alabama Press

Tuscaloosa & London

First Paperbound Printing 1997

∞

The paper on which this book is printed meets the minimum
requirements of American National Standard for Information
Science-Permanence of Paper for Printed Library Materials,
ANSI Z39.48-1984.

Library of Congress Cataloging-in-Publication Data

Mythical trickster figures : contours, contexts, and criticisms /
    edited by William J. Hynes and William G. Doty.
        p.   cm.
    Includes bibliographical references (p.   ) and index.
    ISBN 0-8173-0857-1
    1. Trickster.   2. Animals, Mythical.   I. Hynes, William J.
II. Doty, William G., 1939–
GR524.M96   1993
291.2'13—dc20   92-19629

British Library Cataloguing-in-Publication Data available

CONTENTS

ACKNOWLEDGMENTS
AND PERMISSIONS

This collection of essays benefitted directly from the work of an international research consultation, the Trickster Myth Group within the American Academy of Religion. Working together for a period extending over five years, more than forty scholars shared insights and honed their individual analyses of various tricksters. In an age all too often characterized by disciplinary isolation and occasional ideological rigidity, such a critical team effort and synergistic process resulted in a cohesive approach, served to sharpen the ways in which we defined the trickster phenomenon, and highlighted areas where it still escapes definition. Many of the best essays from this collaboration are revised here: Hynes (chapter 2), Doty (chapter 4), Vecsey (chapter 6), Pelton (chapter 7), Ellwood (chapter 8), Ricketts (chapter 10), and Hynes (chapter 13). These essays have been supplemented by other important critical essays and an inclusive bibliography.

Works included here from previous appearances in journals are by arrangement; we are grateful for permission to include them. At the early stages of the editorial work, both Mary Douglas and the now-deceased Victor Turner were encouraging to us and helpfully critical. Hynes would like to acknowledge the personal support of Margie Shurgot and the financial support of the National Endowment for the Humanities, Doty the personal support of Joan T. Mallonée, the financial support of the Research Overhead Fund, and material support from the College of Arts and Sciences of the University of Alabama.

So many other people helped make this work possible that we will not attempt formally to acknowledge them here. Instead we acknowledge in their help the presence of the trickster who constantly battles to break down our resistance to chaos, disorder, insight, and new knowledge.

The Mudhead clown used as a design at the beginning of each section of this book is from a photograph of a storyteller figure by Dorothy and Paul Gutierrez, Santa Clara Pueblo, from the collection of William Doty. The basis for the cover design by Paula Dennis is a photograph of David Aguirre's "Trickster" (32 inches high; 1990), initially shown at the Brigitte Schluger Gallery, Denver, and a gift from Hynes to Doty.

We gratefully recognize the following for granting permission to reprint or to print works in this volume:

Presses Universitaires de France, for Laura Makarius' chapter, translated here.

Journal of Religion in Africa 12/3 (1981) 161–77, Christopher Vecsey's chapter here.

For Beidelman's chapter here, reproduced by permission of the American Anthropological Association from *American Ethnologist* 7:1, February 1980. Not for further reproduction.

Soundings: An Interdisciplinary Journal, for Anne Doueihi, "Trickster: On Inhabiting the Space Between Discourse and Story," 63/3 (1984): 283–311, an abbreviated version of which is included here as Chapter 12.

The University of California press, for approximately thirty-five pages, abridged and revised here, from *The Trickster in West Africa* by Robert D. Pelton, copyright © 1980 by University of California Press.

MYTHICAL TRICKSTER FIGURES

ONE

INTRODUCING
THE FASCINATING
AND PERPLEXING
TRICKSTER FIGURE

William J. Hynes & William G. Doty

Well, I tell you dis, ef deze yer tales wuz des fun, fun, fun, en giggle, giggle, giggle, I let you know I'd a-done drapt um long ago.
> —Joel Chandler Harris, Uncle Remus stories, cited by Lawrence C Levine, "'Some Go Up and Some Go Down': The Meaning of the Slave Trickster."

Almost all non-literate mythology has a trickster hero of some kind. American Indians had the great rabbit and coyote, the ravens, and blue jay. And there's a very special property in the trickster: he always breaks in, just as the unconscious does, to trip up the rational situation. He's both a fool and someone who's beyond the system. And the trickster hero represents all those possibilities of life that your mind hasn't decided it wants to deal with. The mind structures a lifestyle, and the fool or trickster represents another whole range of possibilities. He doesn't respect the values that you've set up for yourself, and smashes them.
> —Joseph Campbell, in *An Open Life*

Brer Rabbit, cited in our first epigraph, is just one of many intriguing trickster figures.[1] For centuries, perhaps millennia, and in the widest variety of cultural and religious belief systems, humans have told and retold tales of tricksters, figures who are usually comical, yet serve to highlight important social values. They cause laughter, to be sure, as they profane nearly every central belief, but at the same time they focus attention precisely on the nature of such beliefs.

The diversity and complexity of the appearances of the trickster figure raise doubt that it can be encompassed as a single phenomenon. Perhaps just such diversity and complexity help explain why three decades have lapsed since the first comprehensive portrait of the trickster appeared, in Paul Radin's *The Trickster* (1955).[2] The number of studies of individual tricksters has grown, and the range of trickster phenomena is now such that many scholars argue against a generalizing, comparativist view. Others of us have continued to argue that there are sufficient inherent similarities among these diverse figures and their functions to enable us to speak, at least informally, of a generic "trickster figure."

In the editors' perspective as well as that of many of the contributors, we seek to build upon Radin in a critical manner. While we acknowledge the inherent difficulties in speaking about such a complex figure, we steer a course between those who see the trickster as so universal a figure that all tricksters speak with essentially the same voice and those who counsel that the tricksters belonging to individual societies are so culture-specific that no two of them articulate similar messages. Consequently, in contrast to Radin and his fellow essayists, Carl Jung and Karl Kerényi (Radin 1955), we do not argue for archetypal roots in a transcendental human psyche, and we are less interested in origins than in cultural manifestations. But in contrast to a number of contemporary social scientists, the essays here generally do represent the belief that important aspects of a "trickster figure" can be identified across several different cultures. The fact that trickster phenomena contain similar features in several societies leads us to examine comparative social functions, psychological mechanisms, literary traces, relationships to religious systems, and ritual transformations.

This book presents a variety of tricksters set within their specific sociocultural settings across a wide variety of cultures. Some of the tricksters to be encountered include the African Ananse, Eshu, and Legba; Western tricksters such as Hermes, Saint Peter, and Herschel; Native American figures such as Coyote, Wakdjunkaga, and Manabozo; and such Asian tricksters as Susa-no-o, Sun Wuk'ung, Agu Tampa, and Horangi. Readers will find many examples of trickster episodes in this book, appearing across a wide range of contexts.

Published collections of African or Native American tales usually include segments devoted to the trickster, and an inclusive collection of trickster tales ranging worldwide would require several volumes (Apte 1985: ch. 7 provides a convenient summary of trickster tales). The figure is central in many European materials and in the Orient, but because trickster myths are focal in nine of the eleven Native American regions (Bierhorst 1985: 17–18), contemporary American scholarship in particular ignores the figure at the risk of irrelevance.

Here is a sample tale, involving the Southwestern trickster, who is often Coyote:

> Hearing a strange sound coming from an old elk skull, Coyote looks inside and finds a village of Ants (or Wasps) having a Sun Dance. He makes himself small in order to get inside the skull and see better, but presently his body returns to normal size and his head is stuck inside the skull.
>
> He wanders into a village and announces, "I am holy; I have supernatural power; you must give me something!" The awe-stricken people pass him in a procession, marking him with pollen as is customary in that region [as a blessing]. But the last person in line is a smart aleck boy who is carrying a stick behind his back. When he reaches Coyote he brings the stick down with all of his might across the old elk skull, and it cracks and falls off. "That's what you should have done long ago," Coyote tells them, "but instead you wanted too much supernatural power" (Lipan Apache, cited by Ricketts 1964: ch. 8: 18, from Opler 1938b: 169–70).

What does such a story "mean"? Such a question should address initially two sorts of contexts. The first is the specific, local, tribal, historically bounded context that is the province of the ethnographer, the historian of a particular religious tradition, or the critic studying micro-level manifestations of a particular behavior. But there is a second context, less studied today than previously, and that is the broader context of what seems to be the wider phenomena of general human cultural expression. Essays in this book heed the former, but they also engage the latter context, the query directed toward the widest significance, and broadest frame. Here the disciplines of the humanities have long been at home, and here lie the distinctive contributions of this volume.

In some curious ways representative of *conservative* social teachings, tricksters appear primarily at the points of growth and change that represent "the exponent of all possibilities" (Toelken and Scott 1981: 89). Their stories provide a fertile source of cultural reflection and critical reflexivity that leaves one thoughtful yet laughing; and what a culture does with laughter reflects its vitality, flexibility, and creativity. Certainly humans often take themselves too seriously, a foible Oscar Wilde hit squarely when he suggested that such an attitude "is the world's original sin" (Pearson 1946: 196).

Essays in this volume respect the laughter, as they trace the elusive trail of trickster figures through a number of religions and cultures, myths and histories, individuals and societies. We have sought to go beyond such widely recognized materials on the trickster figure as the essays in Paul Radin's *The Trickster* (1955), Mac Linscott Ricketts's 1966 article on "The North American Indian Trickster," and Robert Pelton's 1980 book, *The Trickster in West Africa*, by presenting data from a wider range of cultures and by approaching them through the views of specialists from several disciplines.

In this initial chapter we introduce some of the developments leading to a volume such as this. We glance at some of the methodological issues in trickster studies, anticipating chapter 2. And we begin reflection on the problematic attitude toward comic figures typical of our own culture—we reject the common assumption that if something is comical or entertaining, it cannot represent socially significant material. After naming some of our biases, we provide an overview of the contributions to the book.

THE METHODOLOGICAL TANGLE

Anyone attempting to study tricksters faces significant methodological issues. For example, at one extreme one finds colleagues trained in Jungian psychology talking about the *the* trickster as a universal archetype to be encountered within each of us and in most belief systems. At the other extreme, some anthropologists have called for the elimination of the term "trickster" altogether because it implies that a global approach to such a figure is possible whereas they find it appropriate to focus only upon one tribal or national group at a time (see Basso 1987, and Beidelman 1980—reprinted as chapter 11, this volume).

Although these methodological issues are raised in a distinctly contemporary manner, they are in fact classical in substance, inasmuch as they form part of traditional epistemological debates about universals and particulars. The West has witnessed such debates from the time of Plato and Aristotle, on through the medieval struggles between the scholasticism of Thomas Aquinas and the nominalism of William of Occam, through nineteenth-century controversies about idealism and realism, and more recently in Wilhelm Dilthey's distinctions between the methods of the natural sciences and those of the human sciences. The underlying question is whether we can attain general knowledge or only knowledge of particular cases.

We appreciate the cautions contributed by some of our social science colleagues who advise us to study only particular belief systems and the testimony about the meaning of those systems elucidated by persons from within these systems. At the same time we also take seriously advice from other colleagues who find hints of common ground and similar human experience among very diverse belief systems; although accepting such advice, we still reject any simplistic universalism that would assert the existence of universal knowledge on the basis of only one or two systems. We also reject being limited solely to particular cases. Hence we oppose a nominalism that holds any given particular to be so radically individual and different from all other particulars that there can be no similarity between particulars and that general knowledge is therefore fundamentally impossible. Surely no one today is prepared to agree with the fourteenth-century William of Ockham and the subsequent severe-rationalist position that each human being is so distinctively individual that we cannot speak at all about "humankind"!

Nineteenth-century philosopher Wilhelm Dilthey attempted to resolve some of the dichotomies when he distinguished between the methodology of the natural sciences, in which a general rule is established only by the repeated confirmation of the particular, and the methodology of the human sciences (which he calls the sciences that deal with "Geist," the human spirit that cannot always be limited to the rule of the particular). How the two approaches complement one another remains to be resolved by the academic disciplines. The one point of view is captured in Beidelman's citation (1980: 27) of Evans-Pritchard (1963: 16): "any claim to universality demands in the nature of things an historical or psychological explanation, and thereby defeats the sociological purpose, which is to explain differences rather than similarities." The noted Renaissance historian G. R. Elton represents the other side of the issue in terms of his own scholarly craft: "Meaningful interconnection in the particular, illuminating generalizations beyond the individual case—these are the marks that distinguish the inspired and inspiring historian" (1969: 126).

In this volume we attempt to tack back and forth from the particularities of specific tricksters within their respective belief systems, on the one hand, and the meaningful interconnection between particulars and elucidating generalizations, on the other hand. One tack counterbalances the other. We believe that the reader will gain here an understanding of both particular and more universal characteristics of the trickster (more technical discussion of these issues appears in chapter 2).

Given the particular methodological tangle that attends studies of anthropological themes or issues today, some may wonder at our temerity in presenting this collection of essays. At an anecdotal level, several of our colleagues have been amused that an academic vice-president and a former department chairperson would focus upon a figure famous for outlandish ploys, irreverent language, and extreme displays of individualism. Likewise more than once we confronted the suggestion that our analysis must be suspect because we or our readers might enjoy the materials too much! But through our charting of matters tricksterish, we came to appreciate fully the Renaissance dictum *serio ludere*—play seriously! We find a direct ratio between the degree of seriousness attending a given belief and the degree of laughter and play necessary to hold the first in check. (We discuss trickster-laughter further in chapter 2.)

CRUDE AND LEWD MORALISTS

The rude mockery, even scatology, present in trickster stories is not simply anti-religious or anti-social criticism. As Brian Street notes in the case of the Zande trickster Ture, the trickster tales "can be seen as moral examples re-affirming the rules of society; or rather they serve as a model for these rules, demonstrating what happens if the prescriptions laid down by society are not observed" (1972: 85). Street suggests that we ought not to exclude entirely the possibility that such figures may voice anti-social feelings, insofar as the trickster often represents the obverse of restrictive order (86–90), but we must remember that tricksters or cultural clown-figures are not, as they would be considered in our culture, individually motivated deviants, but socially sanctioned images or performers (Tyler 1964: 195–96). John Bierhorst (1987) recognizes the moralistic, social-sanctioning aspect of trickster materials in his collection of Coyote tales for children when he concludes each one with an Aesop-like moral saying.

So far this introductory chapter has already highlighted some reasons for carefully heeding trickster materials: they are often entertainments involving play or laughter, but they are entertainments that are *instructive*. Tricksters map for some societies just how one "ought" to act just as formal moralists inform members of a Western society about proper roles, but tricksters are not stuffed shirts in the bargain: indeed tricksters are comical if not marginal figures, and they represent sacred beings in some cultures, but not in others (Bierhorst 1985: 13). There may be moralistic instruction, as when the myth-history by which approved behaviors have come about is recited; or when deviant speech patterns on the part of the principle characters signal that they are transmitting specifically heightened information (emphasized by Beidelman 1980: 31).

Ellen Basso's *In Favor of Deceit: A Study of Tricksters in an Amazonian Society* (1987) has taken seriously Beidelman's advice to focus upon specific analysis of trickster language. Basso claims that her "discourse-focused and socially contextualized" study is the first "to show the connections between the content of trickster stories, their tellings, and lives as actually lived" (3–4), although Anne Doueihi has analyzed one text where "there is a flagrant juxtaposition of the discursive, signifying aspect of the narrative and the referential, signified aspect of the text as story" (1984: 284). Earlier, more global approaches are being supplemented today with more specific context-respective analyses that take into account the full narrative and performative textures of the tellings.

Besides presenting examples of trickster tales in various contexts, and the ways these tales are interpreted variously, we suggest that such study of mythical materials is useful within our own contexts: frequently the breaching and upending process initiated by tricksters in their challenges to the accepted ways of doing things highlights the possibilities within a society for creative reflection on and change of the society's meanings. (See the extensive study of "nonsense," Stewart 1979, and of the modern "outsider" figure, Wilson 1956, as well as Babcock-Abrahams 1975 on marginality and 1984 on clowning, and 1978—a strong collection of essays on social revisioning.)

Barbara Babcock-Abrahams's sympathetic account reveals just how such stories promise to expose dimensions of human creativity: "As Trickster travels through the world, develops self, and creates for mankind haphazardly, by chance, by trial and error without advance planning, he reenacts the process that is central both to perception and creation, to the constant human activity of making guesses and modifying them in light of experience—the process of 'schema and correction'" (1975: 181). A similar comment by Ellen Basso, applied to questions of the functioning of human intelligence, reinforces such "real world" aspects in trickster materials: "The very attributes that make such tricksters inventive heroes and clownish fools in the first place are, after all, natural necessities of human intelligence, operating in practical, concrete face-to-face relations that people negotiate all the time, sometimes with considerable immediacy" (1987: 8; cf. 183–84, on Taugi's intelligence). As examples of trickster figures surface across the essays in this book, these observations by Babcock and Basso will be illustrated many times.

PERSPECTIVES AND STRUCTURE OF THIS VOLUME

Several biases surface in this book. First, the editors are scholars trained in the humanities, primarily in the study of religions, but with additional training in the classics, historiography, literature, psychology, and anthropology. We adopt a broadly based, interdisciplinary approach toward human phenomena and literary texts rather than any one specialized perspective.

Second, we take explicit issue with a central theme of the work of Paul Radin and others, when they view the trickster as representing an important but very *primitive* stage in the progressive or evolutionary development of humankind. For example followers of Carl Jung would say that this development occurs culturally as well as individually (the most intellectually stimulating study of Western culture using such a model is Neumann 1954; see Belmonte 1990 for a revisionist-Jungian position). Although not a Jungian, Greenway (1964: 90) also speaks of the *evolution* of the trickster into the culture-hero and later (1965: 58) refers to the earlier levels as representing those of "retarded children." Many other examples of such ethnocentric developmentalism could be cited.

Third, we are persuaded that plurality, plurivocity, and ambiguity are essential to the trickster Gestalt: this mythological figure encompasses many different social positions, is utilized by different societies to inculcate various types of behavior, and may have manifold modes of appearance even within one culture. After the figure was named within analytical disciplines, it began to be used as a helpful descriptor for a very wide range of characters. A more monochromatic figure would provide a simpler treatment, but with "the kaleidoscopic nature of trickster and his tendency to metamorphose into surrounding types with variant or different orientations" (Beecher 1987: 7, n. 4), we are repeatedly led toward greater, not less, typological complexity. (Some of our own interest in typological characterization surfaces again in chapters 2, 3, and 13.)

The reader will find that this book reflects several levels of trickster studies: it includes (1) traditional sketches of trickster figures within specific societies, (2) summaries and surveys across more than one culture (crosscultural or crossnational), and (3) considerations of the trickster within the overall perspective of religious figures, both as mythological models and in terms of the ceremonial clown or clown society whose representatives often have significant roles in supervising ritual performances.

Essays here also contain (4) methodological reflections about how best to study such figures, (5) critiques of the traditional methodological approaches, and (6) revisionist pieces, for example Beidelman and Doueihi, the former from an anthropologist's perspective that distrusts the comparative, the latter from the perspective of literary deconstruction influenced by narratology. No one essay should be seen as representative of a single methodology or theoretical perspective, because most of them engage more than one of the levels listed here, and frequently more than one culture area.

Insofar as truly interdisciplinary work can be initiated by persons working from different locations and academic perspectives, we feel such work is begun here. We do not argue naively for the value of cross-disciplinary or cross-cultural attention, but seek to present a case for it as the "problem of universals" resurfacing in contemporary ethnography (for example, Beidelman's 1980 essay uses terms that reach back to Greek and medieval philosophy—universalism, nominalism, literalism, and realism).

Trickster studies have matured to the point where it is necessary to review their history, and Doty and Hynes do that in chapter 2, "Historical Overview of Theoretical Issues: The Problem of the Trickster." To review the history is also to engage theoretical and methodological issues, and we begin with those most specific to tricksters and conclude with the widest matters of interpretation.

In chapter 3, "Mapping the Characteristics of Mythic Tricksters: A Heuristic Guide," William Hynes offers a cross-cultural typology of common features of the trickster selected from a wide range of examples; these can serve as an orienting guide to some of the complexities of the trickster that will be encountered throughout the book. It is heuristic (helping one to discover or learn) because the application of this guide will cause revision of the guide itself.

In chapter 4, William Doty's "A Lifetime of Trouble-Making: Hermes as Trickster" presents an extended analysis of the iconography of Hermes, his rich role within the original Greek context, and his early and continuing centrality to Western mythology, particularly in determining characteristic features according to which tricksters have been studied.

One frequently cited essay in trickster studies is translated into English for the first time in this volume: the French anthropologist Laura Makarius's "The Myth of the Trickster: The Necessary Breaker of Taboos," chapter 5, suggests an ingenuous argument that tricksters such as Manabozo, Maui, Legba, and Eshu develop out of the role of the magician who is able to violate divine taboos in order to gain and pass along essential cultural gifts for society. Pelton (1980: 243−48) discusses this essay as a "neo-Durkheimian approach."

Mac Linscott Ricketts, a scholar who has been influential in trickster studies ever since his 1964 University of Chicago dissertation directed by Mircea Eliade, offers here "The Shaman and the Trickster," chapter 6.

Utilizing a wide range of Native American materials, he argues that the trickster is a humanistic parody of sacred shamanistic activities.

Christopher Vecsey's "The Exception Who Proves the Rules: Ananse the Akan Trickster," chapter 7, probes the social-cultural contexts of African trickster myths and suggests that in breaking the rules, the trickster confirms the rules.

The work of Robert Pelton is now central in scholarly study of tricksters thanks largely to his *The Trickster in West Africa* (1980). Pelton's chapter here, "West African Tricksters: Web of Purpose, Dance of Delight," chapter 8, proposes a philosophical-theological case that the trickster figure serves as symbol for the transforming power of the human imagination and for the transcendence of the human condition.

Robert Ellwood's essay, "A Japanese Mythic Trickster Figure: Susa-no-o," chapter 9, argues a position contrary to that of Pelton and Ricketts, who see the trickster as satirically antagonistic toward the shaman; Ellwood counters that the shaman and the king are closely intertwined.

William Hynes and Thomas Steele collaborated to write "Saint Peter: Apostle Transfigured into Trickster," chapter 10. They investigate one of the rare exceptions to the paucity of tricksters in much of western Christianity by exploring a noteworthy example in Mexico and the American Southwest where the Yaqui create a full-blown trickster out of Saint Peter.

T. O. Beidelman's "The Moral Imagination of the Kaguru," chapter 11, develops a strong critique of comparative studies on the basis of examining the complex phenomenon of one set of trickster figures in Africa.

Anne Doueihi discusses Western criticism and (see Doueihi 1984) develops a critique of traditional approaches to trickster materials from a deconstructive perspective in "Inhabiting the Space Between Discourse and Story in Trickster Narratives," chapter 12. She argues that most approaches have misread the trickster as part of Western colonial domination of "otherness."

In the final chapter, "Inconclusive Conclusions: Tricksters—Metaplayers and Revealers," chapter 13, Hynes advances a series of possible explanations for the widespread phenomenon of the trickster and for the apparent contradiction that belief systems maintain such deconstructors as tricksters within themselves rather than considering them out of bounds from the start.

The Bibliography at the end of the volume is comprehensive for English-language studies of trickster materials and includes all references for essays in this book.

The reader may begin reading in this volume wherever desired. Although there is a logical order to the chapters, each can stand on its own. Those unfamiliar with tricksters may wish to begin with the general guide offered in chapter 3 or examine several individual tricksters immediately. Those who are already knowledgable may wish to begin with the history of the methodological issues presented in chapter 2.

Each chapter makes good use of original trickster materials that seem to manifest a life and fecundity all their own. This collection of studies sheds considerable new light upon the traces of this immensely complex, maddening, fascinating, and elusive figure.

TWO

HISTORICAL OVERVIEW OF THEORETICAL ISSUES: THE PROBLEM OF THE TRICKSTER

William G. Doty & William J. Hynes

For almost a century Western scholars have treated the trickster figure as troublesome. More than twenty years ago, Mac Linscott Ricketts, who initiated much of the contemporary discussion, declared that comprehension of the trickster figure is "one of [our] most perplexing problems" (1966: 327). A more recent essay by Karl Kroeber, "Deconstructionist Criticism and American Indian Literature," suggests that, given the degree of noncomprehension of the trickster figure, it is "perhaps the most bewildering to a modern reader" of many poorly understood aspects of Native American literature (1977: 73).

We hope in this chapter to remedy some of the bewilderment, or at least to point to some of the resources that offer a more adequate understanding. After tracing the historical definition of the term trickster, we provide a sketch of the major approaches to the trickster figure; another section discusses some of the problems caused by the very complexity of the figure we are scrutinizing. These include the issue of universals versus particulars that surfaces in any such comparative study as this, a Western cultural bias against allowing humor to represent serious and important cultural information, and several hermeneutical (interpretive) issues.

THE TERM AND THE CONCEPT
OF THE TRICKSTER

A sketch of the ways the term itself came into common use will help to clarify the category "trickster." The first use of the English term trickster appeared in the eighteenth century (according to the *Oxford English Dictionary:* 3402), not as an anthropological category, but to designate morally one who deceives or cheats. In the nineteenth century Benjamin Disraeli employed the term to describe lying political opponents within the Whig party. It appeared in Brinton's 1868 *Myths of the New World* (Ricketts 1987: 50), and, in this century, it has been a technical term for figures from European literature as well as for non-European ethnological phenomena, particularly in North America and Africa.

Carroll (1984: 108–09) gives an exemplary table of seven distinct types of North American tricksters, each with the relevant tribal groups, bibliography for primary source collections, and associated animal figures (for examples of African tricksters, see Evans-Pritchard 1967; Pelton 1980). Today the term "trickster" has become so familiar a designator that an author can refer to the trickster figure in Old Comedy of Aristophanes and in Plautus and Terence, as well as in Renaissance comedy and in contemporary films or literature (Beecher 1987). Subtypes such as the Confidence Man have also added analytical categories to the study of literature; likewise Don Juan Tenorio, in Tirso de Molina's *The Trickster of Seville,* is a trickster, although here the term means roughly "lady-killer." More recent sites where the figure appears would include works such as Ken Kesey's *One Flew Over the Cuckoo's Nest* (1962) and Maxine Hong Kingston's *Tripmaster Monkey: His Fake Book* (1989). Hynes discusses additional contemporary manifestations in chapter 13 of this book.

STUDY OF THE TRICKSTER

Students of religion, anthropology, folklore, and psychology have been particularly interested in trickster myths. "More has probably been written about 'tricksters' than about any other single category of character that appears in the myths and folktales of the world" (Carroll 1984:

105). One of the most influential source books has been Stith Thompson's *Tales of The North American Indians* (1929), which contains groups of trickster myths from various American Indian traditions. Thompson was a giant in his field, but like most earlier folklorists, he was loath to comment upon or to interpret the meaning of the myths or tales he recorded.

Although Norman O. Brown has become well known for his *Life Against Death* (1959) and *Love's Body* (1966), his dissertation, later published as *Hermes The Thief: The Evolution of a Myth* (1947), offered an insightful analysis of a classic Western trickster, a figure treated differently below in chapter 4. However, the single most influential work bringing trickster myths and their analysis into the awareness of the literate public was Paul Radin's *The Trickster: A Study in American Indian Mythology* (1955), a much-reprinted book that includes Radin's rendering of Winnebago informant Sam Blowsnake's myth cycles, an analytical essay on the "primitive" trickster figure by Radin, an essay, "The Trickster in Relation to Greek Mythology," by classicist Karl Kerényi, and finally a brief essay, "On the Psychology of the Trickster Figure," by psychoanalyst C. G. Jung.

The essays in Radin (1955) are united in treating the trickster figure as a transcendental or "archetypal" characteristic of the human psyche, stemming from its most archaic strata. Radin, Kerényi, and Jung consider that the figure progresses developmentally within cultures as within an individual's psychological growth, learning over time to deal with its bodily and sexual appetites. Hence the figure represents a sort of primitive developmental level common to humanity, "an inchoate being of undetermined proportions, a figure foreshadowing the shape of man" (xxiv). He is associated typically with organizing the natural world: "The overwhelming majority of all so-called trickster myths in North America give an account of the creation of the earth, or at least the transforming of the world, and have a hero who is always wandering, who is always hungry, who is not guided by normal conceptions of good or evil, who is either playing tricks on people or having them played on him and who is highly sexed" (155).

Although the Winnebago trickster Wakdjunkaga, to whom Radin devotes over half his book, does "bring culture to mankind . . . It is incidental to his desire to express and develop himself" (126); only gradually does he become fully aware of himself and his environments

(135), as he learns to separate himself from the natural world in which he is initially at home (145). The Winnebago Wakdjunkaga cycle functions as a means of "voicing a protest against the many, often onerous, obligations connected with the Winnebago social order and their religion and ritual. Primitive people have wisely devised many such outlets" (152). In comparison with the mass of narrative material in the volume, Radin's commentary and analysis are rather sparse, but they end on a note that hints that Radin found a deep personal relationship with the profoundly humorous yet culturally important figure that he presents: "If we laugh at him, he grins at us. What happens to him happens to us" (169).

Suggesting that the trickster story in Radin's volume represents "picaresque mythology" (175), Kerényi adduces classical parallels and characterizes Wakdjunkaga as a mixed-form, a "Herculean Hermes" (1955: 175, 186). The trickster in archaic society serves primarily "to add disorder to order and so make a whole, to render possible, within the fixed bounds of what is permitted, an experience of what is not permitted" (185)—echoing Radin's belief that trickster stories serve a tension-releasing function in societies.

In his essay, Jung notes that the trickster figure represents a figure compensatory to that of the Christian saint (196), but in particular representing "the collective shadow figure" that has broken down into a folktale figure during the course of cultural development (202). He considers that the Winnebago and other accounts Radin transcribes preserve "the shadow in its pristine mythological form" (202; the psychological "shadow" represents the dark side of the person or culture that is usually projected onto the enemy or opponent). Jung thinks it culturally important to recognize the therapeutic effect of rehearsing the tales of such figures, since they hold "the earlier low intellectual and moral level before the eyes of the more highly developed individual, so that he shall not forget how things looked yesterday" (207). Ultimately trickster myths gesture toward a savior or self-consciousness ("individuation," in Jungian terminology) at the opposite pole so that they indicate a personal or cultural movement away from the darkness and primitivity of the stories related, toward the complementary bright consciousness of culture (211).

An essay by Estelle Irizarry (1987) represents a particularly clear use of the trickster figure summarized by Jung and Radin in *The Trickster.*

Typically for a literary study, in this case the application of the figure to the extensive fictions of the contemporary Spanish writer Francisco Ayala, there are no references to contemporary trickster studies, but the earlier analysis in Radin provides a very workable pattern from which to chart themes and traits. Figures have a tricksterish phallicism, or serve as messengers, or function as culture heroes, or shift shape or gender. Irizarry argues that the trickster is such a predominant figure in Ayala's work that "it may be said that Ayala's narrative forms *a sophisticated trickster cycle*" (222; our emphasis). Such a figure forms the "Key to Ayala's Narrative World," his "representative character" (228) who appears in tandem with the breakdown of centered values in our own day.

Although Radin's work with Winnebago traditions has been cited so frequently, there have been many criticisms. For example, Åke Hultkrantz (1983) finds Radin inconsistent in methodology and dismissive of the Winnebago material culture, so that consequently Radin writes about the trickster as if it were purely a matter of fictitious oral literature and religious beliefs—"the culture hero of the Winnebago is treated as a fictive trickster created by literary imagination, embodying some primal needs," and such a theory of the trickster "is undoubtedly a pure fancy in view of extant mythological materials from other Indian tribes" (28). In addition, Krupat (1985) criticizes Radin's treatment of Native American autobiographical materials. However the primary problem in this context is Radin's treatment of "the trickster" in simplified and accultural terms. Doueihi (1984: 286–87) criticizes Radin's evolutionary bias as well as his lack of sophistication in examining the literary aspects of Sam Blowsnake's narrative.

One problematic in defining the trickster figure, that of the wide range of characteristic features, is neatly expressed by Roger Abrahams: "Trickster is . . . the most paradoxical of all characters in Western narratives—at least as far as the Western mind is concerned—for he combines the attributes of many other types that we tend to distinguish clearly. At various times he is clown, fool, jokester, initiate, culture hero, even ogre. . . . He is the central character for what we usually consider many different types of folk narratives" (1968: 170–71).

Abrahams seems to follow Radin's approach (accepting, for instance, both the argument that such materials serve as social-tension release valves and that they promote a "regressive infantilism," 172–173), and he can treat the figure as being "as capable of changing shapes from one era and society to another as he is of assuming different forms within an individual story" (177). Hence Abrahams like Radin operates with a globalizing, universalizing concept that is highly suspect today, although one of Abrahams's points deserves emphasis: the confusion of categories may be more a problem indigeneous to Western classifications than one innate to trickster materials. The discipline of ethnopoetics has taught this generation that our literary categories often cloak or miscode the organization of materials that seem "native, natural" in the context of another culture (see D. Tedlock 1983).

John Greenway's two interlinked volumes, *Literature Among the Primitives* (1964) and *The Primitive Reader* (1965), mark some of the beginnings of contemporary analysis. Greenway is clear about the need for context-sensitive translations (1964: ch. 1) as well as about the extremely problematic but frequently used designation *etiological*. Although myth-analysts use this term to classify many types of native tradition, and indeed see explaining the origins of things as a sort of early science, Greenway learned that his native informants mostly used this classification only for feeble stories that needed some external justification (50), rather than to indicate the primary purpose of myths and tales (see also Toelken and Scott 1981: 73).

In Greenway, as in the Radin volume, the trickster is still a figure that "evolves with sophistication into a Culture Hero" (1964: 89), and in fact "most Tricksters are like retarded children" (1965: 57). Greenway's comprehensive survey of examples (1965: ch. 3) is augmented by other references throughout *The Primitive Reader;* in *Literature Among the Primitives,* Greenway adds that the American trickster par excellence is the traveling salesman (1964: 72).

TRICKSTERS IN ANTHROPOLOGICAL AND OTHER STUDIES

E. E. Evans-Pritchard's *The Zande Trickster* (1967) is perhaps the most well known collection of trickster materials besides Radin's. It is a collection of previously published materials that does not claim to be a "cycle" like that of the Winnebago, since the Zande do not have such cycles (20). Evans-Pritchard introduces the tales with social-structural information and insists upon our comprehending the details of trickster stories in terms of specific cultural information; nonetheless he is also insistent that "the tales are not a sensitive celluloid plate which passively reproduces the pattern of social structure" (21). The book marked the outright acceptance within classical ethnological study of what had been denigrated previously as "merely folk material"; Evans-Pritchard argues important points about the nature of folk materials—that they are told in particular contexts (18) and that there are no "original versions" (33)—which subsequently have come to be assumed everywhere.

In a volume of essays dedicated to Evans-Pritchard, Brian Street (1972) provides a reflective analysis of the Zande trickster materials Evans-Pritchard presented and compares them to those in Radin's compilation and analysis. Street's analysis is comparative and thematic, arguing that the role of the trickster is primarily that of a delicate balancing between creativity and destructiveness: "To question everything in society would lead to anarchy; to preserve everything would lead to stagnation; the conflict is presented, and the balance achieved, in the trickster tales which so many societies possess. And in all of them a universal feature of the trickster is his role as both revolutionary and savior" (97).

Street emphasizes the border-functioning of trickster characters: "For the 'meaningful,' the 'differentiated' is implied in the action which Ture [the Zande trickster] copies; he defines the boundaries of that action, as it is defined by his society, by representing what happens when that action is not carried out precisely" (100). Ture omits important aspects of a formula, or gets tired of the performance before its important climax; hence:

> The particular cases presented act as models of the forms which society has differentiated out of chaos and by slightly distorting the form the trickster demonstrates where the boundaries lie. Although he has not himself developed during the course of the story, the trickster has presented a model of the "meaningful" to the audience and shown how it developed and is continually being developed out of the meaningless, the amorphous. By acting at the boundaries of order the trickster gives definition to that order. (101)

Anthropologists Claude Lévi-Strauss, Victor Turner, and Mary Douglas have all commented on the trickster phenomenon. For Lévi-Strauss the trickster is the embodiment of all complementary opposites, but in particular of that between immediate sexual gratification and the demands of civilization (1963: 202–28). Michael Carroll (1981 and 1984) has corroborated that argument, while correcting Lévi-Strauss's ethology and ethnology; Robert Pelton (1980: 236–42) is less positive, denouncing Lévi-Strauss's "corrosive Kantianism" and "stoic pessimism."

Victor Turner regards the trickster as temporarily breaking down and intermingling all categories so as to cause new combinations and anomalies (1967: 106). The Latin *limen*, "threshold," which gives us the word *preliminary*, is used to differentiate three segments, of which the "liminal phase" is the temporal moment and the spatial site at the middle of ritual performances. Just there, suggests Turner, is to be found *communitas*, the ideal social sharing of common values and regard for one another: "Communitas breaks in through the interstices of structure, in liminality; at the edges of structure, in marginality; and from beneath structure, in inferiority" (1969: 128). As the ritual participant moves through the liminality of communitas, the usual social restrictions are in abeyance, new metaphors are born, and the usual perceptions of the world are revisioned creatively. The liminal trickster, the court jester, and the clown are related, according to Turner (125) in that they possess marginal status and bring into the social institution new possibilities for action and self-understanding (see further Doty 1986: 91–95; Pelton 1980: 33–36; and Aycock 1983: 124).

Robert Pelton uses Turner's analysis as the center point of his study of Ananse, the West African trickster, but for Pelton: "the trickster is more than a symbol of liminal man. It seems closer to the truth, rather, to say that the trickster is a symbol of the liminal state itself and of its permanent accessibility as a source of recreative power" (1980: 35). And, "Ananse's love to contradict is a structural characteristic; his inner form is that of a personified limen" (58). Pelton's book frames his detailed analyses of the African Ananse, Legba, Eshu, and Ogo-Yurugu with two theoretical chapters. He determines that "the trickster is not an archetypal Idea, but a symbolic pattern that . . . includes a wide range of individual figures" (3). Basically the figure shapes an image of humankind "as a sort of inspired handyman, tacking together the bits and pieces of experience until they become what they are—a web of many-layered being" (4). Such language marks an attempt to break with the traditional morphology and thematic interpretation, which Pelton considers quite inept: "It is precisely the trickster's earthiness, his popular inelegance, and his delightful inconsequence that have made our intellectual equipment for dealing with him look as ponderously inept as a steam shovel grasping for a grasshopper" (19). Pelton emphasizes the serious attempt of societies to deal with the contradictory and anomalous aspects of life; the figure who embodies a seizure of both aspects will be messy and metaphysically ambiguous because that figure will be opening up the purely structured to the yeast of antistructure, because that figure will be pulling "the most unyielding matter—disease, ugliness, greed, lust, lying, jealousy—into the orbit of life" as it is lived daily (252).

Accordingly, for Pelton the trickster represents the human race "individually and communally seizing the fragments of his experience and *discovering* in them an order sacred by its very wholeness" (255); hence "the trickster discloses the radically human character of the whole cosmos," while at the same time "he shows the holiness of ordinary life" (256). And in causing reflection upon the boundaries, upon the very nature of social order, the trickster represents "metasocial commentary" (266) or "hermeneutics in action" (243; cf. Camp 1988: 16, and Gates 1988: ch. 1), a position that indicates Pelton's basic agreement with standpoints in the discipline of the history of religions represented by Mircea Eliade. Pelton is criticized by Edwards (1984: 83–84) for his inattention to published structuralist interpretations.

British anthropologist Mary Douglas also views the trickster phenomenon as having a social function of dispelling the belief that any given social order is absolute and objective (1968: 365). The anomalous is precisely that realm excluded by rigid classifying systems, and Douglas's works return again and again to categories *between* categories—such as the various trickster representations that reflect repeatedly strong antinomies (male vs. female, good vs. evil) caught into a single figure.

American mythologist Joseph Campbell sees the trickster story as an earlier and less developed paleolithic form of the hero archetype (1959: 274). As a "super-shaman," the trickster is inaccurately conflated by Campbell with the earth diver (275) as well as the fire-bringer. In his later work he has developed a somewhat more sympathetic interpretation (see the second epigraph to chapter 1), perhaps because, as he stated in the series of television interviews with Bill Moyers, *The Power of Myth*, Campbell has always considered himself a sort of "maverick" in American intellectual life.

COMPLEXITY AND COMPARISONS

Radin's approach parallels earlier attempts within the academic disciplines of the history of religions and anthropology to explain the diversity of beliefs by resorting to a unitary, evolutionary model, as if all specific instances of belief represented a position on a single, worldwide scale from the simple to the complex. Many earlier treatments of the trickster figure advanced simultaneously a theory of the evolution or devolution of a Creator, Culture Hero, or similar Founding Figure (as just one example, Lowie 1909: 433). Or they revised Radin's evolutionary sequence by arguing that a figure such as Hermes became what the history of religions terms a Culture Hero, after having had Trickster status earlier. (Masau'u of the Hopi is so represented by Tyler 1964: 34; but see the most recent collection of Masau'u/Maasaw tales, Malotki and Lomatuway'ma 1987). Finally one might argue that the trickster was the generic figure *behind* the later clowns (Tyler 1964: 196).

Today such chicken-or-egg derivations are no longer treated seriously. Our rejection of the evolutionary view, which presupposes that the earliest is the most effective or "originary," is similar to that of Doueihi (1984: 298); her article likewise criticizes the "literary naiveté and . . . ideological posture" (297) found in most studies of the trickster figure. The first half of her essay canvasses (from her own definite analytical and ideological premises) a wide range of earlier studies of the trickster figure, including some not reviewed here, such as Brinton, Eliade, Kock, Kroeber, Makarius, and Pettazzoni.

Various voices other than ours have been raised against seeing the trickster as inferior, as merely potential, or as at most a transitional figure. Trickster imagery often is not so much that of the scamp, but of the naif; it is marked not so much by the childish, but the child-like, although to some degree the figure is a combination of both. Such an image represents a potent source of creativity and insight for even the most sophisticated adult because it is full of "delightful, Dadaistic energy" (Snyder 1977: 81). It represents the "existential Man, / a Dostoevsky Coyote" (S. Ortiz 1972: 15), or "the sheerly spontaneous in life" (Erdoes and Ortiz 1984: 335) that promises contemporary creativity parallel to the figure's primordial contributions in the origins of things. Thus a recurrent theme in trickster tales is that, even after taking into account all the bumbling and anarchic social behavior, the trickster contributes substantially to the birth and evolution of culture.

Nonetheless the trickster's sheer conflations of selfishness and buffoonery, of cleverness and heroic creativity, are often inherently problematic for contemporary critics. Some complain about the combinations of these features (Carroll 1981, 1984) or about the shifting balance that analysts locate within such combinations: "not all substantive traits, such as thieving or rebelliousness, are carried through all cultural traditions or diverse genres through time, and therefore not all jesters, fools, or picaros are tricksters, while the trickster might contain properties common to all" (Koepping 1985: 199).

Polly Pope's paper of twenty-five years ago (1967) argued that the structure of traditional trickster stories was neither casual nor accidental; her paper might have led to subsequent applications of componential analysis, but did not. (Note Toelken and Scott 1981: 80–81, arguing against the structural aspect, and Edwards 1978 and 1984, developing a syntagmatic-paradigmatic-generative structuralist analysis.) The sheer profusion of characteristics has led some critics (such as Bianchi 1961a) to distinguish those that stem from the trickster as culture hero from others that stem from the trickster as demiurgic creator. Other scholars have proposed complex lists of typological characteristics: Babcock-Abrahams (1975: 159–60) lists sixteen, and in chapter 3 of this book, Hynes selects and discusses a smaller cluster of six key features (see also Bianchi 1961b: 435–36; Carroll 1984; Luckert 1984: 5, 7, 11, 18; Thompson 1955: 817 sub "Trickster," and compare entries for "Clever persons"; and the inventory designed for folklorists, Abrams and Sutton-Smith 1977).

At the other extreme from typological comparisons, Beidelman (1980, reprinted here) argues that *no* cross-cultural definition can be valid, and Sabbatucci (1981) attacks the very concept of "trickster" as representing a nineteenth-century artifice imposed as a "monstrous abstraction" that puts the final lie to cross-cultural studies. Perhaps it is perspectives such as these that cause omission of the category in indices to contemporary encyclopedic publications—as for instance volumes 9 and 10 of the *Handbook of North American Indians,* where the closest one comes to the trickster is "ceremonial organizations," under "clown societies." Grottanelli (1983: 117) counters that the concept is no more artificial than most; he sees the trickster as exemplifying the role of "mediator/savior" whose power comes from opposing the central social structures that uphold the cultural rules (120, 136, 138).

Typical identifications of the trickster include: Animal-Person (particularly Blue Jay, Coyote, Crow, Fox, Hare, Mink, Rabbit, Raven, Spider, Tortoise), Anti-Hero, Boundary Figure, Bungling Host, Clever Hero, Clown, Culture Hero, Confidence Person, Demiurge, Lord of the Animals, Numskull, Old Man, Picaro, Selfish Buffoon, Selfish Deceiver, Swindler, Transformer. Submotifs are readily identified in texts and in the notes to Thompson 1946; we have not sought to document the various tribal names here, but the list in Edmunson 1971: 142 is helpful. Collections of Coyote tales are listed in Carroll 1981: 303—see also Carroll 1984: 108–09, and for helpful annotations to source collections of Native American Indian mythology, Ullom 1969. Such a dramatic range of trickster figures vies against understanding a particular manifestation as the exclusive property of a particular society, although a society may well claim that its trickster persona is uniquely reflective of its people.

Sometimes the term "trickster" may be applied to figures who could be described "tricksterish" at best by a strict constructionist, but related figures may be elucidated using the typologies developed to identify features. So for instance the clown of several Southwestern American groups, of the shamanistic healing ceremonies of Sri Lanka, or of the commercial circus tent may have tricksterish functions, may perform in tricksterish manners, without being explicitly "tricksters" according to particular formal definitions. Emphasizing the mediating role of the trickster, Aycock notes parallels between the biblical figures of Jesus and Cain: each has the bodily stigmata that indicate a sacrificial figure. Each represents "the mythic hero who stands at the nexus of mortality and immortality, structure and antistructure, the individual and society" (1983: 124).

Of course any formal definition is applied questionably if it is not used flexibly enough to recognize a range of typological variations when the generic figure is manifested in particular societies (see Niditch 1987: 5). Otherwise the model chosen as archetype can exert an ideological pressure that stifles creative interpretation (or that blocks a nongendered interpretation, as Bal 1988 points out). Often one argues that the trickster represents this or that, or perhaps this *and* that, or one may argue that because the figure cannot be held strictly to only this *or* that, or this *and* that, it is useless. However, most of the studies in this volume focus upon the phenomenal richness of the trickster's mythological persona, and as editors we are less interested in total typological consistency than in a matrix of interpretive possibilities. As the reader moves through the book, it will be apparent that there is no one mode of trickster studies, no one classical model of the figure—in spite of the nearly canonical status that Radin's *The Trickster* (1955) has enjoyed.

Successful analysis will transcend simplistic categories, allowing both for flexibility with which to confront polarities, dualities, and multiple manifestations and for complexity with which to grapple with the ambiguity, border-occupying, paradox, marginality, peripherality, liminality, and inversion portrayed by various trickster figures. That such figures are still usefully pursued according to the general framework of trickster studies that has been worked out informally is evident in several disciplines, as witnessed recently in studies of male and female trickster figures in the Hebrew Bible (see Farmer 1978; Niditch 1987).

Exum and Bos (1988) edited a volume of *Semeia: An Experimental Journal for Biblical Criticism* that relates biblical figures to the tricksters of ethnology. There Edwin Good and Claudia Camp discuss theodicy—the formal defense of the presence of suffering and evil in a supposedly benignly designed cosmos—in a manner that is reminiscent of Diamond's introductory essay to the 1976 Schocken reissue of Radin's *The Trickster*, where Diamond reflected on the biblical figure Job.

Clearly issues of "good" or "bad" behaviors are theologically crucial in trickster accounts or in the myth-ritual frames in which they are related, and at one level tricksters map for the society just how one "ought" to act. They do so no less than preacher-moralists inform members of a society about proper roles, but the modes of diction may be those of inversion rather than mimesis, of modeling by imaging the obverse rather than exemplification. For some societies, the polarities involved in trickster modeling may lead to a splitting of a good from an evil trickster-manifestation (Bierhorst 1985: 14). It is noteworthy in this respect that the British psychotherapist R. D. Laing commented that his own understanding of schizophrenia was greatly enhanced by his study of trickster myths in West Africa and that therapists of several other schools of psychology have found the role of the psychotherapist-as-trickster to be worthy of study (see for instance Kopp 1974 and 1976).

PLAUSIBLE MEANINGS IN THE THICKET
OF COMPARISONS

Accepting the global descriptor "the trickster" implies a certain acceptance by the editors of this book of a cross-cultural comparative enterprise that—as we have noted above—has been criticized in many social scientific studies. Udy 1973 names some of the issues and distinguishes cross-cultural from cross-national comparisons. The traditional distinction—which he attributes to Franz Boas—is named by historian of anthropology George Stocking as "an 'eternal tension' between two approaches to the study of human phenomena—one seeking to subsume a variety of them under a general law, the other seeking to penetrate the secrets of the individual phenomenon," until each particular detail has been isolated (1987: xvi).

Ideological models can easily enter when one utilizes too readily (and often unconsciously) assumptions about universals and particulars; in such a case one fails to distinguish the originary from the earliest, or one grants absolute priority to the beginnings of something, the earliest version, and then (as Doueihi 1984: 286, 292, finds that Radin is doing consistently) looking for "evolution" up to or "devolution" down to the situation of a particular time. Or the manner in which the material is presented—the "texture," or "thick context" of the textual performance, in professional terms—is slighted in preference to those "ideas" or "concepts" that the analyst considers to be the real focus.

When today the rhetorics of a tradition, the discourse-level of a tale, and the texture of a recitation (including recordings of laughter or other audience response) are all extensively documented, we see in operation an analytical framework that recognizes that texts have a plurality of meanings, no one of which is universally or archetypally "correct." Texts represent chains of signifiers, even to the point where the signified "content" of one story represents merely the first of yet another chain of signifiers, a story about the first story. It is likely that traditional literature reflects such enchaining, when epithets fly back and forth as tricksters mock shamans, or when scholars or priests call both tricksters and shamans "primitive."

As Doueihi's article suggests, in such a situation we are betrayed into a semiotic activity in which meanings are produced discursively, a situation in which trickster narratives are narrating what tricksters are and how they function: "Trickster is thus not *a* sacred being, but the way the whole universe may become meaningful, sacred, and filled with 'power'. . . . While traditional studies have sought to establish what Trickster's meaning is, the stories show that Trickster *is meaning(s)*" (1984: 309, emphasis added). Mieke Bal, in "Tricky Thematics," pursues a number of semiotic issues in the relationships between trickery and language—tricksters are "exemplary semiotic units, and as such hold a metasemiotic commentary" (1988: 137 and 148)—a conclusion similar to Gates's suggestion that trickster material engages in "a meta-discourse, a discourse about itself" (1988: xxi).

Various comparative cross-cultural approaches have been used in some of the chapters of this book, but our contributors recognize that one should use comparative procedures only with great caution, not normatively or arbitrarily, but heuristically, that is, always holding the interpretive framework faithful to the data. Within the history-of-re-ligions disciplines, "parallelomania" has long been criticized, and we believe that religious studies scholars can avoid its negative features while continuing to operate comparatively at some levels. We would advocate such a use as Mary McBay finds characteristic of Pierre Vidal-Naquet: "While acknowledging his debt to structural analysis [in the book McBay is reviewing, *The Black Hunter*] Vidal-Naquet uses its methodology heuristically, assuming the underlying logic as hypothesis rather than as universal theory. Thus he offers the interpretations that result from its use undogmatically as plausible perspectives which invite further exploration" (1987: 348; cf. Good 1988: 127).

We look for models that enable the interpreter to hone the interpretive tools, and defensible generic or archetypal analysis does precisely that: it sets up patterns of anticipation for particular works, given the accumulated details of a more or less cohesive pattern found in several similar situations. The interpreter seeks not law-like results, but the most plausible interpretations for the situations.

Ours is a time of infinitely separated bits of data. The hope of a project such as this book is not that of finding the lowest common denominator, the transcendental or phenomenological "essence" of tricksters, or the satisfactory combination by which all the major trickster characteristics are combined (such as trickster-transformer, trickster-creator-transformer, etc.—see Bierhorst 1985: 15). It is rather that such a project, by forcing comparisons, can reveal some aspects of being human that might otherwise not surface at all, and these aspects certainly include tricksterish humor!

A CULTURE'S LAUGHTER

Stanley Diamond (1990: 70) proposes that "why and how and at what people laugh is perhaps the most revealing of human actions," and Oscar Wilde's remark about taking ourselves too seriously, which we cited earlier, ought not to be passed over too quickly, since much of American religiosity (whether pop or formal) has trouble with both the comic and the deceitful. The trickster figures referred to in this volume graph ways of operating that go against the Western grain. Despite Augustine's dictum that good can come from evil, we are taught to reject almost automatically the suggestion that a deceitful figure—by the definitions of our society, morally bad—can bring about good.

We, who find the trickster's antics amusing, laugh not just at the underhandedness of the tricks, but precisely at their unpretentious straightforwardness (as Good points out, 1988: 123). The trickster is sneaky, but overtly skillful about his trickery: if we approve only grudgingly, it is because we lack the respect for the trickster often found in cultures where there is great praise given to the combination of vital survival *skill* and hunting. For example Luckert suggests that for the Navajo the divine trickster was originally a "shrewd exemplary model for human tricksters" who hunted to survive (1979: 11, cf. 10, 218). Likewise we tend to forget that even earlier, hunting was not a matter of leisure-time sport but of the raw trickery, focused attention, and creativity that is necessary for individual and societal survival (Luckert 1984: 10), or that for the Greeks, skill in trickery was part of the ideal for masculine success in warfare, love affairs, and commerce (as Doty demonstrates in chapter 4).

Our own more recent repugnance toward cleverness and jesting stems from an ideology long regnant in the West. In *The Comic Vision*, Conrad Hyers cites, as typical of many other moralists, the eighteenth-century German philosopher Georg Friedrich Meier: "We are never to jest on or with things which, on account of their importance or weight, claim our utmost seriousness. There are things . . . so great and important in themselves, as never to be thought of and mentioned but with much sedateness and solemnity. Laughter on such occasions is criminal and indecent. . . . For instance, all jests on religion, philosophy, and the like important subjects" (cited by Hyers 1981: 11). While it is echoed in many familiar moralistic pronouncements, Meier's position represents a strongly contrasting mentality to the tales of trickster figures, who profane precisely the most sacred dimensions.

The Russian theorist M. M. Bakhtin (1968: 4) recalls the bias against humor in the Romantic rediscovery of folk culture led by Herder, a bias that has left untapped an important dimension of European culture and literature (54), and one that Bakhtin attempts to correct by his extensive demonstration of the sociopolitical aspects of carnivalesque humor, aspects that extend even to the origins of the Socratic dialogues (1984: 109; see all of chapter 4 on carnivalization in European literature). Mac Linscott Ricketts even argues that the trickster figure is to be *defined* by his specific secular mockery of the sacred shaman, and Lawrence Sullivan suggests that in the trickster's parody of "all pretensions to perfections . . . the gods, institutional figures . . . he exposes a penetrable (i.e., accessible, comprehensible) reality" (1987: 46).

As we reflected upon the Trickster's humorous antics, we were reminded that we would have to be on our guard lest our own cultural biases against humor keep us from recognizing other ways a culture's laughter could function. For instance, "in some tribes religious ceremonies cannot even begin until all the people, particularly any strangers, have laughed" (Tedlock 1975: 106), or as Beck and Walters document for Native American cultures, "Laughter—that is something very sacred" (1977: 313). And then there is the striking exchange between folklorist Barre Toelken and the Navajo raconteur Yellowman that brings out clearly the "serious" quality of what is "funny":

> Why . . . if Coyote is such an important mythic character (whose name must not even be mentioned in the summer months), does Yellowman tell such funny stories about him? Yellowman's answer: "They are not funny stories." Why does everyone laugh, then? "They are laughing at the way Ma'i [the Navajo Coyote trickster] does things, and at the way the story is told. Many things about the story are funny, but the story is not funny." Why tell the stories? "If my children hear the stories, they will grow up to be good people; if they don't hear them, they will turn out to be bad." Why tell them to adults? "Through the stories everything is made possible." (1969: 221; cf. Toelken and Scott 1981)

Laughter . . . making possible . . . not funny yet funny: as Hynes suggests in our concluding chapter, many trickster figures are helpfully comprehended in terms of *metaplay*. Metaplay is a sort of inversionary logic that probes and disassembles the most serious rules of "normal" social behavior. The deconstruction is not pursued out of careless spite, but in order to reaffirm for the onlooker a necessary social centrism, a centering not short-circuited or bypassed by the immediate or ethnocentric, but creatively opened up to "the other" and the transrational (cf. Doty 1988).

Nonetheless the idea of "playing seriously" is a concept that in itself perplexes many contemporary readers because our folk culture would have us *work seriously* but *play with abandon*. As informally conceived, "play" represents the absence of ordered rules and intentions, the sphere from which "nothing serious" can originate. The mindset is such a stricture upon our modes of understanding that it took a series of influential works by Roger Callois, Oskar Morgenstern, and especially Johan Huizinga (1949) and Hugo Rahner (1967) to legitimate the use of games or play theory as an analytical tool for the study of culture and especially literature, rituals, and religion (see Miller 1970 and Apte 1985: ch. 5). Thanks to their contributions, cultural historians and social analysts have gained a powerful explanatory tool that can demonstrate social structure and hierarchy, disclose rule-governed behaviors in the most random-seeming events, clarify the identification and interrelation of topical realms and symbolism (i.e., hermeneutical topography or visual poetics), show how social change succeeds or fails and how characters in a situation interact according to roles differentially assigned in workaday and play arenas. If in the work world one plays by any rules in order to win, the ideal of "pure" play is not winning, but a zero-sum situation whose beneficial outcomes are shared equally by all participants.

Play in this extended sense need not enfold the risible, but a certain relaxed play-related humor is frequently indicated. Conrad Hyers, in *The Comic Vision and the Christian Faith* (1981), treats the element of humor in his analysis of religion. Such analysis points to the gamelike dimensions of any number of ordinary performances: they can be seen to have rules applicable only to the game arena, a focal space marked out from mundane activities; they involve specific types of progress toward a goal; they function to influence one's fellow players in the nongame world;

and so forth. Trickster laughter—both the laughter *of* the trickster and *our* laughter at him—may well tap cultural levels we otherwise ignore to our peril. As the first epigraph to chapter 1 suggests (but in the dialectical doublespeak of Uncle Remus), if such materials are *merely* entertainments, they don't remain active in the cultural repertoire for very long.

HERMENEUTICAL BROADENING OF SCOPE

For several decades around the middle of this century it seemed as if the present scholarly generation might be named "the age of hermeneutics." Nearly every discipline faced issues of interpretive methodology and principles of hermeneutics, and for once the academic disciplines were listening to one another, all of them plumbing the depths of classical hermeneutics. More recently, especially because of the influence of Hans-Georg Gadamer, "hermeneutics" has been used to designate one type of hermeneutics, and disciplines such as ethnography are witnessing extensive discussion of their own specific interpretive issues. Marilyn Strathern's Frazer Lecture (1987) reflects the discussion of such issues, particularly as the analysis of "writing culture" has become widespread within some schools of academic ethnography (in the collection of essays edited by Clifford and Marcus 1986, one chapter refers explicitly to "Hermes' Dilemma"). John Van Maanen (1988) explores extensively the problematic nature of "writing ethnography" today—surveyed by Doty (1990).

What has carried forward from the earlier emphasis in the humanities upon general hermeneutical principles is an awareness of the importance of clarifying just what one expects from a culture or text or artifact. "Reader response" theory, and other modes of interpretation theory have emphasized recently the context into which the text or cultural artifact is appropriated or interpreted—meaning not that "everything is relative" so much as that similar materials may carry greater or lesser importance in one or another cultural context (in the cultures of two or more peoples, or within two or more sites of a single culture). Hence Kathleen Ashley summarizes: "Tricksters make available for thought the way things are not but might be; their stories can function as critiques of the *status quo* as well as models for other possible arrangements.

Whether and how such stories activate those functions depends upon the interpretive community in which they are told" (1988: 113).

The interpretive communities of those of us who *study* trickster stories likewise activate certain "functions," although they are not necessarily critiques of the *status quo*. The relevant context in such a case is the relative type of methodological approach that prevails—as for instance within much of the social scientific approach to this type of material that has been dominated by the sociofunctionalists. That approach would emphasize that mythological materials relate to establishing or renewing community cohesion, acceptance of hierarchical structures, and so on (see Doty 1986: ch. 2). Trickster materials would be analyzed primarily or exclusively for the extent to which they reduce chaos or provide means of dealing with social disorder, how they graph normative sexual behaviors (by displaying the results of their inversion), or how they vent frustration with social restrictiveness, or provide entertainment, or how they become sources of metaphor creation and hence creativity in general, or how they lead to reaffirmation of belief systems, and so forth (see Babcock-Abrahams 1975: 182–85 for a key statement of some six functions; Beidelman 1980 begins his rejection of globalizing typology by referring to her statement).

But precisely in such a list there are religious or philosophical or worldview-sustaining functions, and several of our essayists have emphasized such matters. Again it will be clear that this volume extends discussion of the function of the trickster into areas that have not been well covered in traditional treatments. The essays here summarize and analyze both the broad context of the trickster phenomenon and that of particular ethnographic locations. While we have sought in this chapter to scan some of the major issues, other theoretical and methodological issues concerning the historical development of trickster studies will appear in subsequent chapters.

THREE

MAPPING THE CHARACTERISTICS OF MYTHIC TRICKSTERS: A HEURISTIC GUIDE

William J. Hynes

At the start of these essays detailing the complexities of the trickster, the reader may find it helpful to ask the central question: What characterizes a trickster figure as such? Using a diverse selection of trickster myths, this chapter advances six characteristics common to many trickster myths. More characteristics could be chosen, but these six serve as a modest map, heuristic guide, and common language for the more complex individual studies of particular tricksters within specific belief systems that follow. Thus, these initial six characteristics invite and anticipate not only the intricacies of the careers of particular tricksters, but emendations from the reader as well as outmaneuverings by that multicultural and multiform figure, the trickster.

The sheer richness of trickster phenomena can easily lead one to conclude that the trickster is indefinable. In fact, to define (de-finis) is to draw borders around phenomena, and tricksters seem amazingly resistant to such capture; they are notorious border breakers. By the same token, scholars who focus primarily upon the distinctiveness of specific tricksters within particular belief systems may underline the impossibility of any definitive cross-context, common content to the term "trickster."

However, if we steer a course between full delimitation on the one hand and no common content on the other, a number of shared characteristics appear to cluster together in a pattern that can serve as an index to the presence of the trickster. At least six similarities or shared characteristics can be identified to craft an initial guide or typology. The reader should not be deceived into confusing such an initial guide with a unified definition or theory.

At the heart of this cluster of manifest trickster traits is (1) the fundamentally ambiguous and anomalous personality of the trickster. Flowing from this are such other features as (2) deceiver/trick-player, (3) shapeshifter, (4) situation-invertor, (5) messenger/imitator of the gods, and (6) sacred/lewd bricoleur. Not every trickster necessarily has all of these characteristics. Still, more times than not, a specific trickster will exhibit many of these similarities. Several scholars, including Laura Makarius, have suggested that one could use such shared characteristics as a matrix by which to survey all known examples of tricksters and to judge their degree of "tricksterness." This might be a very useful way of testing the degree of commonality of such characteristics, but one should be cautious about the imposition of communality from without.

1. *Ambiguous and Anomalous.* Because the trickster appears as fundamentally ambiguous, anomalous, and polyvalent, this figure might well be the living embodiment of Nicholas of Cusa's fifteenth-century philosophical principle of the "coincidence of opposites." In striking parallel, our contemporary Claude Lévi-Strauss views the trickster as the epitome of binary oppositions, a necessary anomaly incorporating every set of extremes (Lévi-Strauss 1963: 224–26). His cosmic interplay engages unceasing sets of counterpoised sectors, such as sacred and profane, life and death, culture and nature, order and chaos, fertility and impotence, and so on. Still, none of these arenas fully captures or defines the trickster: he is not fully delimited by one side or the other of a binary distinction, nor by both sides at once, nor by a series of oppositions. Anomalous, a-nomos, without normativity, the trickster appears on the edge or just beyond existing borders, classifications, and categories. In several of the accounts referred to in this volume, the trickster is cast as an "out" person, and his activities are often outlawish, outlandish, outrageous, out-of-bounds, and out-of-order. No borders are sacrosanct, be they religious, cultural, linguistic, epistemological, or metaphysical. Breaking down division lines, the trickster characteristically moves swiftly and impulsively back and forth across all borders with virtual impunity. Visitor everywhere, especially to those places that are

off limits, the trickster seems to dwell in no single place but to be in continual transit through all realms marginal and liminal. With regard to the more general phenomenon, we are fortunate to have Colin Wilson's seminal study of the alienation associated with being a creative outsider to society, *The Outsider* (1956).

Robert Pelton has observed that the trickster "pulverizes the univocal" and symbolizes the multivalence of life (Pelton 1980: 224). Embodying this multivocality, the trickster himself eludes univocality by escaping from any restrictive definition: the trickster is always more than can be glimpsed at any one place or in any one embodiment. If one states that he is ambiguous, he will "insist" that this assertion is far too simple, that he is more polyvalent than merely ambiguous. If one then asserts that the trickster is polyvalent, he will "reply" that this is still too simple—and so on and so on. The trickster disorders and disassembles. One might say that his presence is felt in the writing of this book; "the trickster" is constantly disassembling and deconstructing it. Such polynomos perversity could easily earn the trickster the title of masked disassembler of the cosmic order!

2. *Deceiver and Trick-Player.* As his name explicitly states, the trickster is a consummate and continuous trick-player and deceiver. In many cultures and religions, the trickster acts as the *prima causa* of disruptions and disorders, misfortunes and improprieties. All semblances of truth and falsity are subject to his rapid alchemy. His lying, cheating, tricking, and deceiving may derive from the trickster being simply an unconscious numbskull, or, at other times, from being a malicious spoiler. Once initiated, a trick can exhibit an internal motion all its own. Thus, a trick can gather such momentum as to exceed any control exercised by its originator and may even turn back upon the head of the trickster, so the trick-player is also trickster-tricked.

In a number of North American Indian tales, the trickster entices a group of ducks into dancing with their eyes closed, whereupon he wrings their necks, one by one, anticipating quite a nice meal. Almost always, however, the trickster is in turn tricked out of enjoying his newly acquired food. In a Menomini version of this tale, the trickster places the roasted ducks in a sandbar so that he may take a nap to rest from his activities. Once he is asleep, other animals eat the ducks, saving the heads and tails, which they carefully stick back in the sandbar to fool the trickster (Thompson 1929: 54–56).

The African Akan gum-baby and the derivative African-American Br'er Rabbit tar-baby are additional examples where those who are normally the butt of the trickster's trickery turn the trick back upon him. Trickery can sometimes overreach itself, causing the trickster's own downfall, as can be seen in the tale of Horang-i, the Korean tiger trickster who inhabits the liminal area between town and forest. On one occasion, he chases two children who flee, climbing a tree to hide. When the tiger pursues them up the tree, they begin to pray to the God of Heaven:

> "Oh God, please save us. If you are willing, please send us the
> Heavenly Iron Chain. But if you mean us to die, send down the Rotten
> Straw Rope!" At once a strong Iron Chain came gently down from
> Heaven to them, so that they could climb up without difficulty.
> When the tiger reached the top of the tree the children were gone. It
> wanted to follow them, so it too began to pray, but in opposite terms,
> because it was very afraid that it might be punished for its misdeeds.
> "Oh God of Heaven, if you would save me, send down the Rotten
> Straw Rope, I beg of you. But if you mean me to die, please send down
> the Heavenly Iron Chain." By praying in this way, it hoped that the
> Iron Chain would come down, and not the Straw Rope, for it expected
> that as punishment it would receive the opposite of what it had prayed
> for. But the gods are straightforward, and always willing to save lives by
> answering prayers directly, and so it was the Rotten Straw Rope that
> came down after all. The tiger seized the rope, and began to climb up
> it, for in the darkness it could not see that it was not the chain. When
> it got a little way up the rope broke, and so it fell down to the ground.
> (Zong 1970: 7–10)

3. *Shape-Shifter.* The trick-playing of the trickster clearly distinguishes itself from other forms of trickery by its frequent association with shape-shifting and situation-inversion. As shape-shifter, the trickster can alter his shape or bodily appearance in order to facilitate deception. Not even the boundaries of species or sexuality are safe, for they can be readily dissolved by the trickster's disguises and transmorphisms. Relatively minor shape-shifting through disguise may involve nothing more than changing clothes with another. Thus the Tibetan trickster Agu Tompa (Uncle Tompa) puts on the robes of a nun so he may invade a cloister and make love with all the nuns; he is discovered only when there is an

outbreak of pregnancies (Dorje 1975: 17–23). Relatively major shape-shifting may involve the alteration of the physical form of the trickster's body. As William Doty notes in an upcoming chapter, the main *Hymn to Hermes* depicts the infant Hermes as a thief; having stolen Apollon's cattle, Hermes returns home by transforming himself into a mist and sliding through the keyhole so that he can swear that he never "stepped over" the threshold. The Navajo Coyote trickster shifts his form, becoming a dish in order to obtain food, or becoming a tree in which to capture birds. The anthropoidal Winnebago trickster not only shifts among numerous animal shapes, but also shifts from human male to female in order to trick a chief's son into marriage. The trickster is the master of metamorphosis.

4. *Situation-Invertor.* As situation-invertor, the trickster exhibits typically the ability to overturn any person, place, or belief, no matter how prestigious. There is no "too much" for this figure. No order is too rooted, no taboo too sacred, no god too high, no profanity too scatological that it cannot be broached or inverted. What prevails is toppled, what is bottom becomes top, what is outside turns inside, what is inside turns outside, and on and on in an unending concatenation of contingency.

The trickster often turns a place of safety into a place of danger and back again. He can turn a bad situation into a good one, and then back into a bad one. Bad becomes good, good becomes worse, worse becomes better, and so on. Tranquility can become disaster and vice versa. In one Yoruba tale, the West African trickster sets fire to a farmer's house, helps the family get all their possessions out safely, and then gives these goods away to passersby on the road (Mezan 1972: 94). Agu Tompa, finding a farmer despairing because his cursed field did not produce its normal crop but rather a thousand penises, turns the situation into a highly profitable one by arranging to sell the penises to Tibetan nunneries (Dorje 1975: 9–16). He has noted carefully that although it is forbidden that a nun may sleep with a man, nowhere is it written that she may not sleep with a penis!

As will be seen in this volume, the trickster is often the official ritual profaner of beliefs. Profaning or inverting social beliefs brings into sharp relief just how much a society values these beliefs. These profanations seem to exhibit a clear pattern of proportionality: the more sacred a belief, the more likely is the trickster to be found profaning it. For example, given the central importance associated with communal action and shared values within the life of the Plains Indians, it is not entirely unexpected that the trickster tales of these groups often center upon the most outrageous antisocial acts imaginable. The trickster profanes and inverts the preparations for war, gives false alarms, causes disruptions and chaos within village life, and even causes the blind to attack each other.

This inverted profaning associated with the trickster is also evident within the numerous examples of Saturnalia in western European history, including the Feast of Fools, the Abbeys of Misrule, Charivaris,[1] and the Mass of the Ass.[2] In 1444, the Theological Faculty at Paris complained that "In the very midst of divine service masqueraders with grotesque faces, disguised as women, lions and mummers, performed their dances, sang indecent songs in the choir, ate their greasy food from a corner of the altar near the priest celebrating mass, got out their games of dice, burned a stinking incense made of old shoe leather, and ran and hopped about all over the church" (Du Cange 1733–36: 1666).

During the Renaissance the trickster was often incorporated into such literary works as Erasmus' *In Praise of Folly,* Shakespeare's *Measure for Measure, As You Like It,* and *Midsummer Night's Dream,* and Ben Jonson's *Volpone.* Elements of tricksterish activity can also be seen in the Picaro of Spanish literature, beginning with *The Life of Lazarillo de Tormes* (1554), and also in the Luftmensch of German literature.

There are nonliterary parallels in the cognate phenomenon of the court jester. Here the King of Order is balanced by the presence of the King of Disorder. In Hasidic Judaism, where the rabbi can have the status of a minor potentate, there is a very interesting example of a religious court jester: Herschel Osterpoler. Herschel constantly mocks the rabbi, the intricacies of Talmudic learning, and even Jewish motherhood! These tales often turn on the fine meanings of a word or Talmudic glosses. Many of the tales have still not been transcribed. Here is a favorite tale handed down within her family to Joanne Greenberg, the author, best known for *I Never Promised You A Rose Garden:*

[A lot of Herschel's tricking is done against his wife. She saves and he doesn't. He often gets money out of her by different ruses. He once got a burial association to pay for her funeral when she wasn't dead.]

Herschel went up to the attic of his tiny home. His wife heard all kinds of pots banging and clattering, and screaming, thumping and falling. He came down looking ghastly pale. He said, "Do you know

who is up there?" She said, "No, who?" He said, "Destitution."
"Destitution, oh my God! What does he want," she asked. "What does
he want? He wants my life; he was going to kill me!" "Well," she
asked, "maybe there is some way to fend him off." "Oh, yes! He wants
a coat." "A coat?" "Yes, he said that he would beat me to death if I
didn't get him a coat!" "That's terrible!" "Yes, he threatened me, threw
me down, and now he has to have a coat." She asked, "Well, what
should we do?" "We have to give him a coat or he will kill me."
So, she rifled her little money out of a little sugar bowl and gave him
the money, saying, "What's his measure?" Herschel said, "Well he's
about my measure. That's why he chose me, because I was about his
measure. And when he saw that I didn't have a coat, he really got mad
that I didn't have anything to give him." So Herschel took the money,
went out, and got measured for a fine coat.

Several days later, he came back with the coat; he went up into the
attic, and there was more moaning and groaning, frightful screams, and
everything else. He came down again. She said, "Well what
happened?" He said, "The whole thing is off; it's a failure." She said,
"How come?" "Well, the coat doesn't fit him." She said, "I thought that
you said that he was your exact measure, that's why he chose you."
"That's true," he replied, "but now that I have this coat, Destitution has
grown so much smaller!" (Greenberg 1982: 5–6)

Mac Linscott Ricketts has noted how the sacred beliefs and person of
the shaman in North American Indian cultures are subject to the counterbalancing of the profanations of the trickster (Ricketts 1966: 336). The
latter closely mimics the songs and healing ceremonies of the shaman.
However, when shamanistic curing acts are performed by the trickster,
the patient is made much worse or even dies. By the same token, when
the trickster attempts to fly to the world of the spirits in imitation of the
shaman, he crashes to earth or forgets how to get back. Elsewhere in this
volume, Robert Ellwood suggests a number of similar parallels within
Japanese mythology: the trickster, Susa-no-o, for example, is a counter-
figure to the shamanistic character of his sister, Amaterasu. In such examples, the trickster seems predisposed to stand as a ritual parody or
satire of sacred values within a given belief system.

5. *Messenger and Imitator of the Gods.* Often of uncertain or impure
birth, the trickster can be both a messenger and an imitator of the gods.
Admixing both divine and human traits, he can slip back and forth

across the border between the sacred and the profane with ease. He may bring something across this line from the gods to humans—be it a message, punishment, an essential cultural power, or even life itself. Thus, Eshu/Elegba, a trickster with minor divinity status among the Yoruba, is sent by the senior gods to cause trouble for those who have offended them (Bascom 1969: 79).

The trickster is often a psychopomp, a mediator who crosses and resets the lines between life and death; associated imagery may include skulls that get stuck on the inquisitive trickster's head, or skeletons that come alive and give chase. Most often associated with conducting individuals to restored life, he can also be the messenger of death. The Shoshone credit Coyote with bringing death itself into the world; other groups consider death the result of the trickster's fumbling accidents.

The trickster quite regularly brings gifts essential to human culture, usually by breaking a central taboo established in the divine order. Thus he may bring fire to humans by stealing it from the gods, as in the case of the Polynesian Maui. Laura Makarius argues in this volume that the trickster is the unique mythic vehicle through which human culture may acquire sacred powers while avoiding the direct involvement in the necessary breaking of the taboo surrounding the possession of these powers. Because it is the trickster who breaks the taboo, while conveying the benefits of this act to humans, the appropriate consequent punishment is deflected from humankind. Thus, the cosmic boundaries are preserved while a crucial power slips across to human use. As Alan Aycock has argued: "the 'trick' played is to transcend ordinary reality by violating it in such a way (through obscenity and violence) that society is simultaneously disrupted and renewed—an act of creation with death as its inescapable attendant" (Aycock 1983: 124). Furthermore, within this process, the trickster often seems to operate within a perpetual bubble of immunity that protects him from the full weight of retribution.

In short, the trickster's position midway between the gods and humans allows him to function as a cultural transformer. However, even this function is subject to parody. When Hermes steals or discovers fire, he is totally unconcerned to share it with humans. The Winnebago trickster forgets what it is he has been sent to do for humankind. When Eshu/Elegba is sent to punish someone, he often punishes the wrong person or fails to punish anyone at all. Christopher Vecsey notes elsewhere in this volume that the Akan trickster, Ananse, attempts unsuccessfully to keep all wisdom to himself in a small pot. He has the further dubious distinction of having introduced that most ambiguous of cultural gifts—debt.

The trickster's status among the gods is equally unstable. There are numerous examples of his attempting to imitate or to usurp the powers of the gods above him. As Hynes and Steele relate in another chapter, the Yaqui have a marvelous tale that not only provides an example of this usurpation but also shows a noteworthy instance in which the figure of Saint Peter has been expanded by popular imagination into a more full-blown trickster figure.

There are parallel examples of Saint Peter's elaborated role as trickster in earlier medieval European folklore. Italo Calvino's *Italian Folktales* (1980 [1956]) contains a good selection, slightly recast in modern idiom. "Put the Old Woman in the Furnace," one tale of Jesus and Peter traveling through Sicily, evidences the same usurpation-through-imitation theme found in the Yaqui. However, in this tale Peter's effort at imitation is notably unsuccessful. When a man approaches them and asks Jesus to make his aged father strong again, Jesus recognizes the burden of old age and suggests to the son that "if you slip your father into the furnace, he'll come back out as a child!" When the man follows these suggestions, his father emerges from the furnace as a young boy. Peter immediately sees the possibility of his turning "some old soul into a child." Thus, when Peter meets a man seeking to have the Lord to cure his dying mother, Peter gives him the same instructions: "The Lord isn't here yet, but Peter is, and he can help you. Know what you have to do? Fire up the furnace, slip your mother into it, and she will be cured." The poor man, knowing that Saint Peter was dear to the Lord, believed him. He slips his mother into a fiery furnace. However, this old woman is burned to a crisp. The man attacks Peter asking what kind of a saint he can be who burns up old women. When Peter tells the Lord, Jesus splits his sides laughing. However, in response to the son's pleas, Jesus blesses and rejuvenates the woman, sparing Peter "the punishment he deserved" (Calvino 1980 [1956]: 595–96). Calvino comments that "Popular tradition makes of Peter a lazy man, glutton, and liar, whose elementary logic is always contrary to the faith preached by the Lord, whose miracles and acts of mercy never fail to put Peter to shame. Peter, in this sort of common man's gospel, is the human opposite of the divine, and his relationship with Jesus is somewhat like Sancho Panza's with the *hidalgo*" (the nobleman, i.e., Don Quixote; Calvino 1980 [1956]: 742/n. 41).

6. *Sacred and Lewd Bricoleur*. The sixth and, for our immediate purposes, the last characteristic of the trickster is his role as sacred and lewd bricoleur. The term "bricoleur" is here used in the sense offered by Claude Lévi-Strauss (1966: 16–18). The bricoleur is a tinker or fix-it person, noted for his ingenuity in transforming anything at hand in order to form a creative solution. Because the established definitions or usage categories previously attached to tools or materials are suspended/ transcended for the bricoleur, these items can be put to whatever inventive purpose is necessary. Elsewhere in this volume, Robert Pelton speaks of the trickster as "sacred bricoleur." Using the inverse logic of the trickster, I would make the suggestion that the trickster can also be a "lewd bricoleur." The trickster manifests a distinctive transformative ability: he can find the lewd in the sacred and the sacred in the lewd, and new life from both. The *Oxford English Dictionary* suggests a parallel binary contrast here when it lists the original meaning of the word lewd as "lay, not in holy orders, not clerical." Thus, the fuller background against which the trickster transforms may be the contrast between sacred-clerical and lewd-lay.

Accordingly, the trickster traffics frequently with the transcendent while loosing lewd acts upon the world. Gastronomic, flatulent, sexual, phallic, and fecal feats erupt seriatim. Yet the bricoleur aspect of the trickster can cause any or all of such lewd acts or objects to be transformed into occasions of insight, vitality, and new inventive creations. The Chippewa trickster, Wenebojo, transforms his intestines into sweet food for his aunts and bloody scabs from his rectum into sweet tobacco for his uncles; of course, tobacco is understood as a "sacred link with the supernatural" (Barnouw 1977: 22–23, 29–30, 52–53).

The trickster seems impelled inwardly to violate all taboos, especially those which are sexual, gastronomic, or scatological. Most tricksters are forever hungry and in search of food. No prohibition is safe from the trickster, especially if it lies between the trickster and a prospective meal. But when such food is gained it is seldom actually consumed. Although the trickster is represented as being insatiably hungry, on those rare occasions when he does eat, little overt evidence of pleasure or enjoyment is indicated: the process of the search and not its fulfillment is the rule.

Sexual exploits abound in most trickster myths.[3] Some of the most infamous are to be found in the Winnebago traditions. Here the trickster's penis is extremely long, detached from his body, and often carried coiled in a box in his pack. Such detachment allows the penis great mobility and autonomy. The trickster sends it swimming across a lake to lodge in the chief's daughter. On one occasion he attempts to use it as a weapon against a pesky chipmunk, with highly polyvalent results. In order to find and kill the chipmunk, who has retreated into a hollow tree, he probes the tree with his extraordinary penis. Forced to unwind more and more of its length, he probes deeper and deeper with no results. Finally, in frustration, he retrieves his penis but finds that it has been gnawed down in size by the chipmunk: "My, what a great injury he has done to me! You contemptible thing, I will repay you for this!"

Kicking the log to pieces, the trickster finds the chipmunk and flattens him, and discovers the gnawed remnants of his penis. "Oh, my, of what a wonderful organ he has deprived me!" What is left is closer to normal size so that when the trickster leaves the scene he no longer needs the box in which to carry his penis. The episode concludes: "And this is the reason our penis has its present shape. It is because of these happenings that the penis is short. Had the chipmunk not gnawed off Trickster's penis, our penis would have the appearance that the Trickster's had first had. It was so large that he had to carry it on his back. Now it would not have been good had our penis remained like that, and the chipmunk was created for the precise purpose of performing this particular act. Thus it is said" (Radin 1955: 38–40). With respect to the trickster's role as transforming bricoleur, it should be noted that this tale continues with a discussion of the various plants and foods that were subsequently grown from the discarded pieces of his penis.

In both ritual actions and artistic depictions, the trickster sometimes carries a phallus or phallic club. Within Western culture, the public ritual use of such overt sexual objects was largely suppressed by the time of the Enlightenment. John Townsen and William Willeford have noted the devolution of the phallus in clowning and tricksters. Thus the phallus is still discernible in the jester's bauble, with its miniature human head or heads at one end and animal bladder at the other (Willeford 1969: 11ff.). The only vestigial evidence remaining in contemporary clowning may be the large flat, bladder-like gloves of circus clowns (Townsen 1976: 22).

Last and certainly not least, the trickster is closely associated with the most profane of lewd profanations, excrement. Winnebago tradition includes the tale of the trickster being nearly blown to bits by an excess of stomach gas and finally being pushed rapidly toward the sky on an ever-increasing pile of his own feces. The cosmic counterbalancing that can be associated with this most profane profanation is clearly evident in the Tibetan story entitled, in its English translation, "Uncle Tompa Drops Shit on the Ruler's Lap." The story also illustrates the trickster's abilities as bricoleur, transforming shit into sacred object by the use of writing:

> Once there were many rulers in different regions of Tibet. Uncle happened to be a good friend of one of these rulers, and so he got a job as his secretary. The ruler himself was not able to write or read, but he was highly devoted in [sic] the religion of Buddhism.
>
> At first, Uncle made the ruler very happy with his work, but one day he annoyed him greatly. The ruler tried to punish him. He took off all the clothes Uncle was wearing and put him on the palace roof during the coldest period of the year. Poor Uncle suffered from the cold all night long.
>
> Early the next morning Uncle scraped off some of the white lime used to whitewash the palace wall. Soon he had enough to spread out on the floor. Then he shit on the white lime dust, picked up a stick and stabbed it into the shit. It soon froze because of the cold. He picked up the stick which now had the frozen shit on it, and a white bottom from the lime. He wrote some words on the bottom.
>
> Uncle looked down into the skylight in the Ruler's private worship room and saw him sitting cross legged and meditating before a splendid altar of Buddha and all the gods. Uncle dropped the shit right on the ruler's lap through the skylight.
>
> The ruler woke up from his meditation and was very surprised. When he looked at this object more carefully, he saw there was some writing on the bottom.
>
> Since he could not read, he ordered his servants to bring Uncle down into his presence. Uncle, still shivering from the cold, was served a hot breakfast.
>
> Soon after, the ruler ordered Uncle to read the "Miracle Shit." Uncle bowed down three times in respect and sat below the ruler's throne in a very humble posture. He picked up the shit and read the writing on the bottom very loudly:

"WOODEN HANDLED AND WHITE BOTTOMED,
THAT IS THE SHIT FROM HEAVEN. HE IS THE
LUCKIEST RULER WHEN IT DROPS ON HIS LAP!"
Uncle stood up in amazement and said, "Ah! You are very fortunate
because this is shit from heaven and when it drops on someone like
you, you're the luckiest person on the earth. You should eat a little bit
of it to get its blessings."
   The ruler touched it to his forehead, ate a piece of it, and put the
rest on his altar. Uncle Tompa saluted and was dismissed. (Dorje 1975:
41–43)

What a powerful epistemological and metaphysical tool literacy can be
in the hands of a bricoleur!

Beyond these six characterisics or similarities shared by trickster figures, there are others that could easily be elucidated. Nonetheless, these
six are the most common to the trickster figure and probably are most
central to his identity. While many specific trickster figures appear to
have most of these characteristics, a particular figure may occasionally
have only one or two. It is hoped that as the reader enters the following
chapters, this cluster of characteristics may prove a helpful map,
heuristic guide, and common template through which to become better
aware of the complexities of specific trickster figures within particular
belief systems.

In the final chapter, following the intervening chapters on particular
trickster figures, a range of interpretative frameworks will be offered by
which the complex and often puzzling meaning of the trickster can be
more fully assessed.

FOUR

A LIFETIME OF
TROUBLE-MAKING:
HERMES AS TRICKSTER

William G. Doty

In exploring here some of the many ways the ancient Greek figure of Hermes was represented we sight some of the recurring characteristics of tricksters from a number of cultures. Although the Hermes figure is so complex that a whole catalog of his characteristics could be presented,[1] the sections of this account include just six: (1) his marginality and paradoxical qualities; (2) his erotic and relational aspects; (3) his functions as a creator and restorer; (4) his deceitful thievery; (5) his comedy and wit; and (6) the role ascribed to him in hermeneutics, the art of interpretation whose name is said to be derived from his. The sixth element listed names one of the most significant ways this trickster comes to us—as interpreter, messenger—but the other characteristics we will explore provide important contexts for what is conveyed, and how. This is not just *any* Western Union or Federal Express worker, but a marginal figure whose connective tasks shade over into creativity itself. A hilarious cheat, he sits nonetheless at the golden tables of the deities.

We now recognize that even apparently irreverent stories show that some mythical models could be conceived in a wide range of significances, even satirized, without thereby abandoning the meaning-complex in which the models originated. For example an extract from a satire by Lucian demonstrates that Hermes could be recalled with respect, as well as an ironic chuckle:

HEPHAISTOS. Apollon, have you seen the new baby? Maia's little tot,
Hermes? He's beautiful. And he smiles so sweetly at everybody. It looks
as if he'll grow up to be a fine young god.
APOLLON. That tot a fine young god? When it comes to making trouble,
he acts as if he's been at it a lifetime (Casson 1962: 99, translation of
Lucian, *Dialogues of the Gods,* 7).

In the subsequent course of Lucian's staged dialogue between
Hephaistos and Apollon, it is noble Apollon who, characteristically,
knows everything—a theme that sounds like an omniscient echo from a
1940s radio drama. Hephaistos loses some of his enthusiasm for Hermes'
charm when he discovers that "Maia's little tot" has swiped the tongs he
uses in his smithy! The pompous Hephaistos and Apollon need deflat-
ing, and Hermes-Trickster happily obliges.

*Such figures were active in the imaginings of antiquity, and recently
the psychotherapist June Singer has indicated how trickster images have
a similar balancing function in contemporary materials:*

In dreams the trickster is the one who sets obstacles in our path for his
own reasons; he is the one who keeps changing shape and reappearing
and disappearing at the oddest moments. He symbolizes that aspect of
our own nature which is always nearby, ready to bring us down when
we get inflated, or to humanize us when we become pompous. He is
the satirist par excellence, whose trenchant wit points out the flaws
in our haughty ambitions, and makes us laugh though we feel like
crying. . . . The major psychological function of the trickster figure is
to make it possible for us to gain a sense of proportion about ourselves.
(1972: 289–90)

Surely a figure who is so near to hand and so useful for restoring a
more modest view of ourselves deserves our concentrated attention,
even if in a manifestation (Hermes) whose stories stretch backward
several centuries Before the Common Era. While Hermes is not necessarily the master model for figures such as the Native North American
tricksters, a look at this oldest Western trickster will show us many of the
typological elements that tricksters demonstrate in other cultural settings, and modern trickster categories help us identify modes of appearance of the ancient Hermes.[2]

MULTIPLEX MARGINALITY AND PARADOXICALITY

The great range of characteristics of the Hermes figure suggests that the narrow approach that seeks the essence of a figure, its lowest common denominator, may not be most appropriate. Multiplicity and paradoxicality, not singularity and the status quo, are central to Hermes throughout his stories.

Hermes is *marginal:* his peculiar icons—ithyphallic herms (square-cut blocks of stone with an erect phallos on the front, topped with a portrait head of Hermes)—were located at entrances to homes, public buildings, and sleeping chambers, and at crossroads. As the patron of roads and travelers, Hermes guided transitions from one place to another. Because he was particularly active at the twilight margins between daylight and darkness, he was described as the "companion of dark night" (Homeric Hymns 4: 290), or as "furtive Hermes, the nighttime chieftain" (Nonnos 35: 228).

Hermes' spheres are those of change, movement, and alteration, and his activity is rapid, as signified by the wings on his head, shoulder, or feet, or even—in an Arabic manuscript—on his belted waist. He often remains outwardly invisible, sometimes wearing the cap of invisibility that connects him with Pluton/Hades. His primary honors are offered not at the great regional temples, but at local roadside herms and at crossing points of roads and paths (where images of Hekate were likewise). As patron of craftspersons, cooks, heralds, teachers, and servants, his is a facilitating rather than a commanding role, and Hermes' presence was acknowledged primarily after he had been among mortals.

With respect to paradoxicality, Hermes is both an old man (*sphênôpôgôn:* having a wedge-shaped beard, like old men in Comedy) and a baby or youth (*achnous:* beardless, downy-cheeked). He is both the god of thieves and prophylaxis against them; the patron of luck in both commercial gain and accidental loss. He has simultaneously masculine and feminine qualities, if we derive characteristics of the father from his progeny, Hermaphroditos. He is both father and son of the Kabeiroi, and of Priapos; both the son and the lover of Kadmos; the father of Eros by Aphrodite or Artemis, and yet descended from the original triad of Chaos, Gaia, and Eros.

In imagery he is represented as both a country bumpkin and a city slicker; he is conceived of both as a reprehensible thief and deceiver and as a responsible public speaker and attorney; he is both the bringer and the withholder of sleep and dreams. He is the god of language and speech, who nonetheless makes his appearances veiled in silence, or at gaps in our conversations ("Hermes has entered," one said, where in older English usage one might observe, after a lull in chatter: "An angel has brought us something to talk about").

In art and in literature, Hermes is paired with wise Athene in helping heroes, especially Herakles and Perseus, his beloved; or he is paired with home-loving Hestia (see the correlations and contrasts traced by Vernant 1969); but above all, he forms a pair with his bright brother Apollon. In his medieval transformation as Mercurius, he appears as both water and fire, as both Virgin—the passive, feminine aspect—and as Lion or Unicorn—the rampant, masculine, penetrating force, identified with the Christ. He is likewise both the base alchemical substance, the *prima materia*, and its ultimate perfection, the *lapis philosophorum*.

Already in antiquity a cultic Hermes was simultaneously benignantly white and malignantly black—a sharp graphing of the polarizations in the character of a deity who was at ease both on Olympos and in the Underworld.[3] Complex titles reflect his paradoxicality and inclusiveness: he is Hermes *Duplex*, and later Hermes *Triplex* or *Trismegistos*, "super-great." *Pammegistos*, "all-great," was also used; and even the medieval *Multiplex*, as Hermes/Mercurius was represented repeatedly on many a fulsome title-page as the patron of all the arts and professions.

Commentators frequently note how many activities and traits are encompassed in accounts of trickster figures. They often see in the multiple aspects features of the ordinary *human* condition as opposed to the specializations of the shaman or the creative High God/Goddess. Wallis Budge can only make sense of all the activities of Thoth, Hermes' closest Egyptian counterpart, by asking us to "remember that according to the Egyptian texts Thoth was the heart, i.e., the mind, and reason, and understanding of the [highest] god Râ" (1904: 1/415; cf. Derrida 1981: Part I.3).

But it seems important to resist the typically Apollonian rationality whose logical condensation would drive us toward recognizing only *one* "essence of Hermes." It may be important to retain openness toward the polymorphous prolixity of the ways this deity flashes in and out of human consciousness. I suspect that often we fail to gain from figures of antiquity and other cultures precisely what they can best contribute, namely a balance to our obsessive singularity and specialization. We must be wary of the implicit *mono*theistic longing instilled in us by the slant of our own cultural science and theology, lest we miss originative *poly*theisms that may be useful to comprehend our ever-more-complex human condition.

The polytheism of the Greeks was an open-textured religiosity honoring various experiences of power made concrete by different members of the divine family. Its concern was not so much the definition or abstract identification of divine essences so much as providing a practical religion that connected humans with the relevant sources of power and clarified behaviors appropriate for human beings. The sharp differentiation between the human and the divine that was developed in Judaism and Christianity went against the Greek sense of a divine-human continuum. Greek mythology functioned less to develop theological dogmas than to clarify ethical behavior. It explored our all-too-human existence in the gap between what comes to us through history and fate or *luck,* and what we can learn through ethical and cultural training, or *education* (Nussbaum 1986 shows how this problem motivated many crucial reflections in Greek philosophy and literature).

In such a context we ought to scrutinize mythical figures whose interactions with and services to mortals are particularly emphasized. As the Greek "god most loving of humankind" (*Iliad* 24: 344–45), Hermes seems a foil for fallible humans as other Olympians could never be except when romanticized in Hellenistic and Alexandrian syncretisms. But he is recognized as *a god,* the only nymph's son who is, and there is something intriguing about the Greek spirit that could divinize such a figure of marginality and paradox, polyvalence and multiplicity, as easily as it idolized the sharp clear focus of a Zeus or Hera.

A marginal, border-dwelling figure, Hermes stirs up and initiates. He is not the deity of the singular heroic act, but of the marginal and plural subjectivities of tradition breakers, and metaphor makers.

THE DIVINE CONNECTOR

The work of metaphor is the work of making connections between two or more fields, or as one might suggest in classical terms, it is the sphere of *the erotic,* since eros was primarily a matter of how people were drawn to one another (and not just the matter of genital sexuality that "the erotic" has become). An intertwining series of images, Hermes will provide us with a range of types of human connection betokened by this trickster's signature emblem, his staff.

Hermes is sighted as a peacemaker, as the patron of youths, flocks, and the lucky find, and as the original sacrificer or cook—in every case the emphasis is upon *connections* between humans, or between humans and deities. Sexual aspects of Hermes are as near to hand, and as phallic, as for other tricksters, especially in his graphic and plastic representations. At an early date the erect phallos alone served as a symbol of Hermes; it was carried forward onto the front of the shaft-plus-head that became the classic herm, as well as in *petit fours* shaped like male genitals, eaten on the god's fourth-of-the-month feast days, and in polyphallic Mercuric door chimes in merchants' shops in Pompeii.

But the phallos was hardly unique to Hermes in antiquity—compare the explicit phallicism of Dionysos' Seilenoi, the satyrs, actors playing roles in classical Comedy, even secret objects in women's mysteries— and I am not struck by a particularly erotic quality (in modern sexual terms) in either the literature or the visual representations of Hermes (see Keuls 1985). To be sure, quite a number of sexual liaisons are reported for the god (thirty-five women, four men), and he sired a number of children (about forty-four), but such activity is not unusual with respect to the ways the Greeks projected images of their male gods.

This trickster's phallic history does not involve reduction in size, like that of the ass/youth in Lucian's *Asinus*, or that of Apuleius' *Golden Ass*, or that of the Winnebago trickster. Nor is it that of displacement, as when the African Eshu-Elegba's rampant phallos becomes old Legba's crooked walking-stick in Haitian Voodoo, although in some medieval illustrations phallic aspects clearly are displaced onto Hermes' staff *(kêrykeion)*.

The *kêrykeion* or caduceus is more broadly symbolic, and indeed it has received all sorts of mystagogic interpretations: "The wand represents power; the two snakes wisdom; the wings diligence. . . . The caduceus also signifies the integration of the four elements, the wand corresponding to the earth, the wings to air, the serpents to fire and water" (Cirlot 1971: 35).

The staff is a communicative device: one type, the Spartan *skytalê*, was a walking-stick marked by the sender of the message in such ways as to identify the messenger and to remind him of the contents to be conveyed. It is also a device of leadership—the shepherd's staff, the speaker's *skeptron* in the agora, the tyrant's scepter—and an agent of transformation, inasmuch as messages often have transformative power: note Aigeus' suicide after he receives the false visual message about Theseus' death. The staff has the power of magical transformation, and hence the *kêrykeion* was ideally to be made of gold, and Hermes was described as shining-like-gold, gold-winged, and gold-wanded (*chrysophaês, chrysopteros,* and *chryorapis*).

Hermes was thought to function as a *peacemaker,* his staff functioning as the "blameless tool of peace" (Orphic Hymns, *To Hermes* 28.7) rather than the spear that the herald *festialis* hurled into enemy country as a declaration of war (Frazer 1929, comm. on Ovid, *Fasti* 4/155). Ovid refers to Hermes/Mercurius as an "arbiter of peace and war to gods above and gods below" (*Fasti* 5/665–66), and in Aristophanes' *Peace,* Hermes helps disinter the buried Goddess of Peace. Even the usual folklore about looking at copulating snakes—such a sight is what made Teiresias blind—is reinterpreted in this light: "When Mercury, holding [the staff given him by Apollon], was journeying to Arcadia and saw two snakes with bodies intertwined, apparently fighting, he put down the staff between them. They separated then, and so he said that the staff had been appointed to bring peace. Some, in making caducei, put two snakes intertwined on the rod, because this seemed to Mercury a bringer of peace."[4] An anonymous literary papyrus represents Hermes as ending the primeval conflict between the four elements, creating from them the sky and the earth—a motif of normative establishment of characteristics of the present world that is found in stories of several other tricksters (see the third section of this essay).

A story in Plato's *Protagoras* concerns Hermes' role in pacifying fighting humans rather than snakes or the elements: when primitive humankind seemed about to destroy itself, "for they had not the art of politics," Zeus "sent Hermes to impart to men the qualities of respect for others and a sense of justice, so as to bring order into our cities and create a bond of friendship and union" (Hamilton and Cairns 1961, translation of Plato, 322 b & c). These qualities were to be distributed to all persons, in contrast to the few who practiced the arts and crafts (in the Aesopic tradition the latter were held to have received a drug of falsehood, Perry 1965: 103). "Gentle" or "pacifying" *(meilichos)* Hermes lifts his rod to check the fray among the gods in Nonnos (36: 108), resulting in "an end to the gods' intestine strife" (188), and he sees to the "mingling of a league of friendship" between Dionysos and Perseus at the end of the *Dionysiaca* (47: 713).

We begin to see why the Roman traditions emphasized the role of hermetic peacemaker (the career of Augustus is treated by Horace, *Odes* 1, 2: 25–46, as an epiphany of Mercurius), as well as something of the Greek horror at the mutilation of the Athenian herms in 415 B.C.E., during the Peloponnesian War, for it had been precisely those aspects of the Hermes cult having to do with peaceful interactions that had been emphasized during Hipparchos' rule (Eitrem 1912: 783; on the period, see Brown 1947: ch. 6; and for a fresh interpretation of the castration of the herms, see Keuls 1985: chaps. 1 and 16).

At regular intervals on highways, mile-markers or distance signposts took the form of herms. Furthermore, in their function as boundary markers and as directional pointers to towns and springs herms facilitated peaceful commerce, traveling, and communication among all sorts of people. In contrast to Ares, Hermes was never markedly associated with warfare or military activities, which disrupt such peaceful communications.

Hermes' associations with Eros, the personified principle of connectedness, betoken phallic expression in its nurturing dimension, seen in Hermes' patronage of youth, his role as god of flocks, and his creative and artistic application of the lucky find. Indeed Hermes' activities suggest a fostering of associations and relationships, a collecting of people for commerce or for political action (the herald's task) or for education or athletics. Whereas Eros is "hot" or "wild," his "generative arrows" wounding even Zeus, Hermes is "agreeable" and "good-natured," and he facilitates but does not force connections. He fathers Pan (or Pans: five such sons are mentioned) and two sons named Eros (one by Aphrodite, one by Artemis), as well as satyrs (such as Pherespondes and Poimenios), Hermaphroditos, and Priapos—these figures extrapolate the god's more aggressive eroticism.

It is useful when studying a body of mythology to scrutinize any cross-referencing connections and relationships within mythic family structures. In this context, that means looking carefully at the emphatic pairing of Hermes with his brother Apollon, "the dark" with "the light." In the Homeric Hymn *To Hermes*, the two first connect through the results of Hermes' magic and trickery and then in fraternal friendship, after the two gods have defined their respective limits and spheres of acting: "Thus lord Apollon showed his love for the son of Maia with every kind of affection."[5] Subsequently the two are paired repeatedly, in many contexts.

Once his place in the divine family is established, Hermes turns toward mortals, as when he assists heroes. He conveys messages from Olympos to Aigisthos, Atreus, Deukalion, Kalypso, Priamos, and Tros; he takes messages into the underworld, and across continents. Above all he is the intermediary who links deities and humans by inventing sacrifice, which serves to bring together members of the politico-religious community. And since the ancient herald might also officiate at sacrifices, having previously prepared the meat, that function developed into the role of cook, and we learn that kitchen implements were dedicated to the herald-cook Hermes. It is he who introduces Ganymedes to the supreme delight of the Olympian cuisine, *nektar* (Lucian 4: 5).

Hermes also links together both deities and mortals by transporting them for the explicit purpose of erotic conjunctions: Alkmene to Rhadamanthys, Aphrodite to a love affair with Otreus, Eurydike to Orpheus, Ganymedes to Zeus, Helena to Alexandros, and Psyche to Eros. In Roman comedy he becomes explicitly a *leno*, a procurer, a role played for Hermes himself by his father when Zeus steals Aphrodite's sandal as a means of leading her to Hermes' bed.[6]

Hermes' roles show that connectedness comes not just from sexuality but also from peaceful social intercourse, business, religion, travel, education, athletics, politics, and even magic (see Doty 1978b).

CREATOR-RESTORER-HEALER

Trickster analysts have argued whether tricksters are prosocial benefactors and creators or merely negative characters indicating a deity opposed to or in tension with a "high god" creator. Some consider the trickster to represent parody of the religious shaman. Hermes functions as a *creator* deity only tangentially, although many traditions ascribe to him the functions of the figure known as the culture-bringer: such functions include the invention or discovery of the practical use of fire and how to kindle it by means of (phallic) fire sticks, the institution of sacrifice,[7] writing and the letters of the alphabet,[8] the institution of libraries, astronomy (his planet was called Hermaon or Hermes, Mercury), the musical scale, divining, the arts and sports of the gymnasion and palaistra, hunting, weights and measures, coins and finances, the clearing and paving of highways, crafts and commerce, and the cultivation of olive trees. He fashioned the first lyre, which he gave not only to Apollon, but also to Amphion, in which case it was crucial to the creation of the walls of Thebes as a sort of enacted musical architecture—the city was characterized as *lyrodmêtos*, lyrebuilt, and Hermes received the epithet *lyraios*.

His association with speech and language is emphasized in the neo-Platonic conceit that he parceled out tongues when human beings were created (as well as brains, the same amount to each—hence large persons who need more brain-substance are stupid: Aesop, see Perry 1965: 108), and the tongues of sacrificial victims were dedicated to him. In one tradition he gives Pandora her voice; and curse formulae call upon him to "bind the tongue" of—hence to immobilize—the victim, just as erotic charms seek his or Aphrodite's skills in "whispering" effectively into the ears of the beloved (he earns the epithet *psithyros*, "the whisperer").

The list of inventions could be extended, but the Greek "first-finder" traditions are notoriously slippery and duplicative, and always slanted from the perspective of the cult transmitting them. Even the discovery of fire is more usually ascribed to Prometheus' theft. What seem more typically trickster-ish than his creations and inventions are Hermes' *corrections and restorations*, often performed at the behest of another deity, in which he enables humans to reunite or to move to a higher level of awareness or insight. These are similar to the common trickster motif of making the cosmos more habitable for humankind. For example the Winnebago trickster relocates a waterfall so that people can live where it had been: "I am telling you," Trickster says, "that the earth was made for man to live on and you will annoy him if you stay here. I came to this earth to rearrange it" (Radin 1955: 52).

Typically the trickster helps humans adjust by stipulating social boundaries, even if he does so by metonymically transgressing them. He brings symbolic organization to the personal universe by his many exploits of disassociation: his arms, which initially fight one another, get organized into the primal right vs. left cooperation; his intestines are tied efficiently into the body at the anus; his long trailing penis is shortened until it becomes more manageable and does not have to be carried around in a box or basket. Likewise Hermes organizes the social cosmos, working out interconnections among people, boundaries between nations, and realignments of military or political power.[9]

Hermes also plays an important maieutic role—the term is from *maia,* midwife or nurse (personified in Hermes' mother Maia)—and he is termed a "male midwife" (Nonnos 41: 171) because he assists at unusual births and childhoods.[10] He is also a healer and physician, able like Priapos to cure impotence and acute fever; on an inscription he is named as a physician, and in the magical papyri he is paired with the goddess of health, Hygieia. The connection that we would expect would be with Asklepios, because of the symbol of the healing snakes that brought curative dreams; and indeed there is a tradition that Hermes rescued Koronis, pregnant with Asklepios, from the fires at Zeus' manifestation. The snakes in the iconography of Asklepios are similar to those on Hermes' caduceus, which is yet today the emblem of the medical profession.

Master of herbs, Hermes recommends the medicinal herb pennyroyal to Trygaios as a cure for overeating (Aristophanes, *Peace,* 712); he gives his name to the autumn crocus used in medicine, the *hermodactyl;* and he helps Odysseus escape from Kirke by use of the magical herb *moly.* He also knows poisons that cause evil dreams and lethargy.[11] Pausanias reports that he once saved Tanagra from pestilence by carrying a ram around the town's borders. Hermes sharpens Charon's sight (Lucian, *Charon,* 7) by means of an *epôdê,* a spell or charm or song—the *kêryx* had to be a good singer! And Seneca designates Hermes as the divine agent who relieves Claudius of his chronic flatulence (see Athanassakis 1977: 90).

THE SHAMELESS ONE

In turning to the characteristics of *deceit, trickery,* and *thieving,* we encounter traits that characterize Hermes that would be shocking as divine traits in other religions. But religious tricksters are regularly famous for their deceitfulness, and what are sometimes self-assuredly referred to as the "high religions" might learn from such a trait, inasmuch as there is a certain deceitfulness at the heart of all social institutions that may even be beneficial in hiding the unmentionable or indefinable mysteries and limitations at the core of human experience.

Unlike the North American tricksters, Hermes does not often get tricked in return, yet his stories suggest some revisionist consciousness, because Hermes punishes persons who act exactly as *he* might be expected to act in their stead![12] So the "chatterbox" (Battos) who tries to make a profit from Apollon by squealing on Hermes, and from Hermes by promising not to, is turned into stone when Hermes finds him out. Aglauos, who accepts Hermes' gold as the price for admitting him to the bedroom of her sister Herse, is likewise lithocized when she tries a hermetic word-game: "I shall not be moved," she says, since she now wants both the gold and the handsome male god. "Right!" says Hermes, and turns her into a black stone doorstop. And on a herm by a field an inscription reads: "Hermes [the thief!] has made a new law against stealing" (Pallantine Anthology 193)—probably an earlier version of the theme that still recurs in various police dramas, "Set a thief to catch a thief."

As is so often the case with other tricksters, Hermes' deceits are often ultimately beneficent. He causes Alexandros at Troas to suppose that a phantom Helena is the real item, while Hermes removes her to safety in Egypt. Taking on the appearance of the absent Dionysos, Hermes summons the Bacchantes to battle with the "Indians" when they have lost all hope (Nonnos 35: 227–42). First the gods conceive of having him steal Hektor's body, and then they arrange for him to accompany Priamos: Hermes pops up before Priamos like a young ephebic thief before the two steal through the Greek guards like a pair of robbers (*Iliad* 24: 24). Subsequently it is Hermes who carries the bribes ("gifts") to persuade Achilleus, Hermes who coaches Priamos on how to act as a suppliant, and Hermes who later drives Priamos home with Hektor's corpse.

Ovid suggests that Hermes "talked like a metronome for hours," telling stories to Argos until the thousand-eyed monster slept, so that Hermes, after this narrative deceit, could kill him and thereby free Io. The poet Bakchylides suggests that: "Hermes could not / Outwit him in mornings," but had to wait until his full power was attained in the dusk of evening (Godolphin 1964: 269). Another version has Hermes use a golden net to trap the gadfly that was Hera's next punishment of Io for her liaison with Zeus. And in Apollodorus' account of the same story (2.2.3), Hermes is sent by Zeus *to steal* the heifer (see also Nonnos 1: 337).

Certainly Hermes attains positive results through his thieving: he is sent by Zeus to Tantalos to reclaim/steal his valuable watchdog that Pandareus had stolen from the Cretan sanctuary of Zeus and given to Tantalos for safekeeping (Apollodorus). And "with a robber's untracked footsteps," he steals Dionysos from the nursing nymphs after Hera has driven them mad (Nonnos 9: 52). Hera almost overtakes Hermes, who carries Dionysos "in his life-protecting bosom," but Hermes shams the appearance of Phanes, and escapes (141).

The connection between Hermes and thievery, while problematic from the standpoint of many modern religious traditions, was asserted in communal rituals in antiquity. From inscriptions we learn of a festival in Samos honoring Hermes the Joy-Giver, where thievery and pick-pocketing were permitted, and of a Cretan festival where sexual license prevailed, and master-servant roles were reversed, as generally at the various festivals of Hermes named *Hermaia*, one of which forms the setting for Plato's *Lysis*. Like the medieval Carnivals, these may have been occasions of a sort of preventative social medicine, venting the interpersonal tensions caused by the strictures of a highly stratified society.

COMEDIAN AND WIT

That humor and laughter are part of the identikit of a divine trickster should not surprise us. Myths of several nations include comic figures, even stories of sexual improprieties, although they are usually suppressed as formal religious traditions are developed. Although scatological elements are not as prominent in the stories about Hermes as they are in other trickster collections, comic and playful elements are just as frequent. In fact Hermes is *the* playful Greek god, beginning with his cradle scene in the fourth Homeric Hymn, where first he whistles noisily while Apollon makes griping older-brother complaints (4: 280), then sneezes and drops "an impudent message" from his bowels down Apollon's spotless robe, when that very august presence has come to accuse the baby of stealing his cattle (4: 295–96). Even the scene where Hermes invents sacrifice is ironically marked first by his ostentatious refusal to partake of the delicious-smelling roasts even though he is ravenously hungry, and then by his presumption in ritually setting out twelve portions—his own being the twelfth! (Brown 1947: chap. 6, tracks the religio-political significance of this scene).

The fourth Homeric Hymn, as close to a canonical account of Hermes' career as we might wish, is replete with comic traits, distinguishing it from the long hymns to other deities. The very first scene portrays the day-old baby *laughing*—a characteristic portent of the Miraculous Child—as he devises the lyre. Then Hermes spitefully hymns his own genealogy and theogony: he shamelessly explicates Zeus' dalliance with his nymph-mother Maia in such a way as "young men do / at the time of feasts when they taunt and mock each other" (4: 55–56, Athanassakis' translation).

Shortly thereafter, "yearning in his heart for new things," he sets off to steal Apollon's cattle. Why Apollon's? Because Hermes knows that his brother will be less than diligent, since he is infatuated with Hymenaios, the young and handsome son of his own cowherd (not the same Hymenaios with whom Dionysos is infatuated in Nonnos). The baby-god's "crafty conceit" of reversing the hooves of his new cattle, and then making huge wicker skis to disguise his own steps, is pure farce, and a motif known elsewhere in antiquity. Returning home, he slips through the keyhole so that he can swear later, in self-defense, that he never *stepped over* the threshold; later the image of this never-too-literal deity was stamped onto housekeys.

The Homeric Hymn *To Hermes,* while extensive, is by no means exhaustive. We hear of additional tales from other sources: Hermes steals his mother's clothes while she is bathing. Hermes steals Apollon's bow and quiver when that noble god's attention is distracted by the music of the lyre. He fools Hera into becoming his foster-mother and hence his protectress, by disguising himself as her son Ares (the milk that sprays from her breasts as she pulls him away in disgust becomes the Milky Way; the mytheme is usually connected with Herakles, whom Hermes carries to the sleeping Hera). And Hermes invents the panpipes, later associated with one of his sons, the comic Pan.

Hermes' self-defense before the council of the gods on the charge of stealing Apollon's cattle leads Zeus *to laugh aloud,* as Apollon will later, because of the older brother's delight in Hermes' lyre.[13] Earlier Hermes' music had soothed Apollon's anger at his younger brother's performance of magic, a scene that becomes a practical joke: after Apollon has fashioned fetters for Hermes out of willow shoots, Hermes causes them not only to drop off his own body, but rooting quickly (again we confront the hermetic motif of *swiftness*), to entwine and secure the cattle where Hermes wants them.

These are selected examples. Hermes almost always appears *unexpectedly* and in an unforeseen manner *(aproidês); ingenuously:* resolving a tiff among the gods with a joke about his being bested by Leto (*Iliad* 21: 498); *self-effacingly:* he complains in Aristophanes' *Peace:* "I have to watch the little things [the gods leave behind], / Pipkins and panikins and trencherlets"; and *impatiently:* "Mercury wastes no time," but speaks and then vanishes in midair (Virgil, *Aeneid* 4: 96). When Apollo and Mercury, out for a stroll, discover the beautiful Chione, Apollo "thought of meeting her that night," but Mercury "could not wait till evening came," and put her to sleep in his arms then and there (Ovid, *Metamorphoses* 11, Gregory's translation).

Hermes causes laughter at others' expense: as *philokertomos,* he "loves his jokes" or "is fond of jeering," as when he teases Aphrodite, who tries to compete with Athene in weaving (Nonnos 24: 296). Frequently the laughter brings a resolution to a tense situation: "All the Olympians smiled" (ibid., 321). Hermes' own laughter often anticipates a later *connection or profit:* the scandalous situation where he and Apollon discuss how they would like to be trapped under Hephaistos' net where Ares and Aphrodite have been caught in their lovemaking (*Odyssey* 8: 339) prefigures Hermes' own union with Aphrodite. His laughter when he stumbles over the tortoise—he calls it "a lucky symbol" (Homeric Hymns 4: 28)—parallels his use of its shell, transformed by a sort of primal humorous *technê* into the lyre, as "a symbol" (or "token," *symbolon* in both instances) to placate Apollon later.

The hermetic laughter is crafty laughter—Hermes' play is not the casual play of little children. He is god of ephebes, athletes, not of the kindergarten, and childhood toys were dedicated to him when boys left childhood behind and entered higher studies. His play is the *serio lude* of the gymnasion, the serious work of leisure when the ephebes studied not only sports, but also letters, music/poetry, philosophy, law, and oratory.

Crafty laughter, but Hermes is also gentle and easygoing (*akakêsios* and *eukolos*), as he loves the mystery of appearing and disappearing, as well as the incognito: he shelters unrecognized with Zeus at the home of Baucis and Philemon, and with Zeus and Poseidon at the home of Hyreius. When Hyreius was granted a boon in return for his warm hospitality, and wished for a son, the three gods urinated on a bull hide they had commanded their host to lay on the ground. Nine months after it was buried in the earth, a male child came forth: Urion, a name later cosmeticized to Orion.[14]

The fact that Hermes can be presented as such a ridiculous character as is portrayed by Aristophanes, and later by Aesop and Lucian, seems to indicate that this was a deity who was imagined to be especially close to ordinary human lives. Hence comedy and satire were more appropriate for the development of his character than the more elevated genres of tragedy or lyric (Pindar is an exception, but even he revises the genre freely to suit the situation).

No doubt the pronounced connection between Hermes *Chthonios* or *Psychopompos* (in either case, stressing his guiding of the shades of the dead) and the realms of the Underworld added a certain reserve to the picture. But even that link gains comic lightness, as when Hermes, employed as a sort of tourist guide to Hades, shows Menippus the bare skull of Helena, and Menippus quips: "Well! Is *this* what launched a thousand ships from every part of Greece?" (Lucian 18: 2).

"Graveyard humor," perhaps, but it is a humor that is also soul-humor, humor of the psyches Hermes guides to and from the world-beyond. Even there, we are to suppose, there will be arguments about who owes whom what (Hermes and Charon arguing over repair bills for the ferryboat, in Lucian's *Charon*). And wit may be a *pharmakon* (preventative medicine) with which to confront death: Sisyphos comes again "into the light of the sun [from Hades] by means of his manifold wits" (Theognis 702–12).

It is through Hermes that we find hints that the Other Place will involve new discoveries and joys: in Apuleius' *Amor and Psyche*, Mercury guides Psyche herself to Olympos, and in his role as divine cup-bearer, tenders her a cup of ambrosia. After her earthly career, she is wedded to Amor (Eros), all the divine family enjoying the wedding breakfast. The child of their union was, we are told, Voluptas: pleasure/delight/enjoyment.

THE HERMENEUT

Before we look at some of the general contributions that analysis of the figure of Hermes makes to trickster studies, one aspect of the classical Hermes remains to be discussed here, and that is his role as messenger-hermeneut or interpreter. There is an ancient connection between herald Hermes and *hermeneuein,* the verb for practice of the art of hermeneutics or interpretation, which is intensified in post-classical ties between Mercurius and *eloquentia.* Hermes carries messages from one person or deity to another; he does not always originate them, and he may select or adapt what he alone chooses to present, and when. As the divine messenger, he participates in the formidable creative power of Zeus as its facilitator, as the one who provides for bringing into language what was only potential.

Already as a baby he "pondered word and deed at once" (Homeric Hymns 4: 46). He remains *facundus,* "wise of tongue" (Horace, *Odes* 1: 10), the speaker who accompanies his lover Peitho/Persuasion even so far as Hades (Aischylos, *The Libation Bearers* 726–27), and whose daughter is Angelias, the teller of glad tidings (Pindar, *Olympian Odes* 8: 81–82).

Hermes elicits metaphoric insights that startle the recipients of his maieutic messages into action, but he guides them as he guided the aged Priamos: he escorts one to the confrontation, but the subsequent interpretations that lead to modes of behavior, the details of the necessary actions, are not explicit. He brings Odysseus the efficacious herb *moly* to safeguard him against Kirke's wiles (a magical contest of wits, appropriate to the grandson of Hermes), but "crafty" Odysseus still has to figure out on his own when to use it and how to plan his eventual escape. Hermes helps Perseus avoid the petrifying sight of Medusa's face, and he helps Herakles distinguish between the real Underworld dangers and the Gorgon's apparently real "empty image" *(kenon eidolon)* there, but subsequently each hero has to act on his own.

Hermes-hermeneut is an arbitrary figure, in that he is not subject to the control of mortals. Hence one prays for clarifications or improvements "if he wills it" (see Aischylos, *The Libation Bearers* 811), and there is a chance-y element in all hermeneutical interpretation: sometimes the interpreter makes the right choice and intuits the correct solutions, and sometimes she or he does not. Words themselves both express and disguise the meanings they create. Nor are there guarantees that the messages are properly or fully stated, as marked by Hermes' promise "never to tell lies, but not necessarily the whole truth," or that we hear them appropriately. Like revelations, hermetic messages confirm or disconfirm themselves only in retrospect, and no less a figure than the elevated Apollon fears that Hermes "might steal back my lyre and the curved bow" (Homeric Hymns 4.544), indicating that even the gods' messages to one another might be deceitful or misunderstood.

In contrast to Apollon's sweeping oracular powers, Hermes' are limited: Apollon grants him the power of minor fortune-telling by means of pebbles, lots, or the archaic mantic bees (see Scheinberg 1979). And these powers may be fragmentary or partial: there was a market oracle where persons stopped up their ears, asked a question, and then took the first words heard when their ears were unstopped to be Hermes' answer.[15] But in hermetic foretelling, as in politics or commerce, there is always a risky element of chance, the possibility one has been led astray by what one desires to hear, and the danger that the god's real messages will be treated only as obtrusive, unreal fantasies.

Hermes inspires (Dido, in the *Aeneid;* later the bringing of inspiration was a central alchemical activity of Mercurius), but he does not specify particular reactions or applications of the message. He provides a language for transitions and discoveries (the "Eureka!" experience of the inventor, poet, initiate), but he does not guarantee their value, or their universality. The hermetic find may bring riches *or* failure. Kerényi suggests: "Accidental discovery is in itself not yet quite Hermetic: it is merely the stuff of Hermetic activity, which is then shaped to the meaning of the gods" (1976: 24). The lucky find *(hermaion)* can become "Hermes' lot" *(Hermou klêros),* the direct hit in games, or the first and best portion in serving meals, only when the randomly encountered opportunity has been worked into a meaningful context. And then it is still "half-shares with Hermes" *(koinos Hermes)*—said when coming upon a lucky find, but which might best be interpreted in this context as "half luck and half elbow grease."

If Hermes models a hermeneutic, it is an open-ended finding of new meanings that may change interpretive force from one context to another; the values of a way-god must necessarily be flexible and adaptive. It is a hermeneutic that perceives merit within deceit—the bag of gold coins that Hermes carries in late vase paintings—within the "Cunning tales of double meaning / Twisted council, clever word!"[16] And it is an aesthetic hermeneutic: Hermes bears epithets marking him as the male leader of the female nymphs, Charities, Graces, or Muses;[17] he has a deep appreciation of the beauty of Kalypso's home (*Odyssey* 5: 59–75). Appropriately enough, it was only *the most handsome* of the ephebes who enacted his role at Tanagra (Pausanias 9: 22.1–2). And Hermes was the patron of crafts: the "hermoglyphic techne" was the art of a sculptor, the phrase "Hermes in the stone," a reference to the potential shape that the artist might discover within the raw materials.

Without specifying a regulative list of trickster traits, I have explored here, and could explore further, many characteristics that Hermes shares with other trickster figures. They include: magical elements, playful, clownlike aspects, and athletics; the modeling of extreme types of human behavior; the connecting of many of the components of higher culture in order to transform "nature" (the traces of the cows Hermes sacrificed are said to be visible on rocks yet today); zoomorphic aspects (the cock, the ram, the ibis—Eitrem 1912: 757–59 lists fifteen animals associated with Hermes); thievery and deceit as normal modes of appearing; wanderlust (god of the ways, roads, travelers); connections with the realm of the dead, souls, or ghosts, and the underworld; eroticism, especially phallicism; age and gender multiplicity; and involvement in setting limits and boundaries. On an even more abstract level of analysis we might point to social catharsis, symbolic inversion, multiplicity of representation and transformation, and close relationship to the feminine.

In addition to these shared features, the complex trickster Hermes is also a messenger/herald/guide; a god of dreams, education, oratory, law, the servant professions; the slayer of Argos; and the divine worker by chance, change, and luck. He is related also to crafts and commerce: Hermes' Greek epithet *emporikos* went into Latin and then, as *emporium*, into English; the base *emporos* means either merchant or traveler; note also the relationship in Latin between Mercurius and *mercor*, "to engage in commerce," as reflected in the adjective *mercantile*.

The range of features almost overwhelms, yet it reminds us how frequently our obsession with monochromatic simplicity and easily accessible handbooks has desiccated deities by slotting them into overly simplified theological pantheons. One of Kerényi's grandest insights is: "Speaking mythologically, each God is the source of a world that without him remains invisible, but with him reveals itself in its own light" (1976: 55). I take that statement to mean that we confront a pantheon in each deity, as well as that each deity "pantheonizes" all the others within his/her own contours. But that perspective itself may be the insight one must learn precisely through the trickster's ways of playing through individual mythostories, the delicate opportunism of Singer's "sense of proportion about ourselves" with which this essay began.

FIVE

THE MYTH OF THE TRICKSTER: THE NECESSARY BREAKER OF TABOOS

Laura Makarius

[Laura Makarius was very supportive of the Trickster Consultation of the American Academy of Religion, and she contributed to it directly and indirectly several times. Her essay, "Le mythe du 'Trickster'," *Revue de l'histoire des religions* (175) (1969): 17–46, is cited repeatedly, yet it has remained accessible only in French in a research library. An earlier translation by Christopher G. Nichols has been revised by William G. Doty.

An article now over twenty years old cannot be expected to engage most recent scholarship, although we had hoped that Makarius would either revise or supplement her unique arguments for this volume. We can only wish that catastrophic illness had not prohibited the revisions Makarius might have contributed.

One of our publisher's readers cautions us all to remember that several usages that were still possible in the 1960s are presently out of fashion: reference to "the African hunter" would now have to be documented and stipulated (which Africans, in which areas?); and an earlier generation of anthropologists sometimes failed to distinguish actual praxis (such as incest) from ritual or symbolic references.

Makarius seeks to refute Radin as she sets the trickster into the sphere of ritual magic; the trickster-figure is the magician, the taboo-transgressor—but the reader can see how Makarius' interpretive contexts led her to her unique perspectives. The bibliography to this volume lists several of her other essays on tricksters and magic.—W.G.D.]

I

Recent works of African ethnography (Evans-Pritchard 1967; Marshall 1962; Wescott 1962; Wescott and Morton-Williams 1962, after Herskovits and Herskovits 1933 and 1958, and Tegnaeus 1950) have contributed new documents to the dossier of research on the problem of the mythic hero called "the trickster."[1] At first believed to be only Amerindian in scope, with the works of Luomala (1949, on Maui, the trickster of Polynesia and New Zealand) and Warner (1958, on Bamapama, the trickster of Arnhem Land, Australia), the problem became apparent in Oceania, and now involves Africa as well. While the discipline of ethnography has accumulated the requisite materials, it has not taken us very far on the road to their comprehension. It could even be said that some interpretive efforts—such as those of the psychologist Jung, [the classicist] Kerényi, and the ethnologist Radin, working together to decipher the enigma of the Winnebago Indian trickster (Radin 1955, cited from French ed. of 1958)—have thickened rather than dissipated the obscurity of the subject.

Ethnologists, psychologists, mythologists, and historians of religion taking a sympathetic interest in the trickster are faced by a mass of contradictions. The mythic hero transforms nature and sometimes, playing the role of a demiurge, appears as the creator, but at the same time he remains a clown, a buffoon not to be taken seriously. He checks the course of the sun, cleaves monsters asunder, and defies the gods; at the same time he is the protagonist of obscene adventures from which he escapes humiliated and debased. He brings humankind the arts, tools, and civilizing goods; at the same time he plays abominable tricks for which humans have to pay much of the price. He dispenses the medicines that cure and save—and he introduces death into the world.

Admired, loved, venerated for his merits and virtues, he is represented as thievish, deceitful, parricidal, incestuous, and cannibalistic. The malicious practical joker is deceived by just about anybody; the inventor of ingenious stratagems is presented as an idiot; the master of magical power is sometimes powerless to extricate himself from quandaries. It is as though each virtue or defect attributed to him automatically calls into being its opposite. The benefactor is also the fiend, the evil-minded one. Finally, in his most boorish as in his most contemptible aspects, in his greatness as well as his viciousness, the trickster is represented as being "sacred," a quality that no ridicule or abomination succeeds in effacing.

If one limits oneself to examining this mythic complex in and of itself, without referring to extraneous realities, one can only choose between two paths: to strive to explain the coexistence of contradictory traits within one character, or to consider him as the result of the overlapping of two different characters. Those who have taken the first path have worn themselves out in psychological reflections without arriving at acceptable results. The second path starts by presupposing capriciousness and ends by disintegrating the mythical character, but without accounting for the two resulting figures or their presumed overlapping. For our part, we will follow a third path. We will search for what, in the social life of the people who possess these myths, may be the reality of experience of which they are the emanation.[2] This reality can be only strongly contradictory, a richly contradictory phenomenon that places itself at the center of the magical and ritual activity of tribal societies: it is *the magical violation of prohibitions.*

Ethnographic observation shows that those taboos that are generally the object of the strictest respect are sometimes deliberately violated by individuals who anticipate getting favorable results by means of transgression. The belief that grounds these types of behavior has not been explained, and its explanation can be sought only in the study of the taboos that are transgressed in such a manner.

Such taboos are measures tending to protect individuals and the community against dangers that are most often imaginary, taboos that present themselves under diverse forms, but that in our opinion derive from a common source, the dangerous quality of blood. When it is not invested with a specific significance that wards off danger,[3] spilt human blood is considered to be *the* malignant, frightful, and dangerous element among all human beings. A particularly acute fear is demonstrated toward the blood of the female sexual functions, the blood of the menses, defloration, and childbirth (Durkheim 1897: 41 ff.; see also Makarius and Makarius 1961: 50 ff.). The fear of blood is extended likewise to fetal materials (placentas, umbilical cords, membranes, and the like), to newborns, who have been soiled by the blood of birth, to the complications of childbirth—multiple or abnormal births, miscarriages, and abortions—and finally to anything whatsoever coming from a cadaver. All these materials are subject to taboo: that is to say, they are removed from contact with or the proximity of others, or even from public view, because of the danger they represent to the community. The same applies to persons stained by blood or contaminated by others, to objects soiled with or found associated with blood, and so forth.

But the frightful and malignant effect that the imagination imparts to blood's *impurity* appears reassuring and benignant when its destructive powers turn against that to which it is adverse: a hostile army, influences that cause illness, all that threatens and harms and ought therefore to be driven away and destroyed. Diverse authors have indicated the efficacious value of blood in this type of magic: the type that leads to having a menstruating woman run through the fields in order to destroy infesting vermin, or that causes menstrual rags to be tied to the neck of sickly children to keep sickness at bay (cf. Gaillois 1939: 38–39, 52 ff., 130).

In pressing our analysis a bit further, we learn that from such a conception of the negative power of blood—which could be summed up by the formula "blood banishes all that is bad"—one passes imperceptibly over to belief in the positive power of blood—"blood provides all that is good." While we might say that the first formula has a rational basis, the second is an extension of the benignant power ascribed to blood, which ends in overdetermining its power and attributing to it the capacity of producing all desirable results and effects, and of dispensing every good thing. Blood will provide not only security and health—as it were, "negative" qualities because they represent only the absence of danger and sickness—but also those "positive" qualities represented by luck, power, wealth, prosperity, and success, as well as knowledge, wisdom, clairvoyance, and the extraordinary powers of creativity. And because such an extension is improper—because it implies forgetfulness of the fact that the benignant power of blood comes uniquely from its ability to drive away evil—and because it does not come up to the conscious level, blood will dispense all these qualities in an unknown, mysterious manner: it will provide them *magically.* It is above all from such an *overdetermination* that the well-known ambivalence that marks the power of blood is derived (on the magical violation of taboos, cf. Makarius

1968: 33 ff., Makarius and Makarius 1968: 222 ff., and Makarius and Makarius 1969).

Mastering this power for efficacious magic inevitably leads to transgressing the taboo that forbids contact with it. Hence magic acting by means of the power of blood has as its essential procedure *the violation of taboo*. The force that redeems the violation of taboo, the force inherent in blood, is the magical power, the *mana* that is, like blood, dangerous, efficacious, and ambivalent. And, like blood and the power supposed to reside within it, it is at the same time concrete and abstract, localized and not localized, visible and invisible, having at the same time the properties of materiality and those of a force.

Such a conception of magic explains the use of medicines based on blood and organic matter, the use of talismans smeared with blood, and the bloody unctions that often necessitate human sacrifices. It explains also the magical usage of fetal matter—embryos, fetuses, abortions, clots of blood from miscarriages, umbilical cords, and so forth—as well as the belief in the magical role of miscarried or stillborn infants and the whole complex of ideas attached to multiple or posthumous births. Fetal materials are inseparable from lochial [postpartum] blood, and they participate in the anguish that blood inspires (cf. Makarius 1968: 32). Aborted fetuses also partake of another source of anxiety, death, likewise inseparable from the fear of blood, because the substance of the latter is the fear of death itself. A parallelism between the magical use of blood and the magical use of materials from cadavers can actually be found. The latter are used under the same conditions, for the same ends, and in the same spirit as blood charms and become confused with them.

The concept of the magical violation of taboo also permits us to explain belief in the magical value of incest, which is found in the most diverse ethnographic areas. Reichard (1950: 180), for example, writes with respect to the Navajo: "Dogma links witchcraft to incest between father and daughter"; other examples given by the same author point out the relationship between magic and fraternal incest. The most well-known example is that of the African hunter who, before leaving for the elephant or hippopotamus hunt, believes he assures himself luck by committing incest (Dobe 1923: 41; Junod 1936: II.60–62). In order to account for this belief it is necessary to understand the reasons motivating the prohibition of incest. Here we can refer to Durkheim, who shows the general fear inspired by blood, the particular fear of blood derived from the female sexual organs, and the even greater fear of bleeding on the part of consanguineous relatives. Thus Durkheim has rendered the fear of incest intelligible on the plane of subjective motivations (1897: 47 ff.; cf. also Makarius and Makarius 1961: 62 ff.). Committing incest is equivalent to putting oneself in contact with the most dangerous sort of blood, that of consanguineous women. "Whoever violates this law [exogamy]," writes Durkheim, "finds himself in the same condition as the murderer. He has come into contact with blood, and its awesome properties are transmitted to him. He has become dangerous both to himself and to others. He has violated a taboo" (50).

These "awesome properties" of blood are precisely those that the violator of the blood taboo intends to master and to direct to his own advantage. From this perspective committing incest deliberately and manipulating blood with a view to fashioning powerful charms from it are acts of the selfsame order that imply a similar danger, which necessitates similar precautionary measures, aiming for the same results. In myths and narratives, as in rituals of violation, the two acts are often associated.

"The incestuous one," to cite Durkheim again, "finds himself in the same condition as the murderer." The parallel would be still more exact if we referred to the murderer of a consanguineous relative instead of just any murderer. Like incest, but more concretely, the murder of a blood relative causes contact with that most dangerous type of blood, namely consanguineous blood. Like incest, such a murder represents the violation of the fundamental taboo of the society, and like incest it is supposed to confer great magical powers. Magical rites of diverse people actually do include, along with incest, the murder of blood relatives. "The assassination of a close relative," writes Kluckhohn, "belongs to the general *pattern* of witchcraft" (1944: 58), and that is true wherever magic is practiced. The life of a blood relative is frequently the price necessary to enter into sorcerers' societies.

The magic founded upon operations of this type—manipulations of blood, incest, murders, and murders of blood relatives—is considered to unleash a "high voltage" power that is extremely dangerous both to the person who sets it going and to his entourage but that produces results of great efficacy. Such magic constitutes the essential activity of sorcerers as well as the rituals of secret societies. It is distinguished from imitative magic in that it does not resort to imitation (although sometimes some imitative rites are mixed up in it) and above all because of its dangerous character. The rainmaker who resorts to imitative magic throws buckets of water into the air; he who resorts to transgressive magic causes an "indisposed" woman to appear in public, commits incest, or violates a tomb, exhuming corpses in order to eat them. If the aims are the same, the means employed in the first instance are inoffensive, while those set in motion by the second are unlawful and dangerous. This example demonstrates that "white magic" and "black magic" are differentiated more by the means to which they have recourse than by the aims they have in view.

Because the blood taboo is the main pillar of social order, magic that can be practiced only by a violation is necessarily considered antisocial and in some way subversive—in fact, it must be occult. On the other hand, by its very nature it constitutes an act that can be only singular, rare, and exceptional: the magical act that draws its force from the danger attached to blood, and from the strength of the taboo covering it, and the taboo must be maintained generally, violated only by way of exception. This contradictory necessity articulates itself in the concept that one violation of taboo annuls another—which prevents the repetition of the transgressive act (see Makarius 1968: 33).

Although by definition it is *the* singular and asocial act—because in flouting prohibitions it flouts the social order—the magical violation of prohibitions is sometimes accomplished on behalf of the society, for the society, as well as the individual, needs the proper magical power to satisfy the essential desires of the group for security, health, protection, victory in war, success in hunting and fishing, and so forth (Davy and Moret 1923: 129 demonstrate that the Amerind hero is the inventor of the magical secrets of hunting and fishing that will assure the provisioning of the group). Inasmuch as the impulse to transgress prohibitions for magical ends clashes with the necessity of respecting them, the society that wishes to violate its own law can do so only through the action of a great magician who accomplishes the violation individually and is then considered the society's hero.

Thus we have the outline of the violator figure who separates himself from the society and transcends its law through devotion to the cause of humankind. He takes upon himself the culpability of all, and from the start he is condemned to atone so that the social order may triumph, to come to terms with the contradiction that has temporarily endangered it.

In such a context we may suggest that the trickster is a mythic projection of the magician who in reality or in people's desire accomplishes the taboo violation on behalf of his group, thereby obtaining the medicines or talismans necessary to satisfy its needs and desires. Thus he plays the role of founder of his society's ritual and ceremonial life.

It is in this vocation as violator that trickster accounts are surcharged with acts of rebellion, disobedience, defiance, transgression, and sacrilege: all these manifestations are intended precisely to explicate, in the symbolic language of myth, the nature and function of the hero. Authors who have studied these myths in diverse ethnographic areas have well recognized the transgressing and profaning character of the trickster hero, but they have not perceived that it constitutes his essence and his sole reason for existence in the mythic universe. For example Radin sees clearly that the Winnebago trickster is presented by the narrator as "a perfect fool who breaks the sacrosanct taboos and destroys the consecrated objects" (1955: 111), but Radin thinks that these violations are attributed to the trickster to make manifest his asocial nature, while it would be more consistent with the facts to invert this remark: an asocial nature is attributed to Wakdjunkaga and his ties with the community are broken because of the taboo violations he commits, and cannot commit, since he exists as a mythical character only in order to violate taboos conspicuously.

It suffices to envisage the trickster hero in this light to dissipate the enigma constituted by his contradictory nature: if the character's texture makes explicit the nature, the vocation, and the destiny of the violator of prohibitions, it can only retain the contradictions inherent in the violation itself. Examination of some trickster myths from different areas should permit us to verify our thesis.

II

Manabozo. Manabozo, the trickster and civilizing hero of the Algonquian Indians of North America, is often represented as having had *an impure birth*—abnormal, multiple, and posthumous birth itself already representing a violation, albeit involuntary, and a sort of predestination to a career of being a violator (cf. Makarius and Makarius 1968: 224; [reference ought to be made also to Makarius 1973, an essay that is an important complement to this entire essay—W.G.D.]). In an Ojibwa account Manabozo is born from a blood clot of his mother who died after having conceived by the wind following an act of disobedience; her womb was torn apart by her children who quarreled in it even before entering the world (Jones 1917: I.3–7 [1]). In a Menomini version, she dies after being hacked to pieces by a splinter of rock generated at the same time as a baby wolf and Manabozo (Skinner and Satterlee 1915: 239–41). Another version from the same tribe describes the bursting of the mother's body: fragments of flesh and blood, gathered together and put under a bowl, generate a rabbit, which will become a human, Manabozo (Hoffman 1892–93: 114). In another Ojibwa variant, he is born, not from the blood of his mother, but from his own placenta, which had been thrown away after the birth of a former child. This birth from a taboo substance will be evoked by the hero in order to justify his decision to abandon his grandmother and his brother. He says to the latter: "In any event, we two have not had the same kind of birth. . . . You, my brother, are like a true human being; as for me, the source from which I've sprung is that which was thrown away" (Jones 1917: 467 [no. 63]).

In the Ojibwa tales we see Manabozo pretending to be dead in order to commit incest with his sister—a customary trickster theme (279 ff. [no. 33]). One account seems to allude to incest with his grandmother, whom he undresses, washes, and then seizes. Afterwards the grandmother hunts up a large amount of meat and prepares for the boy an excellent meal: a favorable result follows the evocation of a violated prohibition (203–05 [no. 27]). Another story mentions Manabozo's indecent behavior when he forces the old woman to relieve herself in front of him (447 ff. [no. 58]).[4]

A Menomini legend attributes to Manabozo the origin of menstruation and miscarriages. After having slain the bear who is his grandmother's lover, he offers his grandmother the flesh of the dead animal, which she refuses. Taking a clot of blood from the bear, he throws it on her belly while saying "Here! Catch that!" She replies: "Because of that your aunts [women in general] will always have troubles at each moon and they will give birth to blood clots like this one" (Hoffman 1892–93: 175).[5]

Manabozo, contrary to all the rules, goes into a menstrual tent to choose his spouse. He ignores the warnings given him, for—as the Ojibwa account puts it—"he was very desirous of entering and he entered there." He spends the night, and the next morning he asks the young woman he found there to marry him. A few days later, having met her again in the same place, he weds her. The myth seems to say that this type of marriage befits the violator of prohibitions (Jones 1917: I.423–29 [no. 54]).[6] "Henceforth," adds the text, "he will give himself up solely to the hunt, and he will have great luck catching game." We need not be surprised, since we know that taboo violation leads to luck, and in particular to luck in hunting.

In a Menomini myth, Manabozo—having sent his brother back to live among the dead—condemned humans to mortality (Michelson 1911: 68–88, 72). The same motif is found in a Sauk tale concerning another Algonquian trickster, Wisaka, who is often identified with Manabozo (Skinner 1923: 38–40). The motif of the introduction of death into the world is constant in the myths of taboo-transgressing heroes. That motif is self-explanatory because the magical power with which they are invested is that of dangerous blood, which cannot be dissociated from death. The origin of tricksters' power residing precisely in the mortal danger constituted by blood, tricksters can never be granted immortality—that is the limit of their beneficent power. Thus we may understand the significance of a frequent tale in Amerindian trickster cycles: several men come to ask the hero to confer upon them the power to conquer women, luck in hunting, luck in games of chance, or the ability to cure the sick. Their desires are satisfied, for these are gifts dispensed by the magical power of blood, but the individual who asks for immortality is rejected brutally and transformed into stone.[7]

Manabozo, in Menomini myth, is initiated by Manitous who give him medicines to cure humans and who instruct him in the performance of the Midewiwin ceremony. All through the great tribal ceremony that bears this name, the narrators sing the praises of Manabozo, founder of all the aspects of the ritual.

The medicine used in the course of the Midewiwin is symbolically associated with blood, although in his transactions with the Manitous the hero speaks only of herbs and roots. The myth states that Manabozo slew with an arrow the bear Owasse, a supernatural animal, and that the blood of the latter flowed onto the side of the mountain and stained it so that it is still visible today. "Thence," adds the text, "we get some of the medicine used in the Mitawak [the Midewiwin]" (Hoffman 1892–93: 89).[8] But it was in a tale from the same tribe, as we saw earlier, that the blood of a bear was transformed into the menses of the grandmother and caused a curse to be pronounced on her, condemning all women to have menses and miscarriages.

The essential rite of the Midewiwin consists of a gesture in which medical bundles are aimed at the candidates who seek to become magicians; their magical force is such that the candidate aimed at falls full length upon the earth and remains inanimate. This power is attributed to a small shell, the "sacred emblem" of the ceremony, that has been given by "The Great Mystery" to Manabozo, and by him to his people (Hoffman 1892–93: 101). This shell is the *Cyprae moneta*, a widespread symbol for the female sex organs.[9] We do not have to search very far for an association with dangerous blood, which is supposed to produce effects of precisely this kind, destroying the powers of those against whom its power is used. And the bear Owasse is not far away either—he who was slain by Manabozo and whose blood furnishes the medicine used during the ceremony—for the candidates are said to imitate "the growls of the mysterious bear" as they dance (Hoffman 1892–93: 102).

The analysis of the myth, as of the rite, indicates that the Midewiwin is associated with a violation of the blood taboo: the blood of the bear murdered by the trickster furnishes the medicine used in the ceremony. Manabozo is initiated by the Manitous in the usage of the magical medicines and in the diverse aspects of the ritual. He appears as the inventor of medicine and the founder of group ceremonial life. When he leaves the Indians he says to them: "Each time you erect a metawikomik [medicine lodge] think of me. When you mention my name I will listen and whatever you ask, I will do" (Moulding Brown n.d.: 102).

This role of founder of the principal tribal ceremony is still more explicit in the case of the Sauk. The initiation of Wisaka (homologue of Manabozo) in the Mitawigan rite, accomplished by the Manitous, constitutes the prototype of the ceremony, and the candidate for magical power represents Wisaka in person (Skinner 1923: 38–40).[10]

We do not mean to imply that the mythic character of the Algonquian trickster was born with the ceremony of the Midewiwin or that
it is dependent upon it. When certain rituals become institutionalized
tribal ceremonies, these ceremonies probably form an integral part
of the tradition and of the legends of transgressing magicians, those
manipulators of blood medicines who lived in days past. Thus the
transgressing magicians, although acting individually or at least outside the community, play the role of founders of the group ceremonial
life.[11]

Maui. Maui is the great trickster hero of the South Pacific (Luomala
1949: 4); like Manabozo, he is of *impure birth.* According to the diverse
versions of his myth he was born from a clot of blood that his mother
had wrapped in her bloody loincloth and thrown into the sea (Beckwith
and Beckwith 1951: in Hawaii, 128–29), from a drop of blood that had
fallen onto an ornament belonging to his mother (in New Zealand, 27),
from the umbilical hemorrhage of a pregnant woman (in Mangareva,
157), or from a red loincloth that his mother found on the beach and
used to gird her loins (110–11). According to another account, a violation of the alimentary taboo committed by his mother at the instiga-
tion of the god Tangaroa who had possessed her might have caused the
trickster's birth (in Raratonga, 173). And according to still another version (in Tuamotu), a very sacred taboo was broken when Ataraga raped
Hua-Héga, who gave birth to Maui (Stimson 1934: 92, n. 10).

Abandoned by his own kind, Maui is raised by gods who teach him
magical secrets, but he soon defies them, for his power is superior to
theirs. In the course of a series of audacious adventures he pulls up the
Earth, raises the Sky, and catches the Sun in a trap. He succeeds in this
last undertaking only by using a rope made from his sister's hair, or,
according to another version, from the pubic hairs of a female relative
(145, 155). He braves formidable beings and steals fire for humankind.

His taboo breakings are numerous. When he comes back to his family,
he lies with his mother, arousing the jealousy of his brothers (39–40). A
Tahitian account contains an allusion to incest with his sister, who,
when Maui lassoed the Sun, raised her skirt to show him her sexual
parts. One of Maui's children, Fakavelikele, commits incest with his
sister and consequently is banished; he becomes the deity of Futuna
Island, and when his inspiration leads a prince to have great success in
war, he takes the place of his father (107).

The magical murder of blood relatives, often linked with incest, is manifested in Maui's deeds. The sacred Hawaiian chant, the Kumulipo, mentions his combat against his maternal uncles, whom he slaughtered, and the blood that flowed from his forehead on that occasion (Beckwith and Beckwith 1951: 135; see also Beckwith and Beckwith 1940: 227–29, and Luomala 1949: 112–13).

It would hardly be anticipated that in a society with such powerful and rigid religious frameworks as those of Polynesia we would find Maui, rebellious by definition, accorded the center-stage role that the Algonquian tribes attribute to their trickster. Nevertheless Maui possesses an exceptional share of mana and the capacity to make use of it in his undertakings aimed at altering the existing order. For the Maori, Maui is among those who "established mana in the world." He is located with other mythical beings at the center of the inextinguishable sacred mana-fire that circles the Earth and determines the climate (Beattie 1921: 16). Maui signifies "witchcraft" as if to recall the way he acquired the powers that enable him to destroy human lives (Best 1924: I.143).[12] A song called "the chant of Maui, the chant of abundance" is related to sweet potato cultivation: in order to obtain the desired results, the words by which Maui assures himself success in the past ought to be chanted in the present (115).

By lengthening the days, raising up the sky, and giving light to humans, Maui modified living conditions. They could not budge because they had webbed, jointless limbs, so the hero extricated them from their impeding membranes and created connecting joints. He gave them fire to cook their food; he invented harpoons, spears, and fishtraps; he perfected fishhooks and made nets to gather shells (29, 30, 35). Exalting his services, the Maori call him Maui Atamai, Maui the Wise or the Good (29).

Luomala notes that Maui has the physiognomy of the civilizing hero, but in spite of efforts of some storytellers to transform him into a solemn benefactor, he preserves his trickster character. He is the one who challenges the established order, and the changes he introduces "have the look of tricks played upon the authorities" (28). He is represented as the adolescent hero who, trampling down all prohibitions, attacks old and powerful deities in order to snatch from them certain spiritual and material goods, in order to confuse them, to destroy them (30). He is beaten only by his grandmother Hinnui-te-po, the goddess of death, when he perishes in an attempt to pit himself against her. After all, the text says, Maui was not a god and could not upset the order of life and death (35). We find here the same limitation on the power of the trickster that we found in the Algonquian stories.

Luomala grasps very well the "antisocial" character of Maui in representing the human race in its conflict between its conventions and its ambitions: "to his human neighbors, his chronically aggressive conduct was antisocial" (28, 29, 34). Furthermore, "for the Polynesians Maui is the divine scapegoat. Thanks to him, they escape the weight of their rigid taboos. . . . They punish him for the crimes they themselves committed in inventing and recounting myths referring to a god who is not a god but who dares to defy the gods and ancient, atrophied conventions" (28–29). In other words Maui takes upon himself the culpability of the group for breaking taboos for the sake of humankind, and he is punished subsequently for defiantly committing transgressions that corresponded to the secret desires of the community.

Legba. "This arch-individualist," write Herskovits and Herskovits about the Dahomean trickster Legba, "can be considered the personification of the being who delights in creating trouble ('a lover of mischief'), ignores inhibitions, recognizes no taboos, and dares to attack and denounce injustice even when it is the work of the Creator. He is moral only when it agrees with his caprices to be so. . . . He has a partiality for humankind, in opposition to the *voduns*" (Herskovits and Herskovits 1958: 36).[13]

Legba is manifestly a taboo breaker: he sleeps with his mother-in-law (41, 145), he copulates with the corpses of three women he has slain (144), and he commits incest with his sister Gbadu and with her daughter Minona (44). He dallies with Gbadu in front of their mother Mawu, and he justifies himself by asserting that Mawu is responsible for his misconduct, for in order to punish him for his incest she has endowed him with an insatiable sexual appetite (44, 175–76). He seizes all the women who pass within his reach. He deflowers a chief's daughter who had remained a virgin because Legba had amused himself by rendering impotent her husband and all the men of his entourage when he switched certain medicines he was supposed to administer. When Legba takes charge of the job his immediate success is recounted in terms of symbolic exaggeration: "There was blood all over the house" (42, 146).[14]

A phallic dance is associated ritually with this event; it is called "the dance of Legba" in the same way that "the drums of Legba" are linked with the sexual act (39, 147). In one account Legba appears as the chief of all the gods because he has succeeded where all his brothers have failed: in a contest Mawu instituted to decide who would be chief, Legba alone was able to dance and to play four instruments simultaneously (139–41). Legba first conceived of and made magical charms; he taught a man, Awe, how to prepare them (ibid). Their magic is both benignant and malignant "because the magical arts have been given also to those who do evil, to sorcerers. . . . Awe gave some of the magical charms to pregnant women in order to prevent them from giving birth. He did harm to little children, but his reputation grew to the point that kings came to consult with him. So magic was spread abroad and both benignant and malignant medicines were given to humanity" (38, 141).

Awe (who is in some ways Legba's double) ascends to the sky in order to test himself against Mawu in knowledge and magical talent. He is forced to return to earth, when pursued by Death, whom Mawu has sent after him. Death attacks, and it is only when Mawu threatens to take away fire that Death gives up the combat "so that humans can cook their foods" (39). Once more we find a relationship between the trickster's deeds and the appearance of mortality.

The origin of divination, a very important aspect of the worship of Fa, is attributed to Legba during a visit to the temple of Fa. Legba had committed double incest with his sister and with his niece (44), and he obtains the "writing of Fa" wherein the fate of each human is recorded. For this reason Legba must be venerated, for "if he wishes, he can change things" (177).

Eshu-Elegba is the homologue of the Dahomean Legba among the Yoruba. Like Legba he is an instigator of trouble. He delights in encouraging humans to offend the gods and also in helping the gods obtain retributive vengeance. He sows discord among humans and plays bad tricks on them. Myths underline his disobedience: Eshu refused to follow the commandments of Olorun, god of the sky and supreme being. He persuaded the Moon and the Sun to switch their abodes, thus upsetting the order of things. "He is the incarnation of defiance, willfulness, irreverence. . . . His lack of respect for authority and his irascible character make him an asocial creature" (Wescott 1962: 62, 340). He has a marked phallic character: his hairdo and his club are phalloform, and the refrain of his ritual chant refers to the long phallus he flings as a bridge over the river—it breaks and causes wayfarers to fall into the water (Wescott 348 emphasizes that the phallus is not considered the symbol of generative power).

However Eshu is not only a mean god. The Yoruba say that even if he has committed many misdeeds, caused wars, displaced the Moon and the Sun, and caused the gods to fight among themselves, he has nevertheless brought them their most valuable possessions: the oracle of Ifa and the Sun. Without him no field would produce. And they add that without Edchou [Eshu] the other gods would be incapable of carrying out anything whatsoever. They recognize in him "a particular kind of superiority" (141; Frobenius 1949: 238–42).

Hence the trickster Eshu-Elegba appears as the founder of divination,[15] the principal aspect of Yoruba cult. One essential trait is missing from the picture: the role of medicine giver. Nonetheless what is not clear to us from the narratives (at least those we know about) is indicated in Yoruban sculptures wherein Eshu is represented with small calabashes placed in his hair or exactly above his forehead. The calabashes represent the calabashes used to hold medicines and indicate magical power (Wescott 1962: 346). Sometimes the trickster holds a calabash and a spoon, symbols of his cult. Another symbol appearing on sculptures is a broken calabash, the fragments of which are carried in a bag held in his hand. The significance of this symbol is clear if one knows that the Yoruba maintain a cult association whose members violently oppose Eshu, whom they consider exceedingly bad and contemptible, "an entirely negative force." One of the principal symbols of that cult is a whole calabash (344–46). The broken calabash then would be the symbol of medicine obtained in violation of taboo, consequently asocial and bad. In this case, also, we have established a relationship between the trickster and magical medicine.

III

It is evident that each of these myths from three different continents should be examined in itself and in relation to its respective society, remembering that meaning can be inflected differently according to each local social situation. In the framework of this chapter we can treat only the most salient traits of each cycle. Hence we need not attempt a full analysis of the myths of Manabozo, Maui, and Legba, but only seek to discern what they have in common.

Whether he be Amerindian, Oceanic, or African, the trickster hero commits such flagrant and scandalous violations of taboo that he seems to be constrained by indefeasible necessity. He incarnates lack of discipline, disobedience, and rebellion, while defying simultaneously the rules of the society and those of the Superior Beings. Maui's transgressive character emerges in the rebellion that leads him audaciously to attack the gods, while Legba defies them by his disobedience and his desire to humble them (Herskovits and Herskovits 1958: 149–50). Manabozo does not play the role of rebel against the gods because Algonquian society does not possess a divine pantheon to be defied. He wages a vague war with the Manitous and the Subterranean Beings, and after the obscure vicissitudes of his struggle he is initiated into the Midewiwin and becomes its founder among humans (Michelson 1911: 72).

Manabozo and Legba are directly related to the magic of their own societies, Manabozo because he was initiated, distributed medicines, and founded the tribal ceremony, Legba because he fashioned the first magical charms, initiated malignant and benignant magic, and established the oracular cult of Fa. In a society with highly developed religious institutions such as Polynesia, Maui cannot appear as the founder of an important cult, but his relationships to magic and witchcraft cannot be questioned. Like Manabozo,[16] Maui is a civilizing hero. Like Legba, Maui befriends humans: he takes their side against the gods, gives them the magical charms that cure the sick, protects those who desire protection in war, and dispenses wealth (Herskovits and Herskovits 1933: 60).

These three trickster heroes are strongly marked by *impurity,* and they are stamped with ambivalence. All three clash with death's ineluctable supremacy. Finally all three are conceived of as beings located between the human realm and that of deities. Manabozo is a tribal hero, having acquired supernatural qualities; Maui is said to be less than a god but more than a human—not a god but "a god who is not a god" (Luomala 1949: 28–29, 35; she also says: "He was torn between the human and the divine. . . . He wanted . . . to destroy the line of demarcation between spirits and human beings" [32–33]). Legba as well as Eshu is classed with the gods, but his role as mediator between the two realms is underlined persistently (Herskovits and Herskovits 1933: 55).[17]

The theory that sees in the trickster the mythic projection of the magician/taboo-violator allows us—in unraveling the contrasts and contradictions between the aspects of the practical joker-buffoon and those of the civilizing hero—to go beyond the controversy concerning this character's unity or duality.[18] The trickster is well named, for he knows the trick, the essential magical *knack* that enables him "to play tricks," to enjoy laughter himself, as well as to instigate laughter at the expense of others. It is completely comprehensible that he who knows the secrets of magical efficacy also gives humankind its most ingenious tools and its most useful information. He may well be the giver of magical medicine and the founder of the ritual activity that ensures the well-being of the group. From him come all other human benefits; and finally he who can change the state of things by exercizing his magical power can modify existing conditions and transform nature as well. We can see that in the end he who possesses such powers may sometimes be regarded—even if hesitantly and after confronting in full those contrasts derived from that being whose nature is the same as his own, who indeed often appears as his double—in the functions of demiurge and creator.

The asocial character of the taboo violation explains how the trickster, represented as the friend of humans, he who struggles with gods in order to ameliorate the human lot, may also be represented as an asocial being, he who ends up being banished from the community. Because he takes upon himself the gravest of social faults—breaking the rules upon which the social order depends—the trickster incarnates embryonically the expiatory being who will take upon himself the sins of humanity and set humans free, by virtue of the familiar process of redemption. The seemingly poorly motivated sentiments of esteem, gratitude, affection, and veneration borne toward the trickster are thus explained in the same way as the physical misfortunes, the insults, and the ridicule that he undergoes and by which he begins to make atonement.

The contradiction between the trickster's quality of "sacred" being and the profanations and sacrileges he commits disappears when we start from the principle that the "sacred" (at least as it is used in ethnology to represent the dangerous, the efficacious, and the ambivalent power with which the hero is invested) is precisely the result of taboo violation, hence the result of profanation and sacrilege, the forms in which the violation is made explicit in myth. It is truly and uniquely because he accomplishes assorted profanations and sacrileges that the trickster is a sacred being. This quality cannot be called into question by his immoral conduct, his blundering about, or his grossness, for sacredness has nothing to do with virtue, intelligence, or dignity: it derives from his violations, which make him the possessor of magical power—that which is identified with "the sacred." And the ambivalence of this power makes clear the ambivalence with which the hero is invested and which comes to be joined to the numerous other contradictions of which he is the focus.

Invested with the power given by the magical violation of prohibitions, the trickster transcends the human condition, without, for all that, attaining to the divine, because of the limitation inherent in his power, namely the denial of immortality. This condition of being more than human and less than divine, of being intermediate between heaven and earth, makes the trickster a mediator—an intercessor like Manabozo, or a messenger like Legba.[19]

Our thesis also clarifies the contrast between the cunning of the hero and his foolishness, between his wisdom and the incoherence of his behavior. The cunning of "the player of tricks" is self-evident, for what "trick" is more cunning than taboo violation, that supreme expedient of magic? But we know that sooner or later the violator must pay the price of his violations, for the magical media that he develops must turn against him in the end. Therefore he must be depicted as falling into his own traps, the victim of his own ruses, and that can be expressed narratively only as being a result of silly and awkward comportment.

On the other hand the violator is supposed to infringe systematically upon customs and rules, doing the opposite of what others do. Therefore he appears as a being who lacks common sense, acting inconsistently and absurdly (the inconsistency is noted by Kerényi 1955: 150). "They are quite right to call me the trickster, the fool!" exclaims Wakdjunkaga, thus coupling two seemingly incongruent terms. A flabbergasting foolishness is attributed to a being upon whom, after all, violation of taboo ought to bestow cunning, intelligence, and knowledge.

Since immoderation is the lot of the being who knows neither laws nor checks nor limits, certain qualities are attributed to the violator: unbridled sexuality, a pronounced phallic character, and an insatiable greediness and hunger. The diverse forms of *impurity*—blood, menstruations, childbirths, excrements, corpses, organs of sexuality and excretion—are the favored domain of the one who is not constrained by taboo. All that which is *impure* is his.[20] Hence we should not be astonished when his behavior is dirty, obscene, and gross.

On the other hand, the trickster is sometimes represented as the unlucky violator whose violation does not succeed, as in the case of Wakdjunkaga, the Winnebago trickster, or of Ture, the Azande trickster. In this case narratives exaggerate the inferior traits of his character, multiply his shameful adventures, and add presumptuousness to the other ridiculous traits.[21]

Finally, in order to stress the significance of the story, mythicizing thought multiplies the taboo violations committed by the hero (we have an excellent example in the first episodes of the Winnebago myth), and it tends likewise to underline its contradictory character, gratuitously increasing the number of opposing traits so that each quality attributed to the hero seems to cause its opposite to appear. Such contradiction, and not the human mind itself as the "structuralists" would have it, would necessarily be expressed by these oppositions. That obscure desire to safeguard that which runs the risk of being lost seems to be a desire to retain the secret meaning of the myth as it accentuates its unique and contradictory character.

This interpretation of the trickster as a mythic projection of the magical violator of taboos has shown that the diverse elements of the mythological *pattern*—*impure* birth, disobedience, systematic violations, audacious undertakings, ridiculous adventures, magical power, ambivalence, the development of ritual medicine, aspects of the player of tricks, founder of the ceremonial life, and civilizing hero—are not heterogeneous traits assembled randomly, but traits that tend to define the nature and function of an organically structured character, the expression of a fixed social reality. Because this social reality is profoundly contradictory—it could even be broadened into a fundamental contradiction between the individual and the society—the contradictory aspects of the character are not only explicable but also necessary.

If our proposed solution to the problem of the trickster is correct, then the interpretation of the "Divine Rascal" that Radin obtained by relying upon the cycle of Wakdjunkaga must be considered erroneous. Radin sees in this whole array of narratives the description of a progressive process of hominization and the coming to consciousness of physicality, starting from a primitive level of being, still undifferentiated and plunged in unconsciousness (Radin 1955).[22] Far from being derived from the depths of antiquity, the trickster can be situated only at a relatively advanced moment of human history, for he is presented as an individual hero, in glaring contrast to his community and acting in opposition to it.[23] If it is true that the myth of the trickster is truly the first myth bringing onto the stage a characterized individual hero, it is precisely this individuation that distances him from a presumed undifferentiated level. The ambivalence and the contradictions that impregnate the accounts of the trickster do not as Radin believed derive from an incapacity to differentiate the true from the false, the good from the evil, the benignant from the malevolent—but from a situation generative of ambivalence and contradictions that has shaped itself in the society, and of which the myth of the trickster is the expression.

SIX

THE SHAMAN AND
THE TRICKSTER

Mac Linscott Ricketts

It is the thesis of this chapter that the shaman and the trickster in North American Indian culture represent two diametrically opposite poles of spirituality. The shaman, the living religious expert, society's first "professional" (combining modern roles of doctor, priest, psychologist, medium, and perhaps philosopher and theologian—as well as actor), represents the religious experience of humility and awe before Spirit; the shaman represents Rudolph Otto's encounter of the *mysterium tremendum et fascinans* (1950), which is widely considered to refer to the religious experience par excellence. But I believe that the trickster, the myth figure most popular in the mythologies of the great majority of Native American tribes, embodies another experience of Reality: one in which humans feel themselves to be self-sufficient beings for whom the supernatural spirits are powers not to be worshiped, but ignored, to be overcome, or in the last analysis mocked.

The trickster is also a *religious* figure, inasmuch as he belongs to the sacred time of origins and inasmuch as he provides a model by which humankind is enabled to transcend existence and conquer for itself a unique place in the Cosmos. The trickster, then, is the symbol of the self-transcending mind of humankind and of the human quest for knowledge and the power that knowledge brings. Unlike the shaman, the priest, and the devotee of supernaturalistic religion, the trickster looks to no "power" outside himself, but sets out to subdue the world by his wits and his wit. In other words, as I see him, the trickster is a symbolic embodiment of the attitude today represented by the humanist.

I was led to this conclusion, that the trickster of the Native North Americans discloses a "primitive humanism," by my doctoral studies nearly three decades ago, and subsequent study and critiques have not altered my hypothesis (see Ricketts 1964, 1966). I remain convinced that the North American Indian trickster, if indeed not all tricksters, stands in opposition to the shaman and supernaturalism; that he represents a different apprehension of humankind, the Cosmos, and one's place in the Cosmos; and that he symbolizes an alternative "way of being religious."

The purpose of this chapter is to present some of the more striking pieces of evidence that confirm, in my opinion, the radically opposite natures of the shaman and the trickster. For while it is true that the Indians in general may not have been aware of the logical opposition of the two figures, I think there is ample evidence to show that in the minds of some individuals the conflict was consciously perceived.[1] But whether conscious or not, the two figures afforded the Indian Americans two very different religious options that served the needs of different temperaments and different times.

SHAMANISM

I understand shamanism to be a worldview based on an experience that stands at the opposite pole from that symbolized by the trickster. The shaman has experienced another realm lying parallel to our own, a spiritual realm, into which he himself has been inducted. I concur with Adolf Jensen that it is, very probably, to the shaman's ecstasy that we should look for the origin of the idea that man is a duality of body and spirit (Jensen 1963: 228–29, 284–85).

In his initiation into the spirit world the shaman has realized that for which humans, or *some* of them at least, have longed ever since humans became aware of their limitations *as limitations:* the transcending of the human condition and the attainment of the condition of "spirit." As Mircea Eliade interprets it, the shaman has found the absolute freedom sought by mortals: "The desire for absolute freedom, that is, the desire to break the bonds that keep him tied to earth and to free himself from his limitations, is one of man's essential nostalgias. . . . In the archaic religions, the shaman and the medicine man . . . constitute an exemplary model for the rest of the community precisely because they have *realized* transcendence and freedom, and have, by that fact, become like spirits and Supernatural Beings" (Eliade 1958: 101; the description of shamanism that follows relies principally upon Eliade 1964, especially chapters 2, 3, and 4).

Wherever shamanism is found—in Siberia, Australia, and North and South America, indeed almost everywhere except Africa—it presents a surprisingly uniform structure. The shaman is one who has undergone a personal vocational initiation, individually and without human mediation, into the realm of the supernatural. Later, he or she may be instructed by other shamans in the techniques of the trade and may be inducted into a shamans' society, but the essential thing is the "spiritual experience." Typically, this experience comes unsought: indeed, many shamans say they resisted the initial overtures made by the spirits. But the call to become a shaman cannot be set aside.

One who is becoming a shaman designate often experiences weird dreams or waking visions and hears voices or strange sounds. The elect one is driven by these manifestations of the spirits (as he or she regards them) to go off somewhere alone. Isolated in the wilderness, the candidate falls into a trance in which he or she imagines being taken to the house of the spirits (or gods or ancestors), which may be located in the sky, the underworld, beneath a deep body of water, in a remote part of the forest, or somewhere else "far away." Sometimes the experience occurs in conjunction with a grave illness, when the man or woman has fallen into a coma.

The spirits who have abducted the candidate now proceed to subject him or her to an ordeal: often he or she is killed, perhaps by being torn or chopped to pieces. The flesh may, subsequently, be scraped from the bones and boiled in a cauldron. *The candidate sees this happening to himself or herself:* spirit and body have become separate. After this "death" the body is restored and the initiate is returned to life and wholeness again. Sometimes an additional substance is added to the resurrected shaman's body: a quartz crystal or other such magic object; this object is a gift of the spirits as a token of the greater powers he or she will henceforth possess.

The supernaturals teach their protégé the arts of healing and other skills and secrets, and they promise to come to his or her aid whenever called upon thereafter. The initiate learns from the spirits the words of one or more songs, and if the helpers are animal spirits (as they often are, especially in North America) he or she learns to imitate their cries and perform a dance that mimics their behavior. Special taboos often are given also.

Following the initial experience, the neophyte shaman returns to the land of the living and demonstrates publicly some of the supernatural powers which he or she has gained. He or she may undergo further instruction from older shamans, but it is the journey to the beyond that has admitted the candidate to the ranks of the professionals. As a practicing shaman, the man or woman will function as a mediator between ordinary people and the spirits. By the use of music (often a drum and rattle are employed as accompaniments of the magic songs), the shaman is able to summon divine helpers and enter into trance. In this state he or she goes again to the region of the supernaturals and learns the cause of the trouble (illness, bad weather, etc.) for which his or her services were engaged. The shaman may also become a medium for the spirits, and with the many voices of a ventriloquist, he or she may carry out a seance.

Sometimes the shaman must do combat with the superhuman beings who have caused the illness of the patient. He or she may box the air or writhe upon the ground in great agony during the process, or he or she may be sequestered inside a small tent so that others can only hear his or her cries and see the shaking of the tent while the violent struggle is going on. More typically in North America, however, the curing is effected by less violent techniques, once the diagnosis has been made. Sucking, blowing, and massaging are standard shamanistic therapies among most North American Indian tribes. The sucking shaman, for example, seems to remove a small object from the patient, something the "doctor" had hidden inside his or her mouth before the session began.

Besides acting as doctors in times of illness, shamans undertake journeys into the land of the spirits to discover the cause of bad weather, poor hunting, or the like, and to learn what people must do to set things right with the spirits who have been offended and are responsible for the bad conditions.

The shaman, then, is one who has experienced illness and death and has known a state of existence apart from the body. The ability to leave the body "in spirit" is the defining characteristic of the shaman, according to Eliade. That is, the shaman is more than a possessed medium, although he or she may be that also. It should be emphasized that the shaman *is not insane.* He has been ill perhaps, in our terms, mentally ill—but *he or she has recovered* from that state (Eliade 1964: 27; for an amazingly similar analysis of schizophrenia, see Laing 1967: chapters 5, 6, and 7). He has been to the sources of the powers that determine life and death, he has returned, and now he is able to go and come again at will. He can do this because he has supernatural friends who have endowed him with superhuman powers and who come to his aid when summoned. The common man knows there is a world of spiritual beings "out there" somewhere, but only the shaman is acquainted with that "spiritual geography" and with the beings who inhabit those regions.

In some respects the worldview of the shaman is like that implicit in the mythology of the trickster, a fact that is not surprising if both belong originally to the world of the hunter, but the two differ sharply in their assessment of the human being's place in the cosmos. Comparison of the two is hazardous because we contend in the one instance with an idea embodied in a myth figure and in the other with an ideology based on a specialized psycho-spiritual experience. Yet in both there is the belief that our world is surrounded by beings and powers that affect human existence. Animals (who are also "people" of sorts) possess powers humans do not have, and there are disease-causing spirits ("cannibals" in Indian mythology), controllers of weather, and many others. For the most part, these spirits are unfriendly to humanity or, if kindly disposed most of the time (as are the owners of game), they may become provoked to anger and turn against humans. Trickster mythology and shamanism seem to have in common such beliefs, which are regularly found among primitive hunters.

But the two figures relate themselves differently to the realm of unseen powers. The shaman has been accepted into that other world, and consequently he looks upon it as a potential source of help as well as harm for man. But by contrast the trickster is an outsider whose attitude toward that world of superhuman powers is a negative one. He has no friends in that other world, and for him it is a realm opposed entirely to the will of human beings. All that humans have gained from the unseen powers beyond—fire, fish, game, fresh water, and so forth—have been obtained, by necessity, through trickery or theft. The reason we have these things today, according to the myths, is because the trickster (that is, humans themselves) wrested them from the owners "in the beginning." What the trickster obtained from the supernaturals was their *goods* only; unlike the shaman he did not also obtain superhuman powers or spiritual friendship. The trickster, apparently, sees no need to have powers other than those with which he is naturally endowed: his wits and his wit. These suffice for him to cope successfully with all the problems he encounters. Likewise, he seems to need no friends: he gets along very well by himself, and that's the way he likes it!

The vision quest or guardian spirit vigil, practiced quite widely in North America and usually involving all the boys of a tribe and sometimes the girls as well, was almost certainly a popular adaptation of the shamanistic initiation experience. The major differences were (1) that the youths deliberately sought the patronage of a spirit, whereas in classical shamanism one waited for the spirit's initiative, and (2) that the powers granted to youths were of varied sorts: ability to succeed and excel in warfare, horsemanship, hunting, love-making, etc.; only occasionally were true shamanistic powers given (healing and so forth). Also, the youths were not "killed" by their spirit friends, but their helpers came to them after they had tortured themselves (usually interpreted as a means of attracting the "pity" of the divine being; see Lowie 1954: 157–61).

But like shamans, the youths returned from the vigils having gained a personal contact with the world of supernaturals and having been given superhuman powers enabling them to do what they believed they could not have done in their own strength. Like shamans, too, they oftentimes received a special song and dance, and even more commonly some tangible token of their encounter with the guardian was given them. In the Plateau region of the American Northwest, the long winter nights were devoted to "spirit dancing" and singing, with those old enough to have received guardian spirit power displaying what they had been taught, just as shamans did to proclaim publicly their new status (cf. Ray 1932: 189–200).

The dancing societies of the Northwest Coast were also popularizations of shamanism. In several of the tribes, the most "powerful" series of these was called by a term meaning "the shamans," although true shamans seldom belonged to them. Instead, the wealthy nobility had created a kind of lodge in which degrees of shamanistic spirit possession and frenzy were *simulated*. The Northwest Coast Indians who had these societies carried their imitations of shamanism to great lengths, with stage-managed "abductions" of candidates for initiation, elaborate spirit masks, all sorts of tricks of legerdemain by which initiates were made to seem to handle fire, fly through the air, wound themselves without leaving a mark, etc. (Boas 1895: 331–738).

The Midewiwin of the Central Algonquians was likewise a "club" organized in imitation of shamanism. Initiates were "killed" by having a sacred otter skin pointed at them (a white shell was supposed to penetrate them, like a bullet), and the members then allegedly gained power to cure diseases and to live to a ripe old age (Hoffman 1885–86: 143–300).

Among the Iroquois there were semi-secret masked societies, composed of persons who had been made ill by certain spirits and who, following a dream, had been cured by a member of the masked society associated with that disease-spirit. Periodically thereafter the cured one had to pay for a public performance of the society, in which he also participated (cf. Speck 1949: 56 ff.). The Kuksu Cult of west-central California is still another example of a shamanistic-like society in which the initiation and bestowal of curing powers are not left to the initiative of the spirits, but are "managed" by older members of the society (cf. Loeb 1932).

These examples by no means exhaust the number of ways in which the ideology of shamanism found expression among the Indian tribes of North America, but they should suffice to establish the point that the influence of shamanism was pervasive and dominant. Yet, despite the widespread acceptance of the "spiritualistic" worldview of shamanism, the mythology of the trickster persisted and was very much alive in most regions of North America. Apparently, the myths of the trickster corresponded to some need or perception of reality on the part of these people. Even though (as I believe) the trickster and the shaman represent opposing worldviews, the two are found side by side in nearly every tribe. Evidently, what I see as an inconsistency was not felt to be such by the majority of Indians.

And yet when we examine some of the trickster stories carefully they appear to be perfect parodies of shamanistic experiences and behavior.

In fact, many stories seem to call for such an interpretation. A few tales, additionally, are undeniably intended to ridicule sacred institutions.

SHAMANISM PARODIED

Almost universally the trickster is said to have attempted to fly, either with a flock of birds or on the back of a single bird, but always with disastrous consequences. The ability to fly is, of course, one of the gifts shamans are given. They fly through the air in trances, and they climb poles or trees in symbolic ascent to heavenly regions. The report of Gladys Nomland concerning shamanism among the Bear River Athabascan tribe of the north-coastal region of California illustrates the importance of flying in the shamanistic experience: "Dreams of flying were a positive indication that the person was being tested by the spirits to see if he should become a shaman; they were considered an exceptionally good sign that such a person had supernatural power" (Nomland 1938–40: 94).

The trickster's flight is depicted as a parody of the shaman's spiritual journey. There are two principal types of this story and three major kinds of endings or sequels. Several tribes, including the Shoshonis and some of the Athabascans of Alaska, say that the trickster envied the geese their ability to fly, and he begged them to take him aloft with them. Reluctantly, they gave him some of their feathers and taught him to accompany them in their aerial adventures. They charged him strictly, however, not to be noisy (or not to fly in circles, etc.). The trickster, of course, could not keep the rules of the game, and so the birds took back their feathers and he fell to the ground in a heap.

In the other major type of flight story, Trickster implores Buzzard to give him a ride on his back. At length Buzzard yields to his pleading; but the trickster proves to be a bothersome back-seat driver, and after a short excursion Buzzard dumps him, high in the air. In some accounts, the trickster sings as he falls, just as a shaman might sing when going in trance to the spirit world.

The meaning of these stories seems to be the same: humans were not made to fly, and although birds may give humans their power (bird spirits frequently were shamans' helpers), humans cannot use such power without making fools of themselves. Trickster gains nothing by his flight (except some short-lived fun), and soon he loses the power because he cannot by his nature keep the taboos or adopt the manner of life of the birds. Trickster, like the human being, is an earth-bound creature, and his wish to fly (and to escape the human condition) is shown to be a frivolous fancy.

Three endings are found as sequels to the flight stories and appear intended to ridicule the shaman. Some of the Algonquians and certain central Californians say that the trickster upon landing turned himself into a rotting animal carcass in order to get revenge on the Buzzard who had dropped him (Buzzard gets his head caught while trying to eat the "carcass"). May we not see this as a parody of the shamanistic dream of being killed and reduced to a skeleton by the supernaturals? In another ending (not always told as a sequel to the trickster's flight), he is dropped into a hollow tree from which he escapes (according to some versions) by throwing himself out, piece by piece, through a tiny hole! Again we think of the dismemberment of the shaman in his initiation. The third major type of sequel or ending to the flight tale has the trickster simply fall to the ground and shatter into pieces, after which he has to be revived from the dead. This variant also seems designed to caricature the shaman's initiatory experience.

The ubiquitous motif of the "blundering host," the bizarre tale of juggling the eyeballs, and the silly story of the wasted shots of "skunk gas" are all probably intended to teach the same lesson as the myth of the trickster's flight: that humans ought not aspire to acquire the powers of other beings. Now this lesson is a direct assault on a fundamental tenet of shamanism. The shaman is the one who obtains powers from superhuman sources, mainly conceived of as animals. The trickster, in trying to get his food in the manner of the Kingfisher, for instance (tying an awl to his nose and diving into the water after a fish), or in attempting to juggle his eyes like the birds or the rabbit, or in acquiring the ridiculous "power" of the skunk, is reaching for superhuman abilities. He is, in fact, attempting to transcend the human condition and live in a mode different from that which is proper to humans. Blundering efforts to do what the animals do may be viewed as mockery of shamans and all others who think they can get higher powers from the animal spirits. Even the costumes, masks, and dancing exhibitions are ridiculed: why should a human want to imitate the form and comportment of an animal? See how silly the trickster is when he tries to fit a "beak" to his face or tries to fly with the geese or goes around expelling gas like a skunk!

Other instances of the same theme, apparently, are the following. In California and the Southwest, Coyote frequently wants to do what others are doing, being envious of their abilities which he lacks. When he asks how they do whatever it is they do, they give him false counsel and he comes to grief. On the Plains, Trickster envies the ability of the bison to live by eating only grass, and he arranges to be changed into a buffalo. Soon he discovers that such a life was never intended for him (Dorsey 1890: 68–69). Wisaka of the Algonquians travels with the wolves for a while and they teach him a magic way to make fire. Before long he has broken the taboos and can no longer work the trick (Skinner and Satterlee 1913–15: 253–55).

Mink's foolish marriages with "women" totally unsuited to be his wives (such as the daughters of Spirit, of Frog Woman, of Stone, and of Cloud) seem to be parodies of a type of shamanistic tale widely told in that region in the Pacific Northwest, tales in which a person gains supernatural powers through marriage to a supernatural (cf. Boas 1905: 124 ff.).

As a reward for service rendered to Thunder Man (a supernatural), the Winnebago Hare obtains the power to get almost anything he wants simply by wishing for it, provided that he does not use the power more than four times a day. He loses the power because he calls too many times for a beautiful girl to sleep with, never being content with the one who appears (Radin 1955: 21).

Several local examples of more obvious satires on shamanism may be noted. In an Okanagon version of the widespread tale of Coyote's pretended death in order to return in disguise and rape his daughter, he declares that he has been given prophetic powers like a shaman, and he predicts his own death and the subsequent coming of a handsome suitor (Teit 1927: 72). A Coeur d'Alene narrator said that once after Coyote had deceived his wife she put a ringing in his ears by an act of witchcraft to get revenge, but Coyote was not in the least upset. On the contrary, he was delighted at having a new trick to display at spirit dances (Reichard 1947: 86–90).

It was Mink who pretended to die (in order to obtain some food) and then returned, claiming to have risen with supernatural powers (Boas

1905: 140). I have found two episodes in tales of the Great Basin Shoshoni in which Coyote says ironically, "I wonder if this means I'm going to become a shaman?" In one case Coyote sees lightning flashing and in the other he hears singing. The stories were collected from different tribes by different anthropologists (Ricketts 1964: 80). The Winnebago Hare seems to be mocking a trick of shamans who practice ventriloquism in order to make a room seem to be full of spirits, when he talks in many voices, pretending to have guests for dinner, in order to deceive his grandmother whom he has sent out of the house to avoid having to share the meal with her (Radin 1955: 80).

Evidently, shamanistic healing sessions are being ridiculed in the commonly told sequel to the popular tale of Coyote's rape of the girl bathing on the other side of the river (the "hose-penis" motif). Coyote returns to the village disguised as a venerable shaman and, on pretense of conducting a private and secret ritual (not an unusual shamanistic procedure), rapes the girl a second time in her own bed. His member, which had been severed in the river escapade, is reattached in the process. The same satire is intended, I believe, in the Chinook story of Skunk's pretended illness, in which he and Coyote contrive to kill a number of their neighbors for food by inviting them into Skunk's tent for a curative spirit-singing (Skunk gasses them to death; Ricketts 1964: 383).

At least two tribes, widely separated, tell how the trickster got his head stuck in an old elk skull (while watching some insects performing a sacred dance in one version!) and then passed himself off as a holy man in a village of awed Indians. In the Lipan Apache account, Coyote says, "I am holy, I have supernatural power, you must give me something!" In the Winnebago tale, Wakdjunkaga tells a woman that he is one of the water spirits, and asks her friends to come, bringing him gifts. He says if they will split his head open with an ax they will find materials there for making medicines (Radin 1955: 33–35). The Apache story ends when a smart-aleck boy cracks open the skull after everyone else has worshiped the trickster, and Coyote says, "That's what you should have done long ago!" (Opler 1940: 69–70).

Some of the Salish tribes of coastal Washington tell how Coyote called in his neighbors to sing spirit songs for him (spirit song singing is the chief communal religious ritual in this region). From time to time during the proceedings Coyote excused himself from the house, complaining of diarrhea. On each excursion he robbed one of his neighbor's houses of food (Adamson 1934: 306, 367).

Priestly customs and sacred ceremonies are mocked in still other tales of tricksters. The Tewa (Pueblo) like to tell how Coyote and Bear played a game of "dress up and scare," to test each other's nerve. Coyote steeled himself to show no fright when Bear came rushing at him in a rage, but when Coyote made his appearance garbed as the god Masuwa (Death), he frightened Bear into the next county (Parsons 1926: 280).

In a Pawnee version of the hoodwinked dancers tale, Coyote pretends to be a priest about to die and thus tries to induce a fat turkey to come near him so he can teach him a "sacred dance," which must be performed with eyes closed (Dorsey 1906: 456–57). In the same collection of traditions is a delightful version of the famous story of Trickster's pretended death in order to marry his daughter. When giving her instructions for his burial he says with heavy irony, "Be sure to bury me with my head sticking out of the ground, because you know that I was always religious and looked to Tirawa [the supreme God] for help" (Dorsey 1906: 430–32).

The holy institution of the guardian spirit quest is blasphemed in a tale collected from the Upper Cowlitz, a tribe of Washington state, by Melville Jacobs (1934: 212). A girl was seeking a guardian spirit and asked Coyote's help. He instructed her to go into the woods and sit on a "red thing," which she would find sticking out of the leaves on the ground in a certain place. The "thing" was Coyote's penis, not a mushroom as she supposed. "Thus she received her guardian spirit power," the narrator told Jacobs.

Perhaps the most amusing of all the satires on shamanism is found in the "helpers" Coyote has in the mythologies of many Western tribes. The exact nature of these advisers varies, but most commonly they are two chunks of excrement which Coyote brings forth when he is perplexed as to what to do. Some narrators appear to have lost an understanding of the proper, humorous meaning of the "excrement advisers," and instead regard them as true supernatural assistants. In most texts, however, it is made plain that they are caricatures of the "pains" or supernatural objects which shamans in this region call forth from their bodies as evidence of spiritual endowment. Like the shamans, Coyote has his advisers too. His talking turds do, in fact, give him good advice, but

Coyote will never admit they have said anything he had not thought of already (cf. Boas 1894: 106 ff.).

The Shoshonean myth pair, Wolf and Coyote, are, I believe, representative of the shaman and the nonspiritualistic man, respectively. Although Wolf is the wiser of the two, it is Coyote who is the hero. When Wolf has been killed by apparently supernatural enemies (an episode in a lengthy, mysterious saga peculiar to these tribes), Coyote manages to retrieve Wolf's scalp and "clothing," by means of which Wolf is restored to life. Coyote achieves this feat not by spiritual knowledge or with supernatural help, but by his own cunning and daring (Lowie 1924: 5, 92–101, 161–64). This achievement of Coyote is even more remarkable in view of the fact that there are many other tales told by these people in which Wolf, Coyote's "elder brother," has to revive Coyote when he has been killed on one of his escapades, or help him when he has lost his eyes by juggling them, etc., because Wolf possesses shamanistic power to do such things.

TRICKSTER VERSUS THE SHAMANISTIC YOUTHFUL HERO

The opposition between the shaman and the trickster and between their respective views of life is expressed in some Indian mythologies in stories of rivalry between the trickster and a "youthful hero" type, who seems to embody shamanistic ideals of manhood.

In the Southeast among the Muskogean peoples there is a widely told cycle of stories about Blood-clot Boy, a hero of a kind also well known on the Great Plains. In the Southeast he sometimes is shown in competition with Rabbit, the trickster, and in such instances Rabbit invariably is humiliated. Blood-clot Boy can do truly remarkable things; but when Rabbit tries to imitate him, he comes to grief. The Boy splits an old woman in half and makes two young ones, but when Rabbit attempts the feat on his "old woman," he succeeds only in making himself a widower. Blood-clot Boy swims in the river and stuns the fish by his presence, making them easy to catch, but Rabbit cannot duplicate the feat, presumably because he lacks supernatural power. Rabbit sends Blood-clot Boy diving deep in the water, and while he is gone the trickster steals the youth's clothes and tries to impersonate him in the

village where he is a hero. Rabbit's attempted deception is soon discovered, and he is roundly punished (Ricketts 1964: chapter 19).

In Caddoan mythology, when the young man called Medicine
Screech Owl became chief of the people, Coyote "became bad," apparently because of his jealousy for the new youthful chieftain (Dorsey
1905: 7–13). The Apache also tell of Coyote's hostility toward a young
hero, Killer-of-Enemies. When the latter was instructing the people one
day, Coyote ridiculed him. He told the people to continue to observe the
old ways and have a good time. For this insubordination, the young
chief took away Coyote's powers (as a myth-time being) and made him
just a miserable, despised animal, or, in another version, a disease-
causing spirit (Opler 1938b: 78–335).

The Plains and Southern Miwok tribes (California) have a unique
tradition about Coyote and a youthful hero, Falcon, in which the two
are not rivals, but instead function in perfect harmony (Kroeber 1907:
199, 240, etc.). However, there is a Coast Miwok tradition relating that
Coyote sent a flood to punish Falcon. The latter survived the deluge by
becoming a feather, which floated on the water. After the flood, Coyote
remade the earth (out of his mat-raft) and repopulated the land with
people made from feathers or sticks (Loeb 1932: 113). Probably we are to
understand that the Falcon was reborn from the feather into which he
had changed himself and that he became the deity of the Kuksu cult, a
society common to several tribes of that region, which involves a "death
and resurrection" initiation. In this myth we see Coyote in his usual role
as antagonist to the young hero.

In the Puget Sound area Raven and Mink are found in their customary
roles as tricksters, but some of their culturally beneficial deeds have been
transferred to a noble lunar hero, Doukuibel, the Moon. Moon's origin is
semi-divine: he was born to a girl who wished for, and obtained, a Star
for a husband; the marriage took place in heaven. Although the baby
was born on earth, he was abducted soon after birth and taken to
heaven to be reared to become the husband of heavenly females. Un-
aware of his earthly origin, Moon was living happily in the land of the
supernaturals when Bluejay arrived and informed him of his home
below. Moon returned then to earth, transforming all manner of evil
beings along the way. Eventually he became the moon in the sky
(Ballard 1929: 69–72).

The hero Moon has largely displaced the trickster from the mythology of this small region, it seems, to the extent that almost all stories of creative transformations have been ascribed to Moon rather than to a trickster-transformer (as is the case with neighboring tribes). The Moon is a spiritually endowed youth, made a demigod by birth and later by being the spouse of supernatural wives while a resident of heaven. He is the ideal of manhood *by shamanistic standards,* and in all respects he is an admirable character (in contrast to the tricksters). He is never foolish, never lecherous, and he tricks only evil beings who are a threat to humans.

Very seldom does the Moon-Transformer come into direct confrontation with the trickster in the mythology of this region; however, there is one story of this type from the Klallam tribe (northwest Sound) in which the trickster, here Kekaiax (an amalgam of Raven, Mink, and Coyote as they appear in mythologies of nearby tribes) begs to accompany the transformer on his journeys. The transformer has no use for him and evidently does not relish having his company, so he tries to change him, as he has changed other beings, into something else. But each time Kekaiax is changed, he resumes his old form in a few moments, and at last the Moon admits defeat and has to take the trickster along with him (Gunther 1925: 140–47). Here, at least, the old trickster refused to be abolished. But among most of the Coastal Salish tribes and their immediate neighbors, the anthropomorphic lunar transformer is the dominant figure in mythology. It would seem that he holds this position by virtue of having ousted an older, trickster-transformer figure such as is found in all the tribes surrounding this region, as well as over most of North America.

Occasionally, as is the case with the transformers of the Nootka, Quilleute, and Kwakiutl, some trickster elements occur in the characterization of the hero, but these are not prominent. The "pure" transformer is noble: a semi-divine hero who appears at the close of the myth age or at the beginning of the age of men, preparing the way for mankind. He changes monsters into useful or harmless things. He fixes and assigns the names of the topographical features of the region, turns animal-people into real animals, and puts the finishing touches on human beings.

The pure transformer seems to represent an image of humankind different from that represented by the trickster (or trickster-transformer).

He is a cipher of *ideal* humankind: humans-as-we-might-be, rather than humans-as-we-are. Fully anthropomorphic, the hero-transformer is humankind clearly differentiated from the animal kingdom (as tricksters generally are not). Partly divine and strengthened by an intimate relationship with the world of supernaturals, he embodies a vision of humankind as beloved child of the gods. He does not trick and laugh his way through life: for him, living is a serious business. With help from on high, he strides through the world, claiming it for a heroic human race that will follow him. It is also the trickster's task to prepare the world for human beings, of course, so it is not surprising that when the two figures meet, one must give way to the other.

The Chinookan peoples of the lower Columbia River, the Clackamas, Wishram, and others, are not distant from the tribes whose mythology we have just considered. Among the myths of these tribes appears the youthful hero Salmon, concerning whom many adventures are told. Salmon is the son of a father by the same name who was also a youthful hero. Skunk, Coyote, and five wolves conspire to kill the first Salmon, but an "egg" saved from the Salmon's body produces a new infant hero. When he is grown, he sets out to avenge his father's assassination. He kills the old tricksters, Coyote and Skunk, and turns the other myth-people into wandering animals. Then he embarks upon a career of many adventures (Jacobs 1958–59: 42–45; Sapir 1909: 49 ff.).

To me this myth appears to be a shamanistic-hero story. Salmon, who in a sense has undergone a "death and rebirth," is entirely different in type from Coyote and the other myth-people. The old generation of animal-people try to kill Salmon, but he rises, stronger than ever, in the person of his son, to transform them into mere animals. He represents a new era in mythology, the age of the Hero. The age of the Trickster has passed.

The most widely known narrative of this type, however, centered in the Plateau region, apparently, but found as far south as northern California and to the east among the Crow, Kiowa, Oglala, and even some Caddoan-speaking groups, is that strange story of Coyote's sending his son up a tree or cliff on a false errand. When the boy, usually a married youth, ascends, the trickster makes the tree or cliff "grow" higher by his magical power, until the young man is projected into the sky. In this manner the older man rids himself of the younger and is then free to take possession of the youth's wives. The trick backfires, however, because upon reaching the sky the youth is befriended by spiritual beings. When he returns to earth, spiritually endowed, he takes vengeance upon his father for sending him away and stealing his wives (see Ricketts 1964: 327–28, for an account of the myth and for references).

We recognize that this youth is the ideal man from the "religious" or shamanistic point of view. He goes to heaven and obtains spirit power. Still, even though he manages to get revenge on the trickster, in some versions (those told in the Upper Columbia River region) he does not succeed in displacing Coyote from the center of mythology. In the Plateau tribes where this story holds a prominence greater than it does anywhere else, it serves as an introduction to the main cycle of Coyote stories, those which show him to be both a culture hero and trickster. In order to get revenge, the son causes his father to fall into the river, but instead of eliminating Coyote, this fall only launches him on his career of good deeds for mankind. The hero-son drops out of the story completely. Thus, despite the importance of shamanism and the guardian spirit quest in all of these tribes, the old trickster, who acknowledges no spirits and serves no gods, retains a popularity in the mythology greater than that of any other figure, including the more noble young hero, who would seem to embody the shamanistic ideal.

TRICKSTER AND SHAMAN AS OPPOSITES

Joseph Campbell, who has beautifully retold a number of tales of tricksters in his *Masks of God: Primitive Mythology,* has seen in the trickster the mythological counterpart of the shaman (Campbell 1959: 267 ff.; LaBarre 1970 reaches the same conclusions, apparently without being aware of Campbell's work). Inasmuch as this thesis is the exact opposite of my own, it should be interesting to see how he arrives at this conclusion.

Campbell avoids the mistake of Radin who omitted culture hero myths from the cycle of original trickster stories, and he regards the myth of the theft of fire as a key to the understanding of the meaning of the trickster. However, Campbell thinks that the fire-stealing myth is a shamanistic-type story, whereas I am convinced that it is not. It is true that both the shaman and the trickster-thief go into another world, and both engage in combat with spiritual beings. Nevertheless, there is a difference, a very significant one, I believe, between the shaman's journey and that of the fire-bringer: the former goes with the aid and companionship of his tutelary spirit or spirits, while the trickster goes alone or is accompanied by companions who are as unendowed with supernatural powers as he. Moreover, the trickster rarely fights with the beings he encounters on his journeys: most typically he outwits them with a trick.

As an argument in favor of Campbell's thesis, it may be proposed that the trickster can make his journey alone because he is a divinity himself: a *divine shaman,* the archetype of human shamans. But if the trickster is divine, why is he portrayed regularly as lacking in supernatural powers? Why does he overcome his opponents by tricks instead of feats of power? Also, if he is the great Original Shaman, why do shamans not seek his aid today? Why is he not the most important spirit helper of shamans? It is a very rare thing for the trickster-hero to be regarded as a living spirit, or even for his animal namesake to be considered a strong spirit today.

Campbell has been overly impressed by the tricks shamans perform as a part of their "technique," and by the seeming titanism of the shamans in their willingness to set themselves in opposition to spirits. It is true that the shaman is an individualist, a "solitary, accustomed to hold his own against many and therefore [one who has] his little tricks" (Campbell 1959: 249; citing Ostermann 1952: 98) and to this extent is something of a trickster. The differences between the shaman and the trickster are much greater than the similarities, however.

The shaman opposes only *certain* spirits, not the whole supernatural, divine realm. We must remember that the shaman has friends as well as foes in that other world. The trickster has only enemies there. The shaman is not irreligious, but devout: his or her defiance is a function of "faith," not the antithesis of faith. He or she reverences those spirits who have befriended and helped him or her: they are spirits before whom one stands in awe, and the shaman would undertake nothing dangerous without their companionship. The trickster, on the other hand, looks to no higher power for aid (one can scarcely call his excreta "higher powers"), but using his one weapon, his devious brain, he attacks and defeats the supernaturals, none of whom is his friend.

Much of what Campbell says about the Promethean character of the trickster is, in my opinion, correct, and he is right to contrast this attitude with that of the priest. Campbell's error, I believe, is in not recognizing that the shaman, as mediator between the human and the transhuman world, is the forerunner of the priest, not his antithesis. The trickster is the true opposite of the shaman *and* the priest.

Shamanistic stories, which are usually accounts of visits to the other world on the part of mortal men, abound in Indian oral literature, but the differences between these and the myths and tales of the trickster are obvious when the two are set side by side. Shamans, we might speculate, probably prefer this type of story to the old myths that lack "spiritual" content. Unfortunately, our sources do not enlighten us much as to shamans' narrative preferences. However Swanton was told in 1904 by a Tlingit Indian of Wrangell that Raven stories were on the decline in his area because shamans preferred stories about spirits (Swanton 1909: 154). The same may have been true in other places. And yet it seems unlikely that trickster stories would have disappeared entirely from the traditions of American Indians, no matter how dominant the shamanistic opposition might have become. The trickster was too firmly rooted in the affections of the people, and he served too vital a function in the lives and psyches of the people. For while the shaman and his spirits provided them with an opening to another world and the possibility of transcending the weaknesses of the human condition, the trickster enabled them to endure what even the gods cannot cure ultimately, the absurdity of human existence.

SEVEN

THE EXCEPTION WHO PROVES THE RULES: ANANSE THE AKAN TRICKSTER

Christopher Vecsey

Studies of the trickster in world folklore (Babcock-Abrahams 1975; Makarius 1969, translated here) have indicated his role as a threat to the rules of societal and cosmic order. He is a paradoxical figure whose antics mock the seriousness of rules, the sacrality of beliefs, and the establishment of rituals. He is a vagabond, an intruder to proper society, and an unpredictable liar who throws doubt on the concept of truth itself.

As a folklore figure he is both human and divine, a person and an animal, creative and destructive, a success and failure. His tales are sometimes myths, sometimes legends, sometimes connected with ritual, sometimes not. They can be entertainment, education, a form of humorous rebellion. They can evaluate, explain, and reflect upon realities, thereby making those realities clearer and more profound to the people who tell and hear the tales.

By breaking the patterns of a culture the trickster helps define those patterns. By acting irresponsibly he helps define responsibility. He threatens, yet he teaches, too. He throws doubt on realities but helps concentrate attention on realities. He crosses supposedly unbreakable boundaries between culture and nature, life and death, and thereby draws attention to those boundaries. Not only do societies "tolerate" trickster tales, but also they "create and re-create" them (Babcock-

Abrahams 1975: 186) because they serve the vital purpose of questioning and affirming, casting doubt and building faith upon the most important societal concepts.

It is my purpose in this chapter to examine the trickster tales of the Twi-speaking peoples of West Africa, the Ashanti and other Akan. My interest is not in the stories as folklore, the relationships of their motifs to world folklore (see Clarke 1958; Feldmann 1963); rather, my aim is to discover the meanings of the Akan trickster tales to the Akan. I wish to see them in their cultural context. I know that one can find similar episodes of similar tricksters in the other areas of the world. Elsewhere the same episodes may have a human, or hero, or deity as the main actor. The environment may differ and the society's attitude toward the tale may differ. One can see, for example, how Americans refashioned their African and European tales to suit their new situations in the New World (see Hampton 1967; Pierson 1971). Folklore is a means of cultural communication; I want to see what trickster tales communicate to the Akan.

In West Africa, as throughout the rest of Africa, the most common prose narratives are trickster tales. Hare, Tortoise, and Spider are the chief actors, varying from location to location. Tortoise is most popular among the Yoruba; Hare is more prevalent in the grasslands; Spider is most common in the forest areas (Diarrassouba 1970: 153). There are also human tricksters. Among the two million Akan of Ghana and environs the trickster is Ananse, the Spider.

The Akan are culturally homogeneous, speaking mutually intelligible dialects of Twi. The folklore forms a relatively unified bloc, including proverbs (Christensen 1973: 509), music (Nketia 1963b: 3; see Nketia 1955 and 1963a), and prose narratives (Barker and Sinclair 1972: 16). Not only are the same themes found in trickster tales among the Ashanti, Fante, Brong, and other Akan, but they are told in the same manner, apparently with the same attitudes and applications. With the little available material (there are few collections of Akan folklore), often not indicating the origin, place, people, date, and other important data, it is impossible to reconstruct a regional map of the tales collected and it is worthwhile to think of the Akan as a cultural unit. As many foreign elements as the Akan have adopted, they have incorporated them into Akan patterns, applying their cultural meanings to new rites, gods, and folklore (Busia 1954: 191). It is proper to think of Ananse, the Akan trickster, as a single character whose tales communicate the same basic meanings to the various Akan groups.

The Akan make great use of oral traditions. Their sacred histories have been memorized and recited by trained specialists (Meyerowitz 1952: 19). No specialists, however, are needed to recite the trickster tales or any of the other folktales which the Akan simply call Anansesem, that is, Ananse tales. All Anansesem, whether they deal with Ananse or not, are considered to be untrue stories. They are not myths in any sense of the word. Anyone can tell them, although only at night or at a ceremonial occasion, for example, at the funeral of a respected story-teller (Barry 1961: 18; Courlander 1957: 104). Before the narrator begins his tale, he will say that the story is not true. The one hundred or more trickster tales and the numerous other Anansesem have no apparent connection with Akan ritual; they are simply tales (Douglas 1931: 130; Rattray 1928: 10).

Nevertheless, the Anansesem communicate important concepts to the Akan. In the tales Ananse attacks the very foundations of Akan life, the Supreme Being, and the Akan people themselves. He attempts to undermine the ultimate bases of Akan reality, the sources of Akan being, identity, and meaning. Whether we call these foundations religious or social does not matter; the traditional Akan make no distinction between religion and society. The important point is that Ananse, through his actions, subverts and revalidates the ultimate bases of Akan life.

The first of these bases is the Supreme Being, Nyame, also known as Onyankopon, Otwereduampon, and Odomankoma. He is the creator, the sky-god, the inexhaustible being, the eldest deity, the giver of rain, sunshine, and help. He is master of life and death, the author of sickness and cures, the one who gave order to the universe, who named all things (see Addae 1970: 162–65; Rattray 1916: 17–26).

There seems little doubt but that Ellis was mistaken in 1887 when he claimed that the Akan acquired a belief in Nyame from Christians or Muslims (see Evans 1950: 244). There is evidence for the ancient origin of a belief in and devotion to Nyame among the Akan, through proverbs, myths, drum songs, ancient temples, and art (see Addae 1970: 159–61 and Rattray 1916: 141–43). There is also little doubt but that Nyame is an active deity, not removed from the life of the Akan. There is a cult to him among the Akan, although interpreters differ regarding the existence of a priesthood devoted specifically to him. Each person has the right and ability to communicate directly with Nyame, through household shrines consisting of a tree called the seat of Nyame in which offerings are placed. In addition, a priest comes by periodically to water the tree and make special offerings for the family. Moreover, there are specialists within the compounds of chiefs who perform the cult for a village or state (see Chatterji 1960: 113–16; Evans 1950: 253). Despite the existence of a myth which states that Nyame removed himself from mankind, he apparently is by no means otiose (hidden).

Besides Nyame there exist numerous *abosom*, divinities, nature spirits, and the like, which possess powers applicable to certain circumstances. They are generally thought to be invisible, but manifest themselves through aspects of nature. The most powerful of these are Tano the River, Earth Mother (Asase Ya), and a malevolent deity named Nyankopon Kweku, but the number of abosom is apparently unlimited. At any time a previously unnoticed abosom can make itself known to the Akan (Akesson 1950: 237–40). Once direct communication is established between the abosom and the people, a priesthood is created for it and it is called upon for health, fertility, prosperity, protection from witches, and other immediate needs. Each of the abosom has a priesthood and shrines. There are four main types of abosom: tribal-wide, town, family, and personal. All are worshiped. The Akan state that as a person has many needs, a person needs many abosom; it would be unrealistic and unwise to expect anyone to prosper or even survive without recognizing the many abosom (Rattray 1923: 150).

On the other hand, it appears that the Akan think of these abosom as intermediaries, messengers, between themselves and Nyame. Each of the abosom has powers, but the source of all power is Nyame. Whether this type of theistic belief can best be described as monotheism, monolatry, or henotheism is not important to the present discussion. Clearly the Akan perform what must be described as religious acts in regard to the abosom. It might be argued that such acts are important enough to warrant the consideration that abosom constitute a separate religious base, apart from Nyame. I shall take this possibility into consideration in the following analysis; however, conceptually the Akan treat the abosom as appendages to Nyame. He holds ultimate power, not they (Danquah 1968).

The second foundation of Akan life is represented by the ancestor spirits. The rituals devoted to the ancestor spirits are the most visible of the Akan religious cults and have led observers to claim that the Akan (like other Africans) are ancestor-worshipers.

There are four major ceremonials that communicate with the ancestor spirits: the Adae, at which ancestors are recalled, honored, and propitiated, and at which the solidarity of the state is emphasized; the Baya, at which thanksgiving offerings are made to the ancestors for the rice crop and requests for blessings are made for the upcoming rice crop; the Afahye, at which ancestors are offered first fruits of various crops; and the Odwera, at which the tribe is ritually cleansed with the help of the ancestors. In addition, the Akan believe that ancestors visit their living relatives; in order to house them during their visits, the Akan construct stools. The Akan do not worship the stools; rather, each stool is considered empty until an ancestor resides in it, just as an offering shrine is empty until the abosom or Nyame appear. There are numerous stools: tribal, men's, women's, officials' and family's. Each was designed for certain ancestor spirits (Coffin 1945: 34—41). While the ancestor visits in the stool, the Akan person can communicate directly with him or her, asking for favors, receiving advice, information, and help.

When observers have called the Akan ancestor-worshipers, they have done so in an attempt to demonstrate the supremacy of the ancestors in the religious life at the expense of Nyame. In short, they have said that the Akan worship ancestors, not God. In this sense they have been mistaken; however, if we understand that the ancestors are the powerful symbols of the Akan people themselves, we see that they participate in the foundation of Akan being.

The ancestors are the owners of all Akan land. The living can pass it on to their children but the ancestors actually own it, sustain it, and thus sustain the Akan people. The ancestors represent the political authority of the Akan. They are paradigms of Akan virtue. They promote fertility (no childless Akan can become an ancestor spirit) and pass down the cultural institutions of the Akan (see Fortes 1965: 134). Furthermore, they are the most important symbols of the two Akan lineage systems, the matrilineal, physical line *(abusa)* and the patrilineal, spiritual line *(ntoro)* (see Herskovits 1937: 287—96). Each Akan person belongs to two families, both of them essential to his or her concept of identity, and the ancestors represent both.

I am not speaking of individual ancestors or even collections of ancestors. I am speaking of ancestors as a concept, and as such they conceptualize the Akan people as a whole. The individual Akan sees himself not as a unit who happens to be Akan (although here we should remember that each Akan identifies with his or her nation: Ashanti, Fante, etc.), but as a member of the Akan people. Before he identifies himself he sees himself as a part of his people. Before there is "I" there is "we." In short, the Akan person derives his identity from his people; without them he does not exist and has no reality, no being, no meaning.

In the same way the ancestors derive their meaning and identity from the Akan people as a whole. The ancestor cult is, in reality, a cult of heredity (see le Coeur 1932: 11–34). To say that the Akan ground of being is the Akan people itself is to state a spiritual as well as a physical fact. It is for that reason that the Akan can be said to have two, rather than one, foundations of life: Nyame and the Akan themselves. It would be incorrect to neglect the ultimate importance of the Akan (see Williamson 1965: 87–96), just as it would be to neglect Nyame.

Before examining the trickster's relationships with Nyame and the Akan people in the Anansesem, I wish to discuss the importance of two aspects of Akan life. The first is kingship. The king represents the Akan before Nyame and he represents Nyame before the Akan (see Meyerowitz 1960). Akan histories are usually woven around the deeds of the kings (Kyeretwic 1964: viii). In recent times prospective Akan converts to Christianity have balked at having to renounce allegiance to the king (Parrinder 1956: 111). The kings were until recently sovereign rulers, divinely ordained, charismatic, reigning—in the case of the Ashanti— over a million people or more. The king is the main actor in the Adae and Odwera ceremonials, the intermediary between the people and the ancestors, between the people and Nyame.

Yet he is chosen by the people. In the presence of the ancestors he wears his oldest clothes as a sign of deference. He is a central cultic participant, but he is not the whole of the Akan people by himself. Akan proverbs attest that the king is powerful, but he must know his place, just as the people must know theirs. He is not to think of himself as a great person by himself; to the contrary, he is the holder of a great office, owing his position to Nyame and the Akan people. More important as a symbol of the people is the Golden Stool. Individual kings pass on but the Golden Stool "holds the soul . . . of the nation" (Smith 1927: 14).

Nevertheless, the king's influence should not be underestimated. He mediates between the two bases of Akan life.

The second aspect I wish to discuss is priesthood. The abosom choose people to be their representatives among the Akan. They possess their chosen ones, teaching them how to call upon the abosom when needed. The priest then forms a cult and shrine, gaining local adherents (Field 1958: 14). Priests are intermediaries between the people and the abosom, leading ultimately to Nyame.

We have thus examined the bases and the intermediaries of Akan life. It remains for us to see how Ananse relates to Nyame, the Akan people, the abosom, the ancestors, the king, and the cultic priests.

Ananse is related to Nyame, first, by name. Nyame is sometimes known as Ananse Kokuroko, or the Great Spider (Meyerowitz 1949: 74), and some Akan think of the two as relatives (Barker 1919: 158). They also share characteristics. Ananse, like Nyame, possesses wisdom and prospers by it (Douglas 1931: 130). One Akan storyteller says of Ananse that "The wisdom of the spider is greater than that of all the world together" (in Barker and Sinclair 1972: 25).

Just as Nyame is thought of as the spiritual father of all people, Ananse is said to be the father of the grandfathers, an ancient Akan ancestor (Danquah 1928: 250, n. 2), possibly one of the founders of the Twi-speaking nations. In one Ashanti myth it is Ananse who fashions man but Nyame must give him life (Tegnaeus 1950: 55), although other myths have Ananse as the actual creator of the world and man (Feldmann 1963: 14).

The point to be gained is that Ananse and Nyame are related by blood, by action, and by characteristics, yet they are definitely two separate entities. Nyame is the object of veneration; Ananse is not. Nyame's actions inspire ritual; Ananse's do not. Nyame is considered the provider for the nations; Ananse is not. Nyame is the Great Spider; Ananse is perverting sub-alter-ego.

In the tales Ananse tries to become closer to Nyame. He bargains to become Nyame's messenger (and then proceeds to warp his messages) in order to share in Nyame's prestige, power, and wealth (see Herskovits and Herskovits 1937: 60–62). Moreover, he attempts to form a closer alliance with Nyame by proposing to marry his daughter. It is apparent that Ananse desires to be Nyame's son-in-law more than he desires his daughter. Nyame announces that the first person to guess his daughter's secret name will marry her. Ananse learns the name through a clever ploy; however, he fails to win her because of his attempt to imitate Nyame's stately actions. Rather than say the name aloud, Ananse uses talking drums as messengers, and when Nyame cannot understand Ananse's poor drumming, Ananse sends Lizard with the message. When Lizard says the girl's name, Nyame awards him—Lizard—the girl's hand. It is proper for Nyame to employ talking drums and messengers to deliver his statements; Ananse should not be so pompous (Courlander 1963: 36–40, 114).

Not only does Ananse attempt to imitate Nyame, but he also attempts to usurp his prerogatives. In some cases he is successful. In an often-told tale, Ananse desires to own all the stories belonging to Nyame. He wants the stories to be about himself instead of Nyame. In order to accomplish this, he makes an agreement with Nyame: he will exchange a number of wild animals or nature spirits for the stories. Ananse uses trickery to capture hornets, a python, a leopard, and other animals according to different versions, and brings these to Nyame. Because of his success, all stories are now called *Anansesem* instead of Nyame's stories. Instead of featuring the deeds of Nyame, they recount the escapades of Ananse (Barker and Sinclair 1972: 29–31; Courlander 1957: 3–8; Herskovits and Herskovits 1937: 53–57; Rattray 1930: 4–59).

Ananse's purchase of the tales results from trickery, but not from deceit of Nyame. In another story Ananse fools Nyame and thereby saves his own life after he has failed to save the life of Nyame's mother. Ananse fools Nyame into believing that the abosom want him alive, and so Nyame pardons him (Rattray 1930: 264–67).

Ananse's infringement on Nyame's sovereignty is most plain in his control over death. Among the Akan Nyame is said to be the master of death and life. Metaphorically this implies that Nyame is the master of everything because death is the fact of existence that cannot be avoided. Men are powerless against it, just as they are powerless against Nyame. Nevertheless, Ananse uses death for his own purposes in some instances and escapes from death, thereby mocking Nyame's ultimate power.

In order to gain wealth from Nyame, Ananse promises to take a grain of corn from Nyame and exchange it for a village of people, all of whom he will bring back to Nyame. He travels from town to town, claiming to be Nyame's messenger. He tells the chief of the first town that he has Nyame's grain of corn, which must be kept with the cocks. Of course the cocks eat the corn and to avoid Nyame's wrath, the chief gives Ananse a cock. Ananse employs the same ruse at the next town, saying that the cock—Nyame's favorite—must stay with the sheep. They trample it to death and Ananse thereby gains a sheep. Ananse acquires a cow at the next town, using the same trick. Next he exchanges the cow for a dead child (or woman or slave, depending on the version), promising to bring the child to Nyame. Because of the dead child's stench, the children at the next town beat it while it "sleeps," and to avoid Nyame's wrath for having "killed Nyame's favorite child," the chief brings his entire village to Nyame. Thus Ananse fulfills his pledge. At each step in the progression Ananse uses death in order to further his own ends. He is a veritable master of death in his own right (Appiah 1966: 3–26; Douglas 1931: 132).

In another tale Ananse feigns death in order to retire to his farm, which his family has tended. He has his family bury him on the farm with his eating and cooking utensils and advises them not to visit him for a long period of time. During this time he eats all the crops that ripen (Appiah 1967: 149–57; Courlander 1957: 20–24).

In a third tale Ananse travels to the land of the dead, from which no living person may return. He tricks Death (personified) into giving him treasured gold sandals and a gold broom, then escapes with the gifts. Where no other person could oppose Death, Ananse is successful (Appiah 1967: 61–68).

Ananse is also credited with bringing Death (personified) into contact with humans. Formerly Death ravaged only animals, but through Ananse's greed and disrespect Death finds humans and begins to kill them (Appiah 67: 139–45). Ananse seems to be intimately associated with death. One Akan tale explains why death is everywhere; another explains in an obvious parody why Ananse is everywhere (Douglas 1931: 135). By demonstrating a disrespectful, almost blithely confident, attitude toward death, Ananse flouts Nyame's authority and power.

In addition, Ananse shows no respect for the abosom. He is not awed by their presence when others are afraid. He tries to bully them, to use them for his own benefit, and even to compete with them. When Efu, a hunchback abosom, provides Ananse with rain for his crops, Ananse beats him to death in order to gain even more rain (Appiah 1966: 115–21; Brown 1929: 92–96). When an old woman abosom of the earth gives food to Ananse's son, Ananse attempts to wrest more from her

(Appiah 1967: 18–24). When everyone else is afraid to approach a sacred grove, Ananse tricks the abosom to help him destroy it and plant his crops (Brown 1929: 73–76). Ananse is too proud to respect the abosom; he disregards their commands as he evades Nyame's authority.

The question arises: Do the Akan enjoy vicarious rebellion against Nyame and the abosom through the trickster tales? When Ananse tricks or evades or abuses the sacred, do the Akan identify with him? It would be mistaken to think of the Akan as existentialists struggling to free themselves of supernatural control; however, the stories do offer a more vulgar view of Nyame than one expressed at a family shrine or at a state ceremonial. In one tale Nyame demonstrates a petulant resentment toward Ananse's success in killing a dangerous python. Because Nyame is obliged to give Ananse some wisdom as reward, he throws a pot of wisdom at him, almost splitting him into two pieces (Appiah 1967: 11–18). Ananse certainly challenges Nyame's hegemony. By stating that the Anansesem are not true before reciting them, the storyteller and his audiences can indulge in the exuberance of twitting any ultimate rule.

On the other hand, the trickster tales recognize Nyame and the abosom's powers and authority. When Ananse wants to obtain something, he must go to Nyame to obtain it. In his scheme to exchange the corn for a village of people, Ananse uses the threat of Nyame's power and anger just as he uses the process of death.

Furthermore, Nyame and the abosom punish Ananse for some of his disrespectful misdeeds. Nyame withdraws all water from Ananse because of his treatment of Efu the hunchback. He also decides against awarding his daughter to Ananse because of his pompous behavior. When Ananse refuses to follow the directives of the old woman of the earth, he suffers from sores and scabs. When Ananse disobeys some river abosom, he becomes physically deformed (Rattray 1930: 66–71).

Even with regard to death, on two occasions Ananse finds himself unable to control the powers he attempts to use. In one case a stone abosom kills him when he asks it the wrong question (Appiah 1969: 142–45); in another case he is killed by a witch's sword that refuses to follow his commands (Courlander 1957: 88–92).

The general picture, therefore, that emerges from Ananse's relationships with Nyame and the abosom is one of challenge but reinforcement of authority. The tales indicate Ananse's ability to violate Nyame's rule, but they continue to affirm that rule. In effect, Ananse is the exception who probes and proves Nyame's rule.

Ananse's disrespect for Nyame's authority is matched by his contempt for the authority of Akan society. His relationship with the people of the tales is even more antagonistic than his relationship with Nyame.

In story after story Ananse fools his friends, neighbors, and family members in order to supply his own needs, which usually consist of food. He steals Lizard's garden after Lizard has performed all the work (Courlander 1957: 88–92). He steals the food of Leopard's kingdom (Appiah 1966: 97–104). After he kills Efu the hunchback, he attempts to blame his friend for the murder. Because he so often deceives people, Akan storytellers comment: "Woe to one who would put his trust in Ananse—a sly, selfish, and greedy person" (in Barker and Sinclair 1972: 25).

Ananse is not above stealing a fiancée from his best friend, Donkey. Through a complicated series of schematic episodes Ananse dissuades the girl from marrying Donkey, marries her himself, and moves far away, leaving Donkey to tend his farm (Appiah 1966: 73–87). I could continue to list the numerous antisocial acts of Ananse; let these suffice as examples.

Most frequently he breaks public trust during a famine. While others starve, he wishes to gorge himself (Courlander 1957: 106). Ananse's greed is directed also against his family. When during a famine he finds a magic pot that provides him with food, he keeps it to himself, refusing to share it with his family members. Because of his greed, his children and wife distrust him, and together they destroy the source of food (Appiah 1966: 59–64). As a result, he and his family vie for sustenance through many of the tales, and when Ananse is successful in one of his schemes, he hoards his rewards rather than share with his divisive brood. In a society in which harmonious family life is emphasized, Ananse's family stands out as a disjunctive example.

On occasion Ananse works for the benefit of a particular village or a particular person, as when he saves a village from an attacking giant python. It should be noted, however, that when he does help mankind he is usually acting with the hope of receiving a reward or payment. Furthermore, when he helps people, they find it hard to believe. For example, when he kills a bird that has been threatening a town, he announces his success, but the townsfolk answer: "Oh, that's Kwaku

Ananse, he is a well-known liar, perhaps he is not speaking the truth"
(Rattray 1930: 181). The characters in the tales know about his antisocial
tendencies.

Is there any justification for calling him a culture-hero as well as a
trickster? Whereas it is true that he plays a role in creation and is
considered an ancient ancestor, he is hardly a figure who brings cultural
benefits to the Akan people. Instead he brings death (Herskovits and
Herskovits 1937: 171), contradiction (see Rattray 1930: 106–9), serpents
and monsters (Barker and Sinclair 1972: 89–94), and debt (Courlander
1957: 77–79; Herskovits and Herskovits 1937: 91; Rattray 1930: 4).
Especially interesting is his introduction of debt into the world, because
the Ashanti say that what joins them together, makes them Ashanti,
is debt.

Ananse does introduce wisdom among the Akan, but he does so only
through anger and accident. Indeed, his wish is to hide all the wisdom of
the world from the people. He places it in a pot and tries to carry it to the
top of a tree; however, he makes no progress inasmuch as he is holding
the large pot in front of him and his legs cannot reach the tree. His son,
spying on him, tells him that it would be better if he carried it on his
back. Ananse realizes that he cannot possibly have all the wisdom of the
world in his possession because his son obviously is giving him good
advice. In anger at his own stupidity he throws the pot down to the
ground. It breaks and its contents scatter to the people (Appiah 1966:
149–52; Barker and Sinclair 1972: 32–34).

Ananse is also credited with introducing weaving and the hoe among
the Akan; however, a close reading of the tales indicates that on the
contrary he introduces these two important cultural items to the British
instead of to the Akan. The latter have to wait for the former to arrive
before receiving the devices (Courlander 1957: 86; Herskovits and
Herskovits 1937: 66; Rattray 1930: 42). Tricksters in other folklore also
play the role of culture-hero, but not Ananse. For the most part he
brings the people destructive and dangerous innovations. On two occasions he prevents cultural items from reaching the Akan. The one case in
which he provides the Akan with a useful item is through an accident,
veritably against his will.

Ananse is not a culture-hero. He certainly is not a paradigm of virtue;
to the contrary, his actions are exceedingly antisocial. He fosters dishar-
mony in the group and in his family; he eats others' food; his actions

contradict the ideal of solidarity expressed by the Akan. Why, then, are his tales so popular? Part of the answer lies in his contradictions regarding Akan ideals.

I have tried to show that the Akan feel a very strong obligation to the social order. The Akan individual sees himself as a member of society before he sees himself as an individual. Akan society has a closely knit structure, each person having a sharply defined position in the matrilineal blood clan, the patrilineal spirit clan, the village, and the state, all within the framework of nature's laws and in relationship to Nyame's power (cf. Debrunner 1961: 5, 61; Rattray 1923: 368). For each position the individual has rights and duties that are clearly prescribed. These are not simply the obligations of citizenship. Far more important, they are the obligations of identity. The person is who he is because of his position within the structure of Akan society. He *is* because he is Akan; he must act in the prescribed manner or risk his very being. Any deviation from the societal norm threatens his existence; banishment is the ultimate punishment because separation from his people means separation from his ground of being.

Ananse, on the other hand, breaks societal rules, violates the trust of his people, and as often as not escapes without punishment; sometimes he even prospers through his misdeeds. He is contemptuous of Akan authority, just as he shows contempt for Nyame's authority. Through Ananse's tales, the Akan individual experiences vicarious freedom from the societal boundaries that bind so tightly. (The boundaries are so tight because they are so necessary.) Ananse gives Akan society the opportunity to mock Nyame's authority; he gives the individual the opportunity to mock society's authority. He is able to do what the ordinary Akan cannot: act unscrupulously with relative impunity. By so doing he calls the most sacrosanct of Akan institutions into question. That is not to say that the trickster destroys the fabric of Akan society. The Akan individual may applaud his successes, but he does not attempt to emulate his antisocial techniques; he enjoys Ananse's illicit schemes but does not approve of them. Ananse does not teach morals when he is victorious. It is when he fails that the Akan draw ethical conclusions (Courlander 1957: 104).

And fail he does. As often as not the persons whom Ananse attempts to trick work their revenge. When Ananse tries to blame the death of Efu on his friend, the friend sees through Ananse's ploy and informs him that Nyame has been displeased with Efu. The friend tells Ananse that Nyame will give him a reward for killing the hunchback. Ananse admits his actions, hoping for gain, and brings the body to Nyame who punishes Ananse for the death. When Ananse steals Lizard's farm, Lizard manages to trick Ananse into returning it.

Not only does Ananse often lose what he has gained through deceit. Frequently he is publicly shamed for his crimes. When he feigns death in order to eat his family's food, his wife finally notices that the crops are disappearing. She suspects thieves. At the advice of a diviner she makes a life-size figure of sticky gum and leaves it in the garden where Ananse finds it at night. Infuriated that someone is intruding into his garden, Ananse challenges the dummy and becomes stuck in it through the familiar "tar-baby" sequence. In the morning his family and neighbors find him and realize his plot. He becomes ashamed and escapes to the dark rafters of a nearby home, a formula ending for the many tales in which Ananse is shamed by his unlawful deeds (Courlander 1957: 21–24). In another version, however, Ananse claims that he has visited the land of the dead and returned because the ancestors have told him that he is not ready to die. The people believe his story and he turns it to profit (Appiah 1967: 149–57).

In addition to presenting Ananse's punishments and embarrassments, the tales offer a picture of a relatively well-functioning society. While Ananse is stealing, his neighbors are cooperating; while Ananse is scheming, his neighbors are planting their crops; while Ananse is violating rules, his neighbors are obeying them.

Hence Ananse's often-successful antics must be viewed in the broader societal context which the tales portray. Ananse threatens societal order, but the other characters in the stories maintain order. Ananse creates doubt about the permanence and power of Akan institutions; the other characters reaffirm faith in them. Ananse breaks the people's rules, but the rules still stand. In regard to the Akan people as in regard to Nyame, Ananse is the exception who probes and proves the rules.

In his relationships with ancestors, kings, and priesthood, Ananse further illustrates his role of casting doubt on sacred institutions. The ancestors play a very small role in the Anansesem; when they are mentioned, however, Ananse is trying to take advantage of them. It is they who provide him with the food-producing pot which he later abuses. He persuades Donkey to tend his farm while he is "away," so that the ancestors may be cared for. Most significantly, when he claims to have returned from the land of the dead, he charges the people in order for them to hear the messages he has supposedly brought from the ancestors to them. He uses the ancestors to suit his devious purposes, but the tales themselves do not throw the ancestors into disrepute.

The stories present a less flattering picture of kings. Sometimes they are lazy, greedy, spiteful, jealous. Ananse challenges their authority more than he does Nyame's and is more often successful. On the other hand, they are often just, regal, and wise, especially in tales that closely resemble stories told about Nyame. In these cases the king appears as the rightful symbol of Nyame on earth. Even when they make errors, their office—kingship itself—is justified.

Priests, like ancestors, play small roles in the Anansesem. They appear as givers of advice, sometimes correct, sometimes not. True to character, Ananse uses the priests for his own ends, particularly when he is feigning sickness and death. In one version Ananse plays the role of a dead man so convincingly that the diviner-priest believes him (Rattray 1930: 140–45). More strikingly, Ananse throws doubt on the institution of diviner-priest when he "returns from the land of the dead" and gets caught in the sticky dummy. By fooling gullible people into paying him to hear messages from their ancestors, he suggests that diviner-priests who carry such messages in real life might be fake, as he is. Aside from Ananse's own perverse actions, however, the Anansesem give no instance of a priest subverting his office. Again, Ananse is the exception.

In his role as bogus priest Ananse brings up a fascinating but tenuous topic: witches. Among the Akan, witches are the counterparts of priests. Like priests, they are powerful individuals, possessed by abosom; however, priests serve the people whereas witches attempt to destroy the people. They are antisocial forces par excellence. They ignore the authority of Nyame and the authority of the Akan in their quest for personal power at the expense of everyone else. They resemble Ananse in their egotism and antisocial behavior. Furthermore, they share characteristics with Ananse and spiders, which are quite suggestive.

First, witches, like Ananse, are unnaturally fond of food, especially meat. Second, they use spider webs as part of their destructive paraphernalia. If a spider web entangles an Akan, he will suspect a witch. Witches walk on spider webs; in addition, they attach them to their doors while they sleep so they will be warned if anyone should enter.

Furthermore, witches hurt each other by cutting one another's spider webs. Third, witches keep their knowledge hidden in a pot in a way similar to that of Ananse when he tries to hoard his wisdom.

I do not mean to imply that Ananse is an out-and-out witch, despite these connections. Rather I am suggesting that Akan society incorporates antisocial elements into its structure, Ananse and witches being two examples. To have an antisocial figure as the main folkloric character seems to me an act of ontological bravado. Accepting witches as part of the system seems to require similar courage (see, on Akan witches, Debrunner 1961; Goody 1957; Ward 1956).

We see, in conclusion, that Ananse raises doubts about the very foundations of Akan life, particularly Nyame and the Akan people themselves. In short, the trickster tales attack and affirm those foundations. We also see that the Anansesem serve to resolve the doubts raised by Ananse. In effect, the Akan eschew "blind faith" in their ultimate realities. Instead they incorporate doubt into faith, making that faith stronger and more profound.

EIGHT

WEST AFRICAN TRICKSTERS:
WEB OF PURPOSE,
DANCE OF DELIGHT

Robert D. Pelton

When I first heard the trickster described during an introductory course in the history of religions at the University of Chicago, I was fascinated. To be sure, I knew of medieval fools, Hasidic rabbis, Zen masters, and the intensity of contemporary religious communities; they all suggested that comedy was an essential aspect of seriously lived religion. Among those especially engaged with the sacred, laughter kept breaking out. Yet until I met the trickster, I had not realized that many so-called primitive peoples delighted in celebrating this disruptive power instead of squelching it or using it to launch some dull theory about institutional stress, cosmic absurdity, or the psychosocial value of playing around. Moreover, while these peoples were discovering laughter at the heart of the sacred, they, like so many Flannery O'Connor prophets and profiteers, were insisting that this discovery of laughter revealed the true being of daily life.

Most of the material in this essay has appeared in somewhat different form in my work, *The Trickster in West Africa: A Study of Mythic Irony and Sacred Delight,* 1980. The interested reader will find there the empirical data, bibliographic sources, and extended analysis that underlie the conclusions and hypotheses presented here. As I explored the ways in which the trickster's antics disclosed the intersection of the transcendent and the commonplace, I saw that he has baffled his interpreters as well as his adversaries because he embodies a purposefully ambivalent language. Through this language the trickster links animality and ritual transformation. He shapes culture by means of sex and laughter, ties cosmic process to personal history, empowers divination to change boundaries into horizons, and reveals the passages to the sacred embedded in daily life.

To look at the Ashanti, Fon, Yoruba, and Dogon trickster figures in their West African context is to see that the trickster exists not as an archetypal idea but as a symbolic pattern embracing a wide range of individual figures. His movement between orders of being helps to fashion a human world that is sacred both as something given and as process, as social enterprise and divine gift. The trickster reflects, in Mircea Eliade's words, a "mythology of the human condition" (Eliade 1969: 157), in which *homo faber*, human-as-maker, is a sacred jack-of-all-trades, tacking together the bits and pieces of experience until they become a dwelling open to heaven and earth. In symbolizing the transforming power of the human imagination as it plays with, delights in, and shatters what seems to exist, until it reveals what it is really, the trickster discloses how the human mind and heart are epiphanies of a holy order of the here and now that encompasses both infinity and the finite mess of actual feces, lies, and even death.

I follow here the ways four West African peoples—the Ashanti, the Fon, the Yoruba, and the Dogon—hear and know their trickster figures. The matrilineal society of the Ashanti, located in what is now southern Ghana, expresses its sense of cosmic doubleness through both a twofold male/female structure of authority and recognition of two paramount deities, Nyame, the male sky-god, and Asase Yaa, "old mother earth." The Ashanti also recognize many divine and semi-divine intermediaries, but in their folklore they play out their cosmic vision through the tales of Ananse, the spider-trickster. The Fon, who live in present-day Benin, also see maleness and femaleness as twin principles of all life, but although their High God, Mawu-Lisa, is androgynous, the female "element," Mawu, predominates. The chief gods are her children, and Legba, the youngest child, is the "linguist of the gods" whom gods and humans must address before approaching his mother.

The Yoruba, an agricultural society like the other three societies I have mentioned, developed towns and a more urban style of religious thought well before most African peoples. The Yoruba have a High God,

Olodumare (or Olorun), and an Earth Goddess, Onile, but their pantheon shows a complex grouping and interplay of sacred energies as well as the expected variety and specialization of deities. Eshu—the "anger" and messenger of the gods, himself the god of the marketplace—keeps this elaborate world spinning by his tricks and schemes that foster every sort of interchange between gods and humans.

The Dogon, much less numerous than the other three peoples named, live on the West African savanna in southern Mali and northern Burkina Faso. They have devised a remarkably subtle and many-leveled mythology, the "amazing word of the world" in which Ogo-Yurugu exists as the chief figure. The Dogon see the world as the fruit of Ogo's rebellion against Amma, the High God, and Ogo's subsequent transformation into Yurugu, the "pale fox." Even though defeated, Ogo-Yurugu continues to shape the innermost patterns of Dogon being, patterns that are not only historical and social, but also intrapsychic and personal.

In Ogo's metamorphosis into Yurugu, as elsewhere, we see that the work of transformation lies at the heart of the trickster's meaning. For example, Ananse overcomes the figure "Hate-to-be-contradicted," whose intolerance of disorder, contempt for social density and biological necessity, and opposition to the multiplicity of nature expresses itself in his physical isolation and his insistence that he can generate his own ancestors (Rattray 1930: 106–9). Ananse destroys "Hate-to-be-contradicted" by composing images of the world apparently more absurd, but in fact more faithful to human reality, than those of his rival.

Ananse's stories about his great penis, longer than seventy-seven poles, his wife's feat of catching a falling pot on succeeding days, and the water that holds the impress of his polygynous family—these are the images of social and biological processes stretched beyond any possibility of truth, except the truth that human life unites order and endless becoming by means of language. When Ananse caps his victory by cutting up his enemy to scatter contradiction among the people, he thereby discloses both his real triumph, the ironic embrace of all antagonism, and his own nature, the embodiment of the dialectic making possible this embrace and social life itself.

It will help to discuss this dialectic and how Ananse embodies it. Ananse's animality, his grossness, and his manic wit are evidence that he is a symbol of the liminal state and of its permanent accessibility as a source of recreative power. Victor Turner has argued persuasively that liminality is a state of radical openness to new forms of being. It is the mid-phase of the "ritual process" in which initiates pass out of normal structure, through a period of nondifferentiation and transformation, and then back into society, which the newly initiated renew by their own transformed being. This ritual process is intimately linked to a kind of "dying into" nature in order to be regenerated by its raw power (Turner 1972: 411). The dialectic Ananse embodies insists that to be human is to possess liminal openness. Ananse's passages from culture to nature to culture, from outside to inside and inside to outside, from potency to act, and from earth to heaven and back, all bear witness to his—and all human beings'—enduring inbetweenness. This inbetween-ness expresses both his neediness and his power to draw new life from every other form of life. Thus Ananse is free to modify his own bodily parts and those of others according to whim or need. He can break social rules by maltreating guests or by having sexual relations with a female in-law. He can disregard the requirement that words and deeds be in some sort of rough harmony, just as he can overlook the demands of biology, economics, family loyalty, and even metaphysical possibility. He shows disrespect for sacred powers and beings, including the High God; his tricks reorder their limits. But Ananse's rejection of human and sacred order leads neither to chaos nor to unchecked individualism. Rather, as he unleashes the forces of the wild or the divine, it is the present world that comes into being, a world unendingly forged by the human capacity to transform what is given from both above and below.

Ananse's style is gleefully oxymoronic. He is not a sweaty meta-physical pioneer hacking the actual out of the jungle of the possible any more than he is a cosmic mechanic revving up the motor of social order by injecting a richer mixture of chaos into its fuel. His foolery yokes together elegance and coarseness so that what now exists appears as a dazzling display of improbability, the result of the trickster's perfect in-ward fidelity to the demands of every mode of social intercourse. Conse-quently, Ananse is the agent of Ashanti doubleness—that interplay between male and female, heaven and earth, King and Queen Mother, Nyame and Asase Yaa, whose embodiment is the Ashanti people. This interplay has many intermediaries, but Ananse's special work is to show that the passage to new life is a story that never stops being told, a story delightful at its very core.

Legba, the trickster-god of the Fon, is even more evidently the master of the Fon dialectic. He not only serves as the High God's linguist, but also mediates among lesser gods as well. His phallic image stands before every human threshold to remind the people that daily comings and goings partake of the transforming power released whenever humans move out of and back into their ordinary spaces. Moreover, Legba exists as the originator of magic, which enables men and women to claim the potencies of another plane of existence for their daily lives. Legba's sexual prowess is the great symbol of his transforming power. Through it he discloses that the world is built on the possibility of human intercourse. The perils of human encounter are great, yet those who meet seek to dissolve boundaries in such a way that the meeting brings harmony, not conflict. Social structures are attempts to create a network of symbolic harmonies that enable people to pass repeatedly through the process of dissolution and reintegration and to move toward the fullness of communion despite the dangers and tensions of these passages. Thus Legba, although subject to his own "nature" as a mediator, ritualizes and consecrates the transactions of Fon life, making them not only safe, but sacred.

Legba plays a still more significant role. The Fon have had an unusually keen awareness of the processes of adaptation through which they have passed in their history, and their mythology has kept alive the memory of the adaptiveness that enabled them to borrow liberally from the religious and political institutions of their neighbors. By understanding their history in mythic terms, they have insisted that such assimilation and borrowing are instances of religious discovery and even revelation. Thus Legba's unflagging movement of renewal from center to periphery and back, justifies adaptation, while disclosing its meaning as the ceaseless recreation of Fon life.

For example, the Fon have so elaborated the passage from dark female inside to bright male outside that the institutions of kingship and family and the inner being of the High God have become mutually reflecting icons of a process that exists both as the stuff and soul of life. In an enormously complex and subtle game, in which the king in the depths of his palace is always both inside and outside, while Mawu in the darkness of the night is always both near and far, vital center and shadowy margin, Legba is a living copula. He joins together the cosmic dialectic and the social process in such a way that the former loses its terror and the latter gains stability, and he does so exuberantly as the laughter he provokes simultaneously humanizes and sacramentalizes the male-female symbolism in which Fon thought is framed.

The link between the trickster and divination in the socio-religious order of both the Fon and the Yoruba represents an even deeper level of meaning West Africans have found in him. Divination rests on the belief that a continuing intersection of physical, moral, and spiritual lines of force causes the world and everything in it. When these forces are in harmony, their intersections create passages into peaceful growth and change. At moments of disruption, conflict, and doubt, intersection becomes collision; order becomes a prison or threatens to dissolve altogether; and the lines tying persons to one another and to ancestors and gods harden and crumble. The passages of life are clogged and finally rupture, and then, as the myths say, all becomes as fluid as water, as destructive as fire, and violence shatters peace. Divination seeks to open these passages of life by transforming them into *limina*, thresholds of larger meaning, ways of turning ordure into order. Eshu, the Yoruba say, turns feces into treasure.

The Yoruba, and the Fon, too, who have borrowed the Yoruba divinatory system and aspects of the Yoruba trickster Eshu-Elegba linked to it, see their trickster as the master of the language of divination: messenger of the gods, disrupter of social machinery (see Wescott 1962: 345). Eshu is a disruptive mediator, provoking trouble to expose and transform desiccated structure. However, in the Yoruba universe he is also a sociotherapist and an iconographer. The Yoruba know very well how to handle disputes and troubles in secular ways, through discussions, advice, and law. For them Eshu's agility, his metaphysical slipperiness, represents a truly sacred power that works through divination and sacrifice to restore lost wholeness.

Religious sacrifice may seem a bargain between hungry man and insatiable divinities. Seen more clearly, it exists as a kind of ritual shortcut, a hastening of the way in which humans always become fully human. The world yields itself to us: in our use of plants and animals, their death is our life. This act of eating not only declares our fleshiness, our inescapable need of something solid to fill our bellies and of somewhere earthly to empty our bowels, but it also supports our unseeable life within. This inner life is lifted from the visible world in thought, word, and silence into communion with the reality that has never sowed, reaped, or eaten, and never will. In sacrifice the exchange happens more directly: Eshu, for example, forges communion by enabling the Yoruba to make their burden of death, through the medium of sacrificial animals, an offering that brings life from the gods and renews the gods' own creative life.

If the system of divination is an *imago mundi,* an icon of the Yoruba cosmos, then wherever that cosmos dissolves or hardens, Eshu brings its rediscovery and redraws its other representations in Yoruba life through sacrifice. In their art and their cities, the Yoruba image their cosmos as a world brought into being by the vital relationship between Sky and Earth, Olorum and Onile, and all their attendant helpers, institutions, and rituals. In complex association with all of these, especially in his mastery of the market, which begins and ends each Yoruba week, Eshu reveals the meeting of these beings and powers as a truly human meeting, a fully Yoruba world. In Carl Jung's terms, Eshu is all synchronicity, and his every-which-wayness embraces everything necessary for Yoruba life. The pattern he endlessly and outrageously recreates is ordinary, but in this ordinariness the Yoruba recognize the shape of their life together.

Space permits review of only one aspect of the elaborate system of correspondences that exist in Dogon life and myth and whose central figure is Ogo-Yurugu, the trickster-like demiurge and pale fox. In both myth and life cycle, Ogo-Yurugu proclaims that the world comes into being and life achieves wholeness through conflict, disorder, and even death, as well as through obedience, harmony, and birth. Amma, the High God, retains his supremacy, but his pure energy becomes visible through the crazed lens of Ogo's rebellion. Ogo's drive to possess his feminine half, by a rape of his own primordial placenta, brings sex and death into creation, making the world truly human even though it must be purified by Nommo, Ogo's obedient male twin. Ogo calls forth the sacrifice out of which human society comes into being, and his disobedient failures are an erotic foreshadowing of the careful ritual forms through which the Dogon order their lives. He is the cosmic antagonist who stirs his protagonist twin to accomplish the world's completion, which is Amma's great *agon.*

The imagery of drama is fitting here, for Dogon custom and myth insist that life is a story always beginning, developing, climaxing, ending, and beginning again. This story is embedded in the Dogon personality itself. With Nommo, Ogo is both the aboriginal source of that personality and its present inmost image—its entelechy, irresistible force, and goal. Ogo's persistent attempts to gain control over his own destiny have molded the human psyche so that, willy-nilly, men (and women also, in a related but different way) must experience Ogo's aloneness, anxiety, and search for wholeness. Especially in their sexuality, men relive Ogo's anguished search, for Ogo's cosmogonic odyssey has been stamped on the human self as an insatiable lust for the unrecovered twin who would make his life whole. Moreover, the Dogon male bears in the depth of his selfhood the whole cast of mythic figures in constant interaction. Within him are Ogo-Yurugu—itching, rebelling, losing, still prodding; Amma— generating, delaying, opposing, shaping, growing silent; Nommo— obeying and achieving dominion, castrated and endlessly fecund; and not least of all, the primordial matrix itself—torn and whole, sun and earth, both memory and hope. This manifold being is inherited by each Dogon child.

The Dogon do not experience their situation as tragic. They under- stand the experience of aloneness as the ground of communion, and they know each of life's expulsions from bliss as preludes to coming home. Thus we can begin to see Ogo-Yurugu as a revelation of Dogon irony, especially in the joking relationship in which "laughter, insult and mockery abolishes the generational system and the ties of rela- tionship, denies the reality of the passage of time, and turns the world upside down to enable it to proceed rightside up" (Calame-Griaule 1966: 401). The inescapable is always pregnant with escape because Ogo-Yurugu knows the trick of harnessing dissolution to rebirth, of passing beyond order through anti-order to transformed order, of yoking in a single dance the twin movements of life and death. Above all he calls forth the endless retelling of the story bearing his name, whose every repetition answers the riddle of the world in a burst of joy.

Mary Douglas's insight into the way traditional peoples try to make contradiction, defeat, and death—anomaly in any form—compost for life itself, helps to show how the trickster embodies the spiritual logic by which peoples seize, and delight in, whatever is contradictory (Douglas 1966: 49–53). The trickster's messy and metaphysically ambiguous pres- ence—in story, dance, phallic image, divination, or "soul"—symbolizes an informing of structure with the energy of rawness and a boundless confidence that such a trick is truly possible. Because the trickster pulls the most unyielding matter into the orbit of life, and because, especially in divination, he links these bits of social dirt into the forms of communal life, he reveals how it is precisely on the plane of the daily and the specific that time is cooled down, social order enlarged, and all experience opened to transformation.

By choosing to handle religion as an interpretable but finally irreducible language, recent students of traditional religions have tried to leave room for absolute ambiguity—rightly called "mystery"—at the center of human spiritual experience. The trickster discloses such mystery by uniting "high" and "low" in a language of sacred ribaldry. Moreover, the trickster embodies the process of symbol creation as an image of the "symbol-making machine" (this phrase was suggested to me by Charles H. Long) that is the human mind in perpetual motion, even in sleep and other subliminal states. For this reason, some interpreters have seen the trickster as emblematic of humans at work to master the earth. A deeper interpretation is possible. To see, for example, the Dogon siting of Ogo-Yorugu's activity simultaneously within the human soul and on the boundaries of human life, in the present and in the deepest past, in solitary rebellion and in complex relationship with every other force, indicates that the trickster discloses humanity's imaginative participation in a "universe impregnated by sacredness" (Eliade 1963: 157). The phallic imagery of these West African tricksters shows this impregnation to be human play as well as divine work, for the organs so unmistakably linking human generation to the animals and the power of the wild also symbolize the ultimate source of creativity.

The trickster displays our human juggling of the fragments of experience as a sacred order disclosed in the transforming power of imagination. As the trickster reveals the radically human character of the cosmos, the daily world is shown to be more than meets the eye, a sacred web of multidimensional planes of being, a dance in which all beings, human and nonhuman, meet and move together in a single pattern.

Does such an exaltation of human imagination surrender to the post-Kantian assumption that religion exists simply as a human project? Certainly, as Eliade has said, the logic of symbols "goes beyond the sphere of religious history to rank among the problems of philosophy" (Eliade 1963: 453). However, if one understands the trickster as a link between imagination and iconography, one can recognize that "discovery" need not be the antithesis of "revelation." When Eliade insisted that "to have imagination is to be able to see the world in its totality" and to grasp "all that remains refractory to the concept," he implied that human life exists as an epiphany of the structures hidden beneath the surface of thought as well as of matter (Eliade 1961: 20).

The "imaginers" of the trickster assume that a spiritual anthropology is not only possible but necessary in order to know the final truth of human being, and I believe we can understand the sense of such an assumption even if we cannot deal here with its metaphysical foundations. In his analysis of the Dinka religion, Godfrey Lienhardt explored the self-awareness of the Dinka in an effort to penetrate their experience of *nhialic*, or "divinity." The Dinka do not experience themselves as separated from the world by their minds, so that extrahuman reality exists only as an object for them. Rather, they know the world as an active subject. Thus the sacred "powers"—the High God and other transhuman beings—are, in effect, the images of human *passiones;* that is, they are active reciprocals of those events in which humans are acted upon by life in a way surpassing their understanding. Lienhardt used the Latin word *passio* because the Dinka know "divinity" so frequently in their painful separation from it and because the word carries the meaning of "being acted upon" (Lienhardt 1961: 149–56). It is important to realize that he is speaking not of what we often term "subjective sentiment," but of events that have specific shape and meaning. The Dinka are able to distinguish between those *passiones* whose answering images are the experience of social structure and those others that seem to them to transcend that structure by providing "the possibility of creating desirable experience and of freeing themselves from what they must otherwise passively endure" (Lienhardt 1961: 149–56).

Thus Lienhardt helps us to see that the trickster is an "image," the reflection in the human mind of the world experienced as an active subject. And what is that specific experience out of which the image of the trickster springs? What is the "active reciprocal" of the *passio* that he imprints on the human imagination? It is the experience of the human mind in its imaginative operation as itself radically ambiguous, essentially anomalous, inescapably multivalent—facing both out and in, linking above and below, animal-like and godlike, social cog and individual solitude; the mind as shaped and shaping, as part of all that is, existing as a subject knowing its apartness and its openness to communion. The trickster is an image of the human power to create icons, but in the sense that the *passio*, the inner experience of this iconographic power, would not exist if there were not a specific active subject to spark it. Even where that subject seems, as among the Ashanti, to reside only in the stories about him, still he is perceived to live side by side—not independently—with the minds that experience and imagine him, reflecting at the same time an inborn quality of those minds and of every other plane of being—animal, transhuman, divine. The trickster exists as a figure of a life that is human because it is more than human.

The one language befitting this image of the human mind and imagination in dialogue with all being is the language of irony. Such irony is a "patterning of facts, a recomposing in which the fact is seen within the creative presence of a contrary" (Lynch 1973: 14). "The task of the imagination," according to William Lynch, "is to imagine the real," above all when it gives body to the sacred and implants it within "the hustle and bustle, the burn and the iron of life" (Lynch 1973: 63). Lynch dissolves the division between the sacred and the ordinary in his "exploration of the ironic imagination," a reimagining of the imagination. It is this same division that the traditional mind bridges with—among other ways, but symbolizing them all—the confident, grossly elegant irony of the trickster.

Irony, Lynch has shown, has its own structure. Neither the mere coexistence of opposites nor the "copresence of contradictory elements" is truly ironic, for the usual quality of irony is the unexpected coexistence, to the point of identity, of certain contraries (Lynch 1973: 84). Irony, then, lies in yoking together in a single figure real opposites, in such a way that they belong together without losing their contrariness, in a dialectic expressing their interdependence and their power actually to transform being and the way we look at it. Thus "the way down is the way up" is an ironic proclamation, and Socrates is an ironic hero, ugly and beautiful, flexible and adamantine, managing the mind's life, but not his wife. In the figure of the trickster, in whom the anomalous and the ordered, the sacred and the profane, the absurd and the meaningful are joined, we have an image of irony and of the working of the ironic imagination itself.

Lynch calls this process, which is style, method, and decision all at once, "composition"; it involves bringing into true relationship the hidden and the manifest elements of life, the low and the high, the particular and the cosmic (Auerbach 1953: 29, 35–40). Such composition will always bring about transformation, because it shatters and reforms both the too-neat structures of the world and the too-smooth images of the mind. This is the ironic mode, which builds on antagonism, finds a passage through one opposite to another, and, always suspicious of tidiness, insists on the doubleness of all reality.

When Ananse defeats "Hate-to-be-contradicted," he both imagines and reflects the meeting of contraries that is the complete expression of truly social life. Legba, Eshu, and Ogo exploit still deeper veins of irony. In divination each of them composes individual and social disorder into new images of the entire network that exists as the sacred universe. Through these tricksters society forges a pattern of life at once more stable and more permeable. Finally, Legba's and Ogo-Yurugu's unending composition and recomposition of the world within the human soul disclose that the *limen*, at once boundary of dailiness and threshold of recreated life, has a real presence in each person.

In short, the trickster reveals that humans themselves are symbols, as Karl Kerényi suggests when he calls the trickster "the exponent and the personification of the life of the body" (Kerényi 1955: 185). Yet in the processes of symbolic thought, the body comes to represent and even to assimilate apparently incompatible planes of being so that humankind becomes "a living cosmos open to all the other living cosmoses by which he is surrounded" (Eliade 1963: 455). The trickster, therefore, in juggling with his own body, in his manipulation of its parts, his toying with its wastes, his fascinations with its orifices, his confidence in its potencies, draws an icon of human openness to every world and every possible transformation.

In an ironic way, the trickster symbolizes the reality of human beings, that "freak," as Pascal calls him, who is the "glory and refuse of the universe" (Lynch 1973: 87). Freakily, the trickster can image human openness to the sacred by lust, gluttony, lying, and flatulence. His satiric mimicry of shamanic rites and practices is not a sign of popular hostility to priestly arrogance. Rather, like Ogo's rebellion against Amma or Legba's phallic dance, his satire affirms the doubleness of the real and denies every one-dimensional image of it. If he struggles with the High God and causes pain and death to enter the world, spoiling primordial bliss, his quarrel is not with the divine order as such, but with a false human image of the sacred, one that cannot encompass suffering, disorder, and the ultimate mess of death. If death is allowed to remain an anomaly lying outside all the patterns of life, then, immobilized by death's presence, life will become stasis. Death seems static because it manifests—with breath leaving, bowels voiding, words escaping into silence, movement fleeing, spirit vanishing, flesh decaying—such total collapse, a perfect centripetality. However, if this centripetality is captured for the center and for the classifications of life, then death's absoluteness of movement will guarantee life's external re-irruption.

Thus it is that so often the trickster's actions make death part of human life. For example, Eshu's ironic use of death, to shatter incomplete order and renew the act of sacrifice that ends the starvation of the gods and their killing of men, discloses the doubleness of the trickster's work. He uses death to stop death—social stasis or breakdown, cosmic rivalry and noncommunion. So, too, Ogo's incest ultimately guarantees human life by fully separating male and female, while Legba and Ananse accept death as the price of cooked food and sex, the transformations that establish the human world. Yet the trickster is no stupid merchant who gets the worse of a slick deal. Just as Ananse trades a stinking corpse for a king's daughter, so the trickster composes an image of humankind exchanging changelessness appropriate only to the High God for an immobility, death, that ironically gives humankind the possibility of new life. The other face of the centripetal quality of death is the centrifugal quality of sex and cooked food, symbols of the life-giving center that humans can become when they open themselves to every surrounding force and mode of being. Therefore in death, which most completely dissolves and fragments humans, the traditional peoples we have studied here see themselves in the trickster as laying hold of the transforming power of the ironic, dialogic imagination whose true stability exists in its capacity to compose new images of life out of every form of death.

This ability of the trickster to turn on its head every idea and event, and death above all, accounts for the humor he provokes as he embodies the radically metamorphic character of humans and their imaginations. His is the irony of wit in the old sense of a truth-seeking power that gives delight by its exposure of the sham of the obvious in the very act of uniting surface and depth. But the trickster both transforms and exploits; when he exposes, he recomposes. When he waves his excrement like the emblems of a shaman, slays elephants with his magnificent flatulence, or simultaneously purges and cuckolds a rival, he is not issuing a manifesto about the overthrow of shamanism, the superiority of the small, or the rightness of adultery. His mockery includes himself, for he literally makes fun of the hidden underside of life, even his own. As the trickster both exposes and transforms that dirty bottom, he invites humans to contemplate what they will become and to hope for what they already are—a world large in its intricacy, spiritual in its crude bodiliness, multiple in its ironic wholeness, and finally transcendent in the absurdity of its pretensions.

The trickster, then, shows that the task of imagining the real is an exercise in sacred irony, because the "real" itself is more than incoherent dailiness or changeless sacredness. The trickster tale lays bare the inner being of social order, and thus becomes, in Clifford Geertz's phrase, "a story [people] tell themselves about themselves" (Geertz 1972: 26). In this sense, tricksters are metasocial commentary. They are a language about every sort of language, and their extravagance, their "wandering beyond" the borders of ordinary discourse—whether ritual, cosmological, or familiar—is an act that both repudiates and affirms this discourse. Like Ogo-Yurugu engaging in unending conversation with Amma, Nommo, and the social order in the depths of the human personality, the trickster makes real the openness of each language to every other language. He makes all experience human experience as he reveals the point at which fluidity and structure, web and dance, become one.

Moreover, because that revelation takes place in a most particular sort of ritualized glee, the trickster shows that the societies that imagine him do not accept the separation between word and event, art and reality, made by our neo-Cartesian culture. The trickster evokes a laughter of truly disillusioned delight. Human dread begins with the suspicion that the project that is life will fail, that every human trajectory will fall short of its goal. Tragedy is the discovery that this failure has its own magnificence, while systems of salvation deny the finality of the failure. The trickster, however, launches himself beyond the boundaries and rules of all structure only to splash down again in the world he left with such boisterous nonchalance, a world he refashions both by his departure and by his return. He displays human order as an enduring system precisely because it is an ironic language where every bit of "non-sense" can be woven into some sort of sentence. Just because the trickster is all synchronicity, he discloses that the irreversible diachronicity of the world, its relentless successiveness, exists as a symbol of dynamism and renewal, not death.

How can such a disclosure be more than mere ideological spinach? In playing creatively with the radical untidiness of a world always moving, breaking apart, and running down, the trickster shows that its leftover fragments and irreconcilable forces are themselves forms of life-giving energy. His scatological bent "exploits the symbol of creativity . . . contained in a joke, for a joke implies that anything is possible" (Douglas 1968: 373). For the premodern mind, the possibility of anything is in itself a threat, not a promise. Human life is seen to be so porous, so vulnerable to forces that will dissolve it, like so much food turned into feces, that only carefully maintained social structures can arrest and control this wasting process. However, these structures too become clogged with waste, and thus the trickster lays hold of them and shakes the stuffing out of them. He celebrates life's porosity, revealing its open-endedness to be hilarious. Anything is *possible;* even feces can be turned into treasure.

In this composting of the products of open-endedness, the trickster acts very much like Thomas Kuhn's scientist faced with challenges to his received paradigms. Both seek to befriend the strange, not so much striving to "reduce" anomaly as to use it as a passage into larger order. Moreover, trying like the scientist to encompass the unencompassable, the trickster yokes just *this* world to a suddenly larger world. His stories and myths are always particular, and the deeper order his passages lead into is always just *here.* Even as he embodies universal qualities of mind and spirit, his work is inescapably specific. Ananse comments on a world carefully balanced between Nyame and Asase Yaa. Legba translates the purposes of Mawu and her offspring to enable the Fon to change and discard form as well as content without ceasing to be Fon. Eshu shatters and reforms the complex image of the divine order that is Yoruba society to move it through mythical and historical time, while Ogo-Yurugu challenges Amma and Nommo to speak the "word of the world" according to its proper Dogon specifications. Even as the trickster may reflect the psychic anxieties and social decisions of a community both tightly ordered and innately porous, he also embodies the power of the ironic imagination to use waste as medicine and to reveal how human vulnerability is, at bottom, liminal openness. Through this power dissolution itself is dissolved, and formlessness becomes the passage to new form.

It is of crucial significance that, as the trickster speaks extravagantly in the specific language of any given people, he joins the energies of the individual imagination and the expressiveness of the transcendent. If the human word in symbol, ideal, ritual, or custom is necessarily many-faced and ironic, then, says the trickster, so is the word of the "really real." The trickster is neither a god nor a man, neither human nor animal; he is all of them. In that "ensemble of texts, themselves ensembles" (Geertz 1972: 29), which exists in the culture of any people, the trickster is only one text among many, yet as master of language he is the ensemble of ensembles, the meeting place of all words. If he is the image of the ironically imaginative mind of polymorphous humans, he is equally the image of the adaptability of transcendence, for which no material thing is too trivial to become a hierophany, not even that little gust of tongue-shaped breath known as the human word.

This word may seem too puny to make anything as large as a world happen, yet in the end it is as possessor of all stories, linguist of the gods, embodiment of divination, and metaphor of social conversation that the trickster reveals the human cosmos to be language. Whether as image or as active reciprocal of the human capacity to converse with every other mode of being, the trickster exposes humans in their inmost and most daily realities. He is a composition of the human flip-flopping needed to hold in balance the words arising from all the conversations in which we are engaged. As the trickster's myths are told, his mastery over form and language also discloses a mastery over time, and suggests that life as it is and life as it might be are ironically joined in the present, a sacred *now* never finally imagined.

It is the quality of this permanently uncompleted *now* that is the trickster's greatest revelation. Peter Berger has seen that humor is rooted in the ultimate incongruity—the "discrepancy between man and the universe." The tragic vision is one response to this discrepancy; yet laughter, the other response, "relativizes" that vision and suggests that "the seemingly rocklike necessities of this world" can be transcended and even transformed (Berger 1969: 87–89). The trickster incarnates discrepancy until it evokes laughter, yet by reveling in contingency itself—in clasping the broken word, the contradictory relationship, the deal gone wrong, the food that never fills—the trickster welds together necessity and brokenness in a composition displaying the hidden ener-getics of the ordinary. His sleight-of-form emphasizes that the necessity of the present exists as a necessary incompleteness always open to a movement at once gross and subtle enough to carry humankind beyond what he sees and knows. Eshu's penis breaks, the travelers fall into the river, and the people shout with glee: the destination is never reached—and therefore it is here.

In large measure, the language composed by the trickster strikes the temporary ear as paradox, perhaps as sheer nonsense. Yet the trickster's is an open body, a body that is also the whole social order experienced as a transforming passage to a cosmic order truly, if not merely, human. Thus the trickster's language is that of analogy, of corresponding levels of being yoked together in an irony demonstrating its own truth by its capacity to realize life's doubleness in society and history as well as in the mind.

Such doubleness, however, is just the problem. Since the Reformation, when the heart of the Christian Eucharist, *Hoc est enim corpus meum* ("This is my body") became simply "hocus-pocus" to so much of Europe, Western civilization has been unable to imagine the doubleness of life—holy and ordinary, rooted yet open to transformation, mortal and enduring—that makes possible transhistorical communion. The final vision of Claude Lévi-Strauss' *Tristes Tropiques* captures elegantly our culture's disenchantment in its portrait of the human race's slide into nothingness, with only the Marxist myth to give it a modest hope of slowing the rate of historical dissolution (Lévi-Strauss 1974: 393–98). Yet it seems to me that Lévi-Strauss has asked only the next-to-last question—"What is there, then?"—and received only the next-to-last answer: "Nothing." The two most persistent images of the trickster—his youthfulness and his glee—suggest that those who imagine their own meeting with death in the figure of the trickster would think that Lévi-Strauss lacks irony even more than faith.

The trickster and his tales are an education in wit. They inform the pliant imagination of the child with adult irony and remind the adult consciousness that all barriers are boundaries of the mind that only a child's expectancy can break through. There, within, death will rule if the imagination cannot find a way to question nothingness, which is both the absolute of formlessness and the silence of perfection. The human voice, in male and female wholeness, rises like the sun to give the world a face, and always it retains, no matter how complex its grammar and its imagery become, something of the primal simplicity of a child's voice—filling the silence of the universe with names, demanding to be heard and answered—even as it achieves the adult wit to spell out both question and answer in ever more elaborate webs of language.

The trickster, then, embodies this childlike voice asking and answering the last question: "What is nothing?" His answer is double. Its first part is this: "When I went there, I found myself back here." The humor of the trickster rests finally on his disclosure of the potency, and thus the sacredness, of all that now exists. Ananse reveals that the corners of human life are not dead ends, but junctures in a web of purpose stretching to all beings and all possibilities. The trickster soars into heaven, forages in the wild, captures contradiction for humankind, not as a promethean hero but as the agent of a sovereign irony holding all ·beings in a mutually sustaining life, whose boundaries ceaselessly widen as he seizes and affirms everything negative and anomalous. In reaching into nothingness the trickster touches the ultimate pollution that threatens each something; and in discovering that nothing's power only thrusts him back into what is present, he transforms every potential avenue of corruption into a passageway of rebirth. The least thing, then, like the worst thing, becomes a possible place for the revelation of what is greatest.

The second part of the answer completes the first: "Nothing? When I touched it, it caught me, and filled me with joy." If the trickster's opponent is named "Hate-to-be-contradicted," ought not the trickster be named "Love-to-contradict?" He can speak all languages and embrace every form. Why should he fear nothingness and death? Why should he not, instead, revel in the passage of old forms into new? Indeed, he does. His extravagant glee insists that to be stuck in the sweet viscosity of the world is sheer delight, because this world—in the ambiguity of its sweetness as much as in its unyielding, unclassifiable ambivalence—is the image of a transcendence as inexhaustibly fluid as water, as wholly present as air, as immovable as earth.

In this metaphysics the trickster is neither first cause nor last end. He is an exemplar of wit in action, the most practical joke of all as he pulls the chair out from under the system to keep it moving, as he bounces back from beyond every beyond with a gleeful shout that *there* is really *here*. Other peoples have made similar discoveries, of course. The Buddha's smile, Zen masters' pranks, and especially Jesus' cross—all in various ways proclaim that no-thingness will never have the last laugh. But with his own odd, ambiguous clarity the trickster reveals that the active reciprocal of the apparently bottomless *passio* of human yearning he embodies is nothing—so huge, so dense, so resilient, so ungraspably all-embracing that, once touched, it turns bottomlessness inside out to a fullness that is pure joy.

NINE

A JAPANESE MYTHIC
TRICKSTER FIGURE:
SUSA-NO-O

Robert S. Ellwood

This study explores the trickster figure in Japanese mythology. It is restricted to one figure, Susa-no-o, and essentially to one text, the *Kojiki,* completed in 712 C.E., the oldest extant Japanese book. The trickster dimension of Susa-no-o has been suggested before, for example by Cornelius Ouwehand (1958–59) and Maruyama Manabu (1950), but to the best of my knowledge this figure has not been extensively discussed in light of current trickster theories.

I

A basic purpose of this investigation will be to show how Susa-no-o, while undeniably a trickster figure in any sense of the term, also ends up as an exemplar of sacred kingship, and in the process demonstrates congruence between the trickster role as such and the ritual role-reversals and taboo-breaking that can be part of the "testing" and initiation of a candidate for sacred kingship. These observations may be of general as well as specifically Japanese theoretical interest.

In the course of this study we look at Susa-no-o as trickster in light of categories derived from the landmark works of Paul Radin (1955), Mac Linscott Ricketts (1966), and Laura Makarius (1969). Ricketts cites two groups of traits characterizing the trickster that point suggestively to those which, on the one hand, indicate his "outsider" and merely disruptive nature, and on the other, those which make him, however devious his means, a benefactor of humankind and which suggest the attributes of the archaic sacred king, a magical giver of bounty and culture as well as establisher of order. The first set of traits are those of the trickster as such: prank-playing, erotic, hungry, vain, deceitful, cunning, wandering, breaking of taboos, spoiling, and clowning. The second are those of the trickster as transformer, a culture-hero who changes a chaotic myth-world into an ordered creation: fertility figure, slayer of monsters, thief of light, or bringer of other boons for human-kind.

In the classic Japanese mythology as presented in the *Kojiki*, Susa-no-o can be shown to exemplify most of these features (I follow the translation of Phillippi 1968 and the Japanese text of Kenji 1960). Ambiguous and equivocal, a deity associated with water and storms, this god is both constructive and destructive. Brother and consort of the sovereign goddess Amaterasu, he is also her adversary and spoiler. He is a god of heaven, ocean-born, and lord of the underworld. Giver of ruin and death, at the same time he is slayer of a noxious dragon, rescuer of a maiden (in a variant of the Perseus/Andromeda myth), and bestower of fertility and culture.

Susa-no-o, then, is more than the comic and earthy trickster found among North American Indians, particularly the Winnebago. Certain of the themes emphasized by Ricketts, such as the trickster parodying the shaman as well as stealing goods from heaven, stress the human fool side of the trickster and are muted in the Japanese god. Susa-no-o is genuinely ambivalent: divine yet subject to the most infantile of human passions, destroyer yet culture hero. As Kerényi said of Hermes, Susa-no-o is a "trickster among the gods" (in Radin 1955: 188–89). Thus he disregards boundaries both cosmic and moral, yet is not merely a spirit of disorder. He rages wantonly and incites chaos, yet even this chaos is productive for the development of the divine order in the long run. He is destructive yet heroic and life-giving. Even his "holdfast" role in the underworld is important to the divine economy and to the mythic plot. Unlike some tricksters who may seem to be "locked in" as eternal rebels against all order and propriety, Susa-no-o undergoes transformation.

Two basic theories are offered to explain this state of affairs. One party, represented by the distinguished mythologist Matsumura Takeo (1951), views the god's split character as the result of a confrontation between two groups. Susa-no-o, it is said, was initially the patronal agricultural deity of Izumo. The benign picture of him derives from that region. However, the view of Susa-no-o as a violent and obstreperous opponent of Amaterasu, the Yamato patron, represents the point of view of the Yamato court, which in the end was to write the *Kojiki*. Other scholars, such as Higo Kazuo (1942 and 1943, summarized in Ouwehand 1958– 59), without entirely denying the influence of regional antagonism and of the circle within which the literary versions of the myths were produced, see the apparent contradictions as integral to Susa-no-o and as embodying a complex mythic scenario, itself confirmed by ritual and folkloric reinforcements.

Our present purpose is not to resolve this issue, even though it is acknowledged that on it may hinge the question of whether Susa-no-o is originally and essentially a trickster figure or has become such only by the grace of fortuitous literary juxtaposition. We will content ourselves with the *Kojiki* narrative itself, which is complex enough for this preliminary foray. Our position is that Higo Kazuo has sufficiently demonstrated the viability of the complex Susa-no-o typology in Japanese mythology. In Japan a single deity may be both benign and unreliable. In any event, the *Kojiki* has exercised enough influence in Japan to warrant the examination of its structures for their own sake. Let us then summarize the *Kojiki* account of Susa-no-o, giving some attention to critical and interpretive points.

The background is a myth of the Persephone type. In the beginning the primal parents, Izanami and Izanagi, descended from heaven. At the end of a great bout of procreation, in which these two produced both gods and lands, Izanami, the primal mother, was killed while giving birth to the fire god. Izanagi, her mate, pursued her to the underworld but was unable to bring her back to the land of the living, for she already had eaten the food of the other world. Chased by hideous hags and polluted by the realm of death, he was forced to return above. In the process of purifying himself in the ocean Izanagi generated other deities. The most important of these were the solar Amaterasu, who issued from his left eye; the lunar Tsukiyomi, who came from his right eye; and Susa-no-o, who was produced from his nose.

Izanagi then entrusted these three noble offspring with great missions: Amaterasu was to rule the High Plain of Heaven, Tsukiyomi to rule the kingdoms of the night, and Susa-no-o to govern the oceans. The first two went decorously to take over their charges. However, Susa-no-o—whose name may mean "swift, impetuous male" or simply "the male (god) of Susa," a village in Izumo—immediately showed his cross-grained character by refusing to enter into his watery kingdom. Instead, he sat down and wept. When Izanagi impatiently questioned him, he stated that he wished instead to go to the land of his mother, the underworld. Enraged, the first father expelled his son from the earth. Still quite contrary, the impetuous god now determined to go first to the High Plain of Heaven to take leave of his sister Amaterasu before descending below. In Paul Radin's words, he was a trickster who "is at the mercy of his passions and appetites" and who "possesses no values, moral or social" (1955: ix). Susa-no-o begins to exhibit himself as "the spirit of disorder, the enemy of boundaries," as Karl Kerényi has put it (1955: 185).

His ascent to Heaven causes the mountains and lands to shake and roar, which startled Amaterasu. She muttered that it was to no good purpose that he was coming up. Putting up her hair like that of a warrior's, wrapping herself in the magical *magatama* beads, and taking up a bow and quiver, she stamped her feet with awesome force and greeted her sibling with furious challenges. Some scholars have viewed this performance as revealing a masculine side of the goddess, possibly suggesting a hermaphroditic nature (Sokichi n.d.). However, others propose that we may actually be witnessing a powerful shamanistic dance, appropriate to Amaterasu inasmuch as shamanism in ancient Japan was mostly feminine. In this case the shaman would have been possessed by a militant male deity whose garb and manner were assumed by her (Nobutsuna 1947). The symbols—beads, bow, stamping—in any case were clearly associated with shamanism. If this scenario is correct, we have here a scenario in which Susa-no-o as trickster is set against a shaman figure. We shall return to this point later.

Susa-no-o showed no starch in the face of that warlike apparition. Announcing that he had only the best of intentions, he proposed that his sister and he swear oaths and beget divine children. They achieved the begetting, employing their swords and jewels in a magical manner.

After this orgy of procreation, suggestive of the typical sexual prowess of the trickster, Susa-no-o boasted of moral victory over his suspicious sister, crying out that the beautiful children he had produced proved that his intentions were pure. But then he was carried away with his supposed triumph, and "raged with victory," breaking down the ridges between Amaterasu's rice paddies and strewing feces in the place where she was about to celebrate the Harvest Festival, the Niiname-sai, the most important rite of ancient Shinto and one often laden with overtones of ominous significance. Finally he dropped the body of a backward-skinned pony into a room in the new house of the Niiname where Amaterasu was overseeing the weaving of divine garments by her maidens. One seamstress was so shocked she pierced herself in the genitals with the shuttle and died. Some variants have it that Amaterasu herself was wounded.

All these crude and brazen insults represent the transgression of ancient taboos, revealing Susa-no-o at his height as prankster, spoiler, and breaker of taboos. Amaterasu first sought to excuse her brother and mate. After the last outrage with the pony, however, she became frightened and hid her solar self in the rock-cave-of-heaven. Heaven and earth were plunged into darkness, giving rise to a myriad of calamities.[1]

All the remaining deities met in the river of heaven to discuss this very serious matter. The great solar goddess was finally lured out of the cave by a ribald dance, obviously parodying shamanistic practice. Succeeding in having the lovely deity back in their midst, the assembled gods turned to the business of punishing the obstreperous Susa-no-o. They severely fined him, cut his beard and nails, and once again expelled him from divine society, casting him down to wander the earth.

If we accept the *Kojiki*'s own chronology, once on earth the outcast soon visited a goddess called Ogetsuhime—undoubtedly identical with Toyouke of Ise and other forms of the great food goddess—and asked her for viands. She responded by taking various kinds of food out of her own body. Seeing this, Susa-no-o thought it so repulsive and polluting that he killed her. Out of her body then grew various useful plants—rice, millet, beans, wheat, and soybeans—which were used for seed.

This mythic episode, probably related to the similar and more famous Hainuvele myth of Indonesia, is repeated in the *Nihonshoki* with Tsukiyomi, the moon god, as the deity who slays the life-giving food maiden. Most authorities believe that this passage is inserted here gratuitously and thus has no intrinsic relation to the main narrative (Phillippi 1968). Nonetheless, it could be seen as playing a significant literary role at this juncture, for this suggests a positive, transformative, and boon-giving side to Susa-no-o's violence, which so far had been almost wholly destructive. The violence can now be associated with the mystery of death as the prerequisite of life, a theme that so preoccupied archaic agriculturalists.

The next tale represents Susa-no-o's greatest triumph as a hero. Finding an old couple weeping because their last daughter had to be sacrificed to an eight-headed and eight-tailed dragon who required a maiden every year, the god vowed to destroy the monster. Susa-no-o met the enemy and, like Indra with Vritra, offered wine to each of the eight mouths. When the beast had fallen into a drunken sleep. Susa-no-o hacked him up. In the monster's middle tail, he found a sword. This became the famous Kusanagi sword, part of the imperial regalia. Susa-no-o then married the maiden. Arriving refreshed in spirit at Suga in Izumo, he there built her a palace, where they both dwelt.

This universal story is of considerable Japanese folkloric interest. Through popular religion we can trace the exploits of a great deity represented by a serpent, who is a mountain lord and controller of the waters of rain, storm, river, and flood. Higo Kazuo even suggests that, despite the conflict, Susa-no-o may also be another version of the same deity, reflecting in agricultural society the ambivalent nature of water: now beneficent and now destructive. In field research, Higo Kazuo found at least one shrine to Susa-no-o, fairly popular as an agricultural deity, in which a serpent symbolized the god. At a number of other shrines, springtime rites were held in which straw serpents were "slain" in pulling contests or with bow and arrow, offered to the god, and finally thrown into a river with customs suggesting that a water-god is being propitiated. In some cases the *Kojiki* myth is invoked to justify these practices (Ouwehand 1958–59).

Susa-no-o's final appearance is in the cycle of his son or descendant Okuninushi. Okuninushi is now the principal deity of the Grand Shrine of Izumo and one of the most interesting and sympathetic deities in the Japanese pantheon. He was one of a band of many brothers who, like those of Joseph in the Bible, despised and tried to kill him. However, he showed his worth by healing a rabbit skinned by a crocodile. Twice he was killed by his brothers and twice revived by his mother through quasi-magical means. Some commentators have seen in Okuninushi the figure of the archaic shamanistic healer initiated by passage through death and resurrection; he is certainly the prototype of the Izumo kuninomiyatsuko, the priest-king of Old Izumo (Phillippi 1968: 94).

After the two revivals from the dead and a near escape from his brothers' arrows through the fork of a tree, Okuninushi was advised, apparently by his mother, to go for counsel to Susa-no-o, now lord of the underworld. The latter had finally fulfilled his primal yearning to rejoin his mother. On arriving, Okuninushi met Susa-no-o's lovely daughter, Suseri-bime, and they immediately fell in love and married. But Susa-no-o seems not to have looked benignly on this union, for he directed his apparent heir to sleep one night in a chamber of snakes, and the next night in one full of centipedes and bees. Each time Suseri helped him flee. Susa-no-o sent him chasing an arrow and then set fire all around him. However, a mouse helped Okuninushi escape through a hole. Later, while letting his daughter's mate cleanse his hair of lice, Susa-no-o fell asleep. Okuninushi tied the older deity's hair to the rafters, took his sword, bow of life, and heavenly zither, and escaped with Suseri.

Once awake, Susa-no-o disentangled his hair and tried to pursue the fleeing pair. But he was too late, and he could only call out to them a grudging blessing. He pronounced Okuninushi a scoundrel, but bade him use the weapons of life to subdue his brothers, make Suseri his chief wife, and become *Utsushi kuni tama no kami*, ruler and divine spirit of the land, dwelling at the foot of Mt. Uka. This is the same spot from which Okuninushi still reigns in his great shrine.

The Izumo great deities have a pattern of engaging in tremendous land-making activity, after which they go into quiet retirement as the kami of a shrine. In the *Izumo Fudoki*, the divine protagonist pulled huge blocks of land with a great hawser from Korea to make Izumo. When these prodigious labors were done, he set his staff in the ground and enshrined himself in this sacred spot. Subsequently Okuninushi seems to have become assimilated to Susa-no-o; he became known as ruler of the underworld, psychopomp of the dead, and patron of marriages.

II

What are we to make of Susa-no-o? He has been given a fresh interpretation by the studies of Yoshida Atsuhiko and Obayashi Taryo, which have attempted to link Japanese mythology with Indo-European, especially as the latter has been analyzed in terms of three divine functions in the well-known work of Georges Dumézil (see Obayashi 1977; Yoshida 1961–63, 1977, and works of these scholars in Japanese). This connection would have seemed quite incredible until recently, but archaeological and comparative mythological research has now brought forward evidence that Korea and Japan were probably in contact with Indo-European, Iranian-speaking Scythians in the early centuries C.E. Korean royal tombs of the fourth century have yielded evidence of strong Scythian influence. It is quite possible that, were permission given to excavate them, Japanese Kofun-era mausolea would produce similar results. Perhaps the horse-riding people who, according to one leading theory, entered Japan shortly after 350 C.E. to become the Yamato imperial and aristocratic class were Scythians or at least of a Scythianized culture (see Ledyard 1975).

Their takeover perhaps is reflected in the dynastic and religious changes the *Kojiki* shows beginning in the reign of Ojin, who is portrayed as coming from Korea in the sense that he was born just after his mother Jingu Kogo's return from her historically improbable conquest of that land. Only the post-Ojin emperors are commonly termed *hi no miko*, children of the sun. It seems likely that it was only after the takeover that the imperial solar descent as well as the solar character and supreme sovereignty of Amaterasu became the court ideology (see Waida 1976). Indeed, Amaterasu may be modeled on Jingo Kogo (perhaps the same as the Himiko or Pimiko, Sun Child, of the Chinese chronicles) as shaman empress. Japanese priests and spirit mediums are not well distinguished from the deities they serve. Thus, it is noteworthy that the first mention of Amaterasu within the historical portions of the *Kojiki* after the days of the legendary Jimmu Tenno is a deity who possessed the Empress Jingo, who was in a mediumistic trance while carrying Ojin.

This is not to say, however, that all the myths of Amaterasu, much less the entire myth-cycle with which she is associated or the persons of all the other gods such as Susa-no-o, necessarily arrived in Japan on horseback in the fourth century. All sorts of adjustments are possible. One could hold that a new mythic pattern was superimposed by the conquerors within which old folklore survived only as bits and pieces and names. Or one could contend that the new arrivals needed only to make relatively slight adjustments in existing mythology to suit their own ideological needs. Whatever the case, one can be sure that the official mythology as we have it in the *Kojiki* represents the invading aristocracy's own interpretation of things, after it had jelled a few centuries later and was canonized in court circles.

The Indo-European school tends toward a high view of change imposed by the Scythian-related conquerors, at least in the official *Kojiki* text. The school would see behind the Japanese names and conventions not only isolated Indo-European myths such as those of Perseus and Persephone, but also gods classifiable according to the three functions described by the great Indo-European comparativist Georges Dumézil. These functions are (1) the maintenance of the cosmic order through priesthood and sovereignty, (2) the presence of war and physical prowess, and (3) the power of fertility and production. These corresponded to the classes of archaic Indo-European society: (1) kings and priests, (2) aristocratic warriors, and (3) farmers and artisans. Amaterasu, for example, becomes a heavenly sovereign, and Okuninushi the land master of Izumo, a strong exemplar of the third-function deity. However, it is Susa-no-o who fits into the second function. Like Vayu and Starkdr elsewhere, he epitomizes the wild and disruptive aspect of the warrior's calling, even as Takemikazuchi exemplifies its controlled and benign aspect.

So it is that Susa-no-o's outrages in heaven can be interpreted as the "sins" against the first-function cosmic order common to second-function figures everywhere.[2] The deity's subsequent more benign career in Izumo has to be construed as movement into the third-function role so well limned by his descendant and son-in-law Okuninushi. These theorists go so far as to make the submission of Izumo to Jimmu Tenno, scion of the first-function Amaterasu and Takamimusubi, a reflection of the victorious war of the gods of the first two functions against the third, found also in the Eddic account of the struggle of Aesir and Vanir. It seems undeniable that the *Kojiki*, the ruling class's version of its own self-legitimating mythology, contains Indo-European pericopes and is frequently capable of trifunctional interpretation. The Scythian hypothesis seems a reasonable way to account for that. On the other hand, presumably only the few remaining Shinto fundamentalists would deny that the sources of Japanese mythology are exceedingly complex.

Nonetheless, the three-storied universe, the creation narrative, the High God sending down messengers, and the centrality of shamanistic scenarios, while not without possible Indo-European correlates, are all aspects of the *Kojiki* that seem to me more closely akin to Altaic (Turko-Mongol) models. Southeast Asian and Oceanic mythic parallels to such themes as the murder of the food goddess are well known. With respect to what Higo Kazuo discovered about Susa-no-o's obstreperous behavior in heaven toward Amaterasu, possible folkloric and cultic background for this myth may provide alternative explanations for material that has been interpreted as an example of trifunctionalism in action.

However Indo-Europeanism does much to illumine the *Kojiki*. A basic motif of Japanese mythology is the marriage of heavenly male deities to daughters of land kami to produce an offspring who incarnates both harvest and sovereignty. One is reminded of the amours of Zeus and the royal lines that proceeded from them. However, the Japanese unions of heaven and earth are never interpreted as rape but as proper marriages consummated only after the suitor has passed some sort of test. The child of this union, such as Okuninushi or Susa-no-o, becomes a hero who ultimately establishes sovereignty. Like these two, the child is notable for pushing the limits of the cosmos, pursuing adventures to all levels of the universe, and embodying every extreme of temperament. This role clearly calls for the talents of a combination of hero and trickster, or a trickster among the gods who, when called upon, can rise to the dignity appropriate to a god. In his going from ocean to heaven to earth to underworld, Susa-no-o exemplifies extremes of border breaking, disruptiveness, and fecundating serenity.

To some degree this role certainly parallels the Altaic motif of the shaman, who is supposed to have access to all worlds above and below, near and distant. Here one is also reminded of the Polynesian Maui. But perhaps in this respect Susa-no-o can be seen as most comparable to Indra or a combination of Thor and Loki. These gods all began life as an offspring of heaven and earth, experienced difficulty in finding their proper level, and underwent vociferously wild and obstreperous moods. All explored the various realms of reality, from heaven to the abodes of giants and serpents, and fought with tellurian dragons. As these deities' lives advanced—and their cults developed—all showed traces of moving away from disorder toward becoming more dignified, more related to the bestowal of fertility and sovereignty. In both this area and in his putative relation to atmospheric phenomena such as wind and rain, Susa-no-o can be viewed as cognate to the Indo-European second-function deity, and not simply as an expression of destructiveness.

What is most important to our concern with Susa-no-o as trickster among the gods is his relationship with sovereignty. He seems to have been the founding god and sovereign of Izumo, and by his charge to have passed the dignity on to his descendant. I believe Susa-no-o's trickster qualities and sovereignty-giving qualities are linked. These in turn are also linked to his fertility and agricultural role.

It is Susa-no-o, as an establisher of a kingdom and dynasty, who after his birth from the sea and primal wailing dwelt in three realms with a quite different character in each place. At all times, however, something of the trickster is visible. In heaven he was deceitful, orgiastic, and outrageously destructive. On earth he assumed a different nature. He remained prone to violence but with good results; he used trickery to slay the dragon and rescue the maiden, but nonetheless emerged as the classic hero. He then established his kingdom with his bride. In the underworld, his temperament again changed. He became a "holdfast" deity who tried to keep Okuninushi from marrying his daughter, but his tricks and stratagems always failed, as Okuninushi outwitted the senior lord. Okuninushi then replaced—in effect merged with—Susa-no-o as lord of agriculture and great deity of Izumo. When this divine dynasty later submitted to the Yamato line descended from Amaterasu, it was given control of the underworld as compensation.

Because of his trickster indiscipline and outrages, Susa-no-o was active in all three levels of the mythic cosmos. This activity is important to sacred kingship and links him to that model. A general feature of the sacred king in Japan is that he or his ancestors have done "something" in each realm: in heaven, earth, and the underworld. The same can be illustrated in the accounts of Izanagi, Okuninushi, and Amaterasu. In the ancient Japanese Daijosai accession ceremony, which is still enacted by each new emperor, the sovereign wears a garment called the *hagoromo*. In mythology, this garment is worn both by celestial beings (on their descent to earth) and by the first of the earthly imperial line, Prince Ninigi. The new emperor enters two lodges with white and black lamps, which might possibly include earth and underworld in their symbolism, thus making the rite an enactment of descent from heaven and entry into the two realms. The *Nakatomi no Yogoto*, a liturgy containing very archaic material recited at the Daijosai, refers both to the imperial heavenly descent and to underground waters; these are probably also the waters with which the emperor ritually bathes in the

Daijosai, and in Japanese mythology these waters are closely connected with the underworld (see Ellwood 1973).

Another class of Shinto festival that may have a relation to Susa-no-o and the complexities of his character is the "laughing" and "abuse" matsuri. In these closely related observances, most commonly associated with New Years, participants laugh together in the shrine before the presence of the deity at something the kami is believed to find funny. Often it is, in fact, an erotic burlesque. Alternatively, they heap abuse on each other. Because these maledictions are not taken seriously, they soon lead again to the same end—uproarious merriment. These performances are held to soften the kami's heart with fun and, some add, also allow the god to express vicariously and harmlessly the scorn he must feel for mortals (see Marukawa 1963).

The best known shrine dedicated to Susa-no-o, the Yasaka Shrine at Gion in Kyoto, formerly had a famous custom of this type. In the Edo period the great writer Saikaku described it in these words: "Worshipers go to the Shrine of Gion in the capital city on New Years Eve for the ritual of *Kezurikake*. Lights before the shrine are dark and faces cannot be distinguished, when the worshipers, old and young, men and women, stand apart on both sides and strive to heap abuses of various kinds on one another. It's so funny that the listeners hold their sides with laughter" (*Seken Munazanyo*, 1692: iv; cited in Marukawa 1963: 13).

Susa-no-o's outrages against Amaterasu do not parallel this ritual exchange of insults between men and women quite as obviously as does Izanagi and Izanami's trading of boasts at the gates of the underworld. Further, it was not simply Susa-no-o's outrages that provoked the assembled gods into the uncontrollable laughter that lures Amaterasu out of the cave. But we should bear in mind that all these episodes took place within the context of the Niiname-sai, the Harvest Festival, which in ancient times was assimilated to New Years. The Niiname is the great pivot of archaic Shinto. Unless its paradigmatic themes and customs are fully understood, nothing of Shinto myth or attitudes can be rightly comprehended.

Let us recall that Amaterasu was enclosed in a sacred room preparing for the Harvest Festival at the time of Susa-no-o's unexpected intrusion. Further, the Harvest Festival was, and still is at Ise, celebrated at night (even as was the Gion laughing rite). Here are two *Manyoshu* poems about the Niiname from the same century in which the *Kojiki* was compiled:

> Though it be the night when I make
> offerings of the early rice of Katsushika
> I will not keep you, darling,
> Standing outside the house.

> Away, you who rattle at my door,
> On this sacred night of new rice-offerings,
> When I've sent my man out
> And worship in the house alone.
>   (*Manyoshu XIV:* 3386–87, 3460, trans. Shinkokai 1940)

The Hitachi Fudoki from the same century tells of a wandering deity who attempted to visit the kami of two mountains on the evening of the Niiname. One refused him entrance, saying the interior of his house was taboo on that day, but the other admitted the visitor, offering him food and drink (Shozo and Atsuharu 1940). To this day at the related Namahage festivals of northern Japan, persons dressed as gods go from door to door accepting food and drink and offering, like the American Halloween, "trick or treat!"

Thus, we see that the Niiname was celebrated at night and that offerings were prepared by a woman—a feature doubtless connected with Japan's ancient matrilocalism and powerful female shamans. But these same passages also suggest that on this night husbands left their homes. Later, as it also suggested by continuing custom, "mysterious visitors" would arrive and bang violently on the doors of these houses. These were, of course, the menfolk, perhaps disguised as gods and perhaps not at their proper homes. In time they may have gained admission, perhaps by proving in some more or less ritual way that they were truly gods, as the mythic paradigms suggest over and over. Once inside, they shared in the feasting or even a temporary *hieros gamos* (sacred marriage). The point is that to break a taboo at this particular time, as in the ritual orgy, abuse, and taboo-transgression of so many other Japanese festivals, would be quite intentional and seen as leading in the end to divine laughter and human benefit.

Even though Amaterasu was not amused and Susa-no-o apparently failed the Niiname test, these observations hint at an interpretation of Susa-no-o that—far from making him just a naturally disruptive, negative entity—casts him as really a "good" fertility god and disaster preventer who had to go through an abusive, taboo-breaking performance for the sake of a greater good. This is a role quite appropriate to a trickster, a point to which we shall return. It also fits the actual cultic image of Susa-no-o as chiefly a fertility deity on the order of Toyouke and Inari. But within this type Susa-no-o specializes in disaster prevention. The world-famous midsummer Gion Matsuri, previously mentioned, mounted by the Yasaka shrine in Gion, is intended to ward off plague. Such work is never far removed from the abuse, laughter, and ambivalence so central to Susa-no-o's cultus. When that deity was engaged with Amaterasu in an orgy of procreation before the Harvest Festival on that mysterious night of role reversals, his zeal first surged into obstreperousness before falling back to relative and precarious benignancy again.

Moreover we can see reflected in Susa-no-o the archetypal Japanese myths of both agriculture and sovereignty. The intimate connection of these two motifs is shown by the fact that the most sacred accession rite of a new emperor, the Daijosai or Great Food Festival, is at one and the same time his inaugural performance of the Niiname or Harvest Festival, the same rite at which Amaterasu was interrupted. The paradigmatic myth behind both harvest and kingship characteristically tells of the descent of a heavenly male deity who marries an earthly maiden, probably the daughter of a land kami. After some obstacle has been removed or an enemy of the marital coupling has been defeated, this union then produces an heir. The child is the harvest and/or the founder of a sacred ruling dynasty. In the case of the imperial lineage, the first two heavenly scions sent down to earth failed of their mission. Thus, Ame-waka-hiko was killed by an arrow at the time of the Harvest Festival. A third envoy, Prince Ninigi (Ama-no-hiko-ho-no-ninigi), succeeded in marrying an earthly maiden, but the first child was born in a burning building amid an atmosphere of suspicion. A younger son of Ninigi, Ho-ori, quarreled with the older brother and then went to the realm of the Sea King and married his daughter, but not until he had passed a test involving mounting a throne-couch, like that in the Daijosai lodges, in such a way as to show he was of true blood. (This pattern and particularly the concept of the "disrupter" is described in Ellwood 1973: 45–49, 70–71, and in Sokyo 1956.)

Susa-no-o then clearly has the sort of background appropriate to a sacred king, even if this has been achieved by often unedifying situations into which his trickster character has plunged him. Thus, because he refused to rule the sea, wailing childishly instead for his mother and his more decorous sister, he went to heaven. Cast down again to earth because of his outrages, he apparently ended up in the underworld because of his first immature desire. Nonetheless, he became a ruler, representing heaven in the archetypal marriage of heaven and earth, overcoming the obstacle of the dragon, and producing a harvest and a dynasty through trickery.

Laura Makarius interprets the trickster as the essential breaker of taboos. Drawing from African, North American, and Oceanic material, she demonstrates that he characteristically has an impure birth, commits incest, and violates interdictions. The latter are especially those connected with "dangerous blood," blood which can curse but which also has magical power when adeptly employed (Makarius 1969).

Thus the Algonquian trickster Manabozo slew a bear whose blood was used in the tribe's sacred medicine. However, another myth of the same tribe has Manabozo kill a bear who was the lover of his grandmother, throw some of its blood on her belly, and in the act curse all women with the menstrual cycle. Moreover, violating the most stringent taboos, Manabozo went into the womenfolk's menstrual hut to choose and marry his wife, but this flagrant violation brought him only good luck in the hunt.

It would be easy to picture Susa-no-o as a trickster of the same sort. His birth clearly involved impurity, for he was born of the washings of Izanagi's oceanic purification. It is implied that he desired to commit incest with both his mother and sister. Even though it is probably too restrictive to contend that the trickster's transgressions need to involve "dangerous blood," we may note that blood was, in fact, a matter of very serious taboo in ancient Shinto. As with disease and death, blood could not be put close to a holy place. Remember too that, following several of Susa-no-o's outrages, a maiden weaving in the sacred hall of Amaterasu struck the shuttle against her genitals and died. It can, I think, be persuasively argued that the *Nihonshoki* variant in which it is Amaterasu herself who is injured is probably the older version. In any case, it seems obvious that the connecting of blood with the genitals is at the very core of the taboo-breaking. Furthermore, it is interesting to note that the earlier licentious dance, by which Ame no Uzume aroused the godly laughter that drew Amaterasu out of the cave, apparently included a compensatory positive female genital magic. Later, when Susa-no-o killed the serpent to save the child that was to become his bride, we are told the river Hi ran with blood.

The offenses committed by Susa-no-o seem to have had also a liturgical character. They closely parallel the lists of those sins that are especially ritually polluting. These lists were read aloud at the very ancient rite of Oharai or "Great Purification," performed by the Court whenever ritual impurity was feared and later on a regular basis.

Thus, later in the *Kojiki*, at a significant juncture in Japanese history, while the Emperor Chuai played the trance-inducing zither, the Empress Jingo became divinely possessed. The possessing deity told the imperial couple to go West and seize the treasure-land of Korea. Chuai questioned whether there was a land to the West and whether the possessor might be a deceiving deity. The enraged god cursed the sovereign to death. Until his demise, the sovereign was still playing his zither.

Because of this extremely ill omen, the Great Purification was held throughout the land. We are told that "a thorough search was made for such sins as skinning alive, skinning backwards, breaking down the ridges, covering up the ditches, defecation, incest, and any sexual relations with horses, cows, chickens, and dogs" (Phillippi 1968: 259–60). After the Great Purification was held, the possessing deity was again invoked, with the Empress serving as medium. The possessor now revealed herself as none other than Amaterasu. This is, as we have seen, the first mention of her name since the Divine Age and the days of Jimmu Tenno. The order to seize Korea was repeated with the possessor, adding that the conquered land would be ruled by the child in the Empress's womb, the future Emperor Ojin. This child was reportedly born as the Empress returned from the conquest of Korea.

The first five of the sins exorcized above strongly suggest those committed by Susa-no-o. In the Oharai Norito (prayer) of the *Engishiki*, an important court ritual text published in 927 BCE (see Bock 1972: 85–86), these first five of the *Kojiki* list just cited are cited as among the "Heavenly Sins"; the rest, the sexual sins of incest and bestiality of which Susa-no-o was apparently ironically innocent, plus such pollutions as skin disease, insect infestation, and witchcraft, are cited as "Earthly Sins."

This last peculiar list, which does not include such ordinary crimes as murder and theft, is clearly not a mere moral code. It suggests rather a ritual index seeking to isolate at least representative examples of both intentional and natural events that not only violate the norms of the human community but also flagrantly affront the natural cosmic order itself.

The explicit perversions of the "Earthly" pollutions are obvious. However, the "Heavenly" examples are themselves also highly symbolic pollutions. Skinning an animal backwards may be no great thing in itself, but to the taboo-conscious mind to do *anything* in reverse or backwards is to do it the opposite of how it was *meant* to be done. Any such action constitutes a potentially dangerous insult to the cosmic order. So, too, the abuse of the natural agricultural function of ridges and ditches, or defecating in the wrong place, reverses the positive cosmic order. So it is that Susa-no-o's violent taboo-breaking was of an acutely symbolic character.

We have seen that as a first-class taboo-breaker Susa-no-o's acts are best understood as cosmically symbolic offenses intentionally committed, or mythically placed, within the context of the Harvest Festival rituals. The *Kojiki* narrative, together with other ancient myths, poetry, and rites, hints at lost aspects of the Harvest Festival usage that were central to religion and sacred kingship in the Japan of the protohistoric era. Beyond this hint one can only speculate. However, precisely in this vein let me suggest the following speculative scenario.

Ancient Japanese rulers and chieftains typically had a sister, wife, or other female relative who served as court shaman. This shaman, in a trance, would give advice from the gods on matters of state. This practice is reflected in the mediumistic role of Jingo and survived among Ainu and Okinawans into the present century. A shadow of the *tenno miko* was also perpetuated in the role of the imperial princess who served as priestess at Ise into the Middle Ages (see Ellwood 1967).

The Harvest Festival was apparently a night when heavenly envoys, sacred sovereigns, and aspirants to sovereignty were tested. Let us say that on that night this woman shaman retired together with female servers, like Amaterasu before them, to a new and pure ritual house to prepare the first fruits and sacred new garments.

These offerings would be presented to the kami of the land. The shaman would personify the daughter of the land kami, to whom heavenly male kami would descend to achieve a marriage that would produce a present harvest of food and a future harvest of sovereigns. As the night wore on, she would probably go into trance to allow that princess-goddess *(hime)* to speak through her.

Then a man dressed as a heavenly kami—the ruler or aspirant— would come to the pure house with a great clatter, demanding entry. However, a test had to be met before the sacred door could open and the harvest feast and probably the couch of the "goddess" could be shared. Not all at the Harvest Festival passed this test. Some were rejected and had to leave unsatisfied. Others seem to have died suddenly and mysteriously, like Akme-waka-hiko.

It is likely that this scenario included some sort of abuse and deliberate taboo-breaking that, though dangerous, might through this ordeal assure the worthiness of the male kami as well as the prosperity of the coming year. Perhaps there would be an exchange of insults between those inside and outside the house paralleling the later abuse festivals. Perhaps the visitor would try to desecrate the sanctity of the New House until the shaman, like Amaterasu when Susa-no-o first came clattering up, was possessed by a militant deity strong enough to face the visitor down. If this visitor was unable to transmute his passion from rampage to procreation and to attain the demeanor of a sovereign aligned with cosmic order, he would fail the test.

Clearly that was a job which called for someone with some trickster capacities, able to move with facility among temperaments and cosmic levels. Susa-no-o shows a fascinating ambivalence between successful and unsuccessful enactment of this role. No matter how cross-grained his character and how unorthodox his means, this trickster among the gods manages to bring good in the end. Susa-no-o represents a particularly intriguing window into the religious mind of ancient Japan.

TEN

SAINT PETER:
APOSTLE TRANSFIGURED
INTO TRICKSTER

William J. Hynes & Thomas J. Steele, S.J.

At first glance there would seem little reason to view the Apostle Peter within the context of the New Testament as anything but a straight-forward disciple of Jesus. Furthermore, within the ongoing tradition of the formal Christian interpretation and ritual presentation of Peter, where has it been suggested that he may also be a trickster? However, when popular interpretations of Peter are examined, particularly those within the Christian folklore of the Yaqui, Spanish, Mexican, and New Mexican cultures of the American Southwest, numerous instances of Peter as trickster can be found. How could such a seemingly disparate state of affairs come to be?

Within mainstream Christianity, Peter has most often been viewed both as an exemplar of the *imitatio Christi,* wherein human chaos is conquered by belief in Jesus, and also as an ecclesiastical leader through whom the authority structure of Christianity, particularly in its Roman Catholic form, has been legitimated. At the same time, there are elements within the Biblical picture of Peter that depict him as a bumbler and liar. However, it is only within the unofficial realms of popular Christianity that these elements are subsequently developed. Here Peter has often been celebrated as a trickster who constantly does everything he shouldn't and who upends every situation and authority including that of Jesus himself.

It will be argued here that although there are certain trickster elements in the New Testament picture of Peter, these are used in quite divergent ways by different groups within Christianity after the close of the New Testament canon, in accord with their respective symbiotic interests.

Thus mainstream Christianity, largely intolerant of disruptive behavior in general and of the seemingly chaotic activity of the trickster in particular, often passes over the trickster elements in the scriptural portrait of Peter as anomalous to Peter's real character, or it simply views these elements as aspects of human sinfulness that were overcome by faith in Jesus. Popular Christianity, on the other hand, more enamored of the acknowledgment and celebration of disorder, seizes these same trickster elements and expands the picture of Peter to include a wider range of features typical of a more fully blown trickster figure.

In short, popular Christianity seems far more disposed to appropriate the trickster potential in Peter, extending explicit elements from the Biblical picture and supplying additional components to augment and expand Peter into a more recognizable trickster. There are numerous examples of such stories, particularly in medieval European folklore. In fact, a more extensive treatment of this subject might attempt to trace linkages between European and New World Petrine folklores. However, this chapter will focus mainly upon the Christian folklore of the Yaqui, Spanish, Mexican, and New Mexican cultures of the American Southwest to demonstrate how popular Christian culture apparently supplies a number of components absent in the Scriptural picture of Peter so he can become a more ample and typical trickster figure.

TRICKSTER TRAITS

As is noted in an earlier chapter, tricksters seem to be found at the heart of virtually every religion and culture. Systems normally busy generating firm adherence to their beliefs also maintain within these belief systems, somewhat contradictorily, a raft of tricksters who perpetually invert and profane these same beliefs. In myth and ritual tricksters seem to be officially sanctioned exception clauses by which belief systems regularly satirize themselves.

A border-breaker *extraordinaire*, the trickster is constantly shuttling back and forth between such counterposed sectors as sacred and profane, culture and nature, life and death, and so on. Anomalous, *a-nomos*, without normativity, the trickster typically exists outside or across *all* borders, classifications, and categories. He neither norms nor is normed.

In most cultures and religions where the trickster is found, he acts as the underlying cause of disruptions and disorders, misfortunes and mishaps, importunities and improprieties. All semblances of truth and falsity can be subject to his rapid metamorphosis. His lying, cheating, and stealing from forbidden sectors seem to occur within a perpetual bubble of immunity. Everything he touches is subject to his disassembling and dissembling. He is a postmodernist gone riot!

The trickster can be both messenger and imitator of the gods. At times they may send him for a specific purpose. Other times he may be found parodying the powers and prerogatives of the gods themselves. As Ricketts argues elsewhere in this book, shamans and priests of the gods are favorite targets for his satire. In crossing the border between life and death, the trickster often functions as psychopomp, escorting separated souls to the land of the spirits. It is also quite common for the trickster to bring gifts essential to human culture, usually by violating a border or by breaking a central taboo; thus he may bring fire to humans only after he has stolen it from the gods. While he traffics with the transcendent, he also looses lewd acts upon the world. Yet, in his role as *bricoleur*, the trickster can transform any of these aspects of his character into beneficial contributions to culture and religion.

SCRIPTURAL PORTRAIT OF PETER

The images of Peter found within the New Testament reflect a fairly high degree of anomaly and ambiguity. Although double names are not unusual in the New Testament, and even though there is no consistent pattern with respect to this figure, the appellations Simon and Peter symbolically incorporate much ambiguity and oppositeness. At the very least his name change from Simon to Peter marks the transition from ordinary person to apostle (Mark 3:16).

The ambiguity of this figure is clearly felt when at one moment he is referred to as the *Cephas*, literally, in Aramaic, the rock on which the church will be built (John 1:42), and in the next moment is called Satan because he tries to hold Jesus back from his impending passion (Matthew 16:22–23). He is both a "Peter" of great faith and a "Simon" of "little faith" (*oligopistos:* Matthew 14:31). On the one hand he is chosen to lead and feed Jesus' flock (John 21:15), and on the other hand he is a *skandalon,* an open impediment to faith (Matthew 16:23). At one and the same time he is both the living stone of faith and the stumbling stone of disbelief (Brown, Donfried, and Reumann 1973: 92–94).

The first to proclaim overtly Jesus' identity as Messiah (Matthew 16:16, Mark 8:29), Peter's triple affirmation counterbalances his triple denial (Luke 22:54–62; John 18:25–27). This apostle imitates with inconsistent success Jesus' walking on water and his healing of others (Matthew 14:22–31, Matthew 17:14, Acts 3). Simon Peter can be both a babbling dunce (Mark 9:5) and an eloquent spokesperson (Acts 1–3). He is both a "youth" who girds himself, going wherever he pleases, as well as an "old man" girded by another, empowered to go into fearful areas (John 21:18).

As the chief *apostolos,* Simon Peter is first and foremost a messenger. In this role he clearly attempts to imitate Jesus—if often in a superficial, foolish, and comic manner, such as in the walking-on-water scene. In the face of Jesus' approaching passion, it is this apostle who insists emphatically and enthusiastically that he will lay down his life for Jesus, only to have this assertion challenged directly by Jesus and then inverted quickly and conspicuously a short time later. In John's account of the last supper, Peter's attempt to correct what he perceives as Jesus' undignified action of washing the apostle John's feet is rebuffed by Jesus' statement: "If I do not wash you, you have no part in me." To that the apostle Peter responds impassionately and extravagantly that Jesus should also wash Peter's hands and head (John 13:6–7). When Jesus is about to be taken prisoner in the garden, Peter acts impulsively, drawing his sword and cutting off the ear of Malchus, the high-priest's servant, only to be rebuked again by Jesus for preventing Jesus from pursuing his father's mission: "Shall I not drink the cup the Father has given me?" (John 18:19).

In the apocryphal Acts of Peter, we are offered a marvelous coincidence of *imitatio* and *inversus* when it comes time for Simon Peter to die; he asks that he might be crucified—but upside down (Acts of Peter 37). This disciple is given powers specifically over borders, particularly the borders of death. In imparting to him the keys of heaven Jesus states: "Whatever you bind on earth shall be bound in heaven, whatever you loose on earth will be loosed in heaven" (Matthew 16:19). In rabbinical language, Peter seems to be empowered to declare certain actions as forbidden and others as permitted. In short, he sets and unsets limits or demarcations central to belief and practice.

Peter breaks one crucial pollution-taboo, resulting both in the significant resetting of dietary categories and in the redefinition of who can become Christian (Acts 10:9–16). In a thrice-repeated vision, Peter is instructed by God to eat foods previously considered unclean. In this vision a great sheet, held by its four corners and containing every creature that walks, crawls, or flies, is let down upon the earth. When Peter is instructed to "kill and eat," he refuses on the grounds that he has never eaten anything profane and unclean. He in turn is corrected: "It is not for you to call profane what God counts clean." In this way what was previously profane and unclean is inverted to become what is acceptable and clean. In terms of the thesis of Mary Douglas' *Purity and Danger* (1966), what had been "unclear and unclean" becomes now "clear and clean."

Further, this vision offers a *raison d'être* for Peter's associating and eating with gentiles, especially gentile Christians. He is clearly a cultural transformer, although not by theft or deceit. Peter's attitude is far more overtly respectful than that of most tricksters, inasmuch as he does not plot or connive this transformation, but is explicitly instructed from above to break this taboo. More importantly, it is this action that redefines who may become Christian and unifies previously ritually disparate Jewish/Gentile Christian communities. Yet even in this area, Peter exhibits sufficient inconsistency to warrant a confrontation with Paul (Galatians 2:11–14).

The gift of the keys of heaven also includes certain psychopompic powers. Not only does Peter serve as the rock upon which the church is to be built, but the "powers of death," that is, literally, "the gates of Hades" (*pylai haidou*), will not prevail against it (Matthew 16:18). These psychopompic powers closely parallel those held by the Son of Man who declares that: "I have the keys of Death and Hades" (Revelation 1:18). Nonetheless, Peter's encounters with death are pervaded by ambiguity. Thus, he is perturbed for a period of time by the prospect of Jesus' death (Matthew 16:22). Once reconciled to this, he declares himself ready to face his own death (Mark 22:33), only to have his readiness inverted by subsequent events, as already mentioned. This same ambiguity about death is played out metaphorically in the apostle's struggle with sleep in the garden of Gethsemane. Here Jesus' threefold injunction to the disciples to be awake and watchful is met each time with the response of sleep. Jesus notes this polarity with the observation that "the spirit is willing, but the flesh is weak" (Matthew 26:33).

Peter's denials of Jesus obviously involve both lying and deception. However, even this deception seems relatively ineffective. In Mark's account, Peter's denials are so transparent as to fail to convince the inquirer (Mark 14:66–69). In contrast to the pattern of most tricksters, there are virtually no deceptions directed by Peter toward Jesus. Further, Peter's deceptions seem neither rapacious nor continuous. While a few incidents can be interpreted as implying trickery, they are not generally elaborated upon. Thus Peter twice escapes from prison without the knowledge of his captors (Acts 5:17–19; 12:1–11). Having impetuously committed Jesus to paying the temple tax, Peter is instructed to pay the tax for them both by catching a fish in whose mouth he will find a shekel (Matthew 17:24–27). This action conveniently avoids a confrontation concerning whether it was appropriate for Jesus to pay this tax. In Luke's account of the calling of Peter, there is a partial parallel when Jesus says that henceforth Peter will be "catching men" (Luke 5:10). However, this passage does not overtly allude to any specific trickery.

If there is very little trickery clearly associated with the Peter of the New Testament, there are absolutely no pranks to be found. There are two other areas where the New Testament portrait of Peter is notably deficient with respect to trickster elements. First, there is only very modest and exclusively metaphorical shape-shifting linked with Peter: there are the plays on the double name of Peter as well as the contrast between the living rock and the stumbling stone. However, the frenetic transmorphisms that occur with most tricksters are absent. Secondly, there is clearly no lewd behavior surrounding the picture of Peter in the New Testament.

In summary, the New Testament presents a complex image of Peter as a highly impulsive, impetuous, unrefined, spontaneous, elemental, and exuberant person. He is exceedingly quixotic and is forever buffeted by rapid reversals in attitude and behavior. Peter exhibits the central ambiguities and polarities so typical of tricksters. Further, he is a messenger who frequently attempts to imitate Jesus. While associated with border breaking, situation inversion, and deception, he is not linked with trickery, transmorphism, and lewd behavior.

In confronting the New Testament portrait of Peter, most mainstream Christian commentators have focused upon the office and prerogatives of Peter. A few, including Origen and Augustine, have found themselves touched by the ambiguity at the heart of this figure (Brown, Donfried, and Reumann 1973: 95). Contemporary interpreters occasionally repeat similar observations almost in passing. The Gospels present a "very mixed picture of Peter" (Brown, Donfried, and Reumann 1973: 62, 77, 107). He is both "faithful and faithless," exhibiting "a compound of every strength and weakness among the disciples" (Scherer 1952: 383–84). "Courageous and cowardly," he is one in whom love and pride are "strangely intertwined" (Buttrick 1951: 434). Peter is deeply "ambivalent" (Rustad 1979: 1–25). The special mark of this man is "a queer undependability. He was as sudden and as fickle in his quickly changing moods as his own Sea of Galilee" (Gossip 1952: 487).

In the end, however, the commentators agree that these qualities simply pose an anomaly in the overall portrait of Peter or offer an instructional device for highlighting the struggle between the presence and the absence of faith. It remains for the popular imagination, as reflected through art and folklore, to fill in and embellish more fully the features implicit in the trickster framework. For our purposes here these features can be demonstrated with examples drawn from Christian folklore of the Yaqui, Spanish, Mexican, and New Mexican cultures of the American Southwest.

Of these cultures, only the Yaqui are indigenous to the American Southwest, inhabiting southern Sonora in Mexico and later some areas of southern Arizona. The first contact between this indigenous culture and Europeans occurred in 1533, when a group of Yaqui defeated a Spanish exploration group led by Diego de Guzman. Beginning in 1617, the Jesuits succeeded in convincing the Yaqui to live in immediate proximity to a series of settlements near the coast. Before the Jesuits were expelled in 1767, they succeeded in introducing new crops and livestock as well as *cofradias,* societies that were instrumental in conveying indigenous and Christian religious traditions. One of four major societies, the Judases, was characterized by its *chapayakan* or clowns who "engaged in complete license, mocking every sacred institution." Among the analogues to these clowns is a trickster-like dancer, *pascola,* who maintains "an almost constant patter of comment on current events, dialogue with members of the crowd, absurd narratives in which he was often the foolish protagonist, and pantomine dramas with the Deer Dancer" (Spicer 1983: 262).

SAN PEDRO IN SOUTHWESTERN FOLKLORE

Each of these cultures evidences a series of tales centering upon the picaresque adventures of San Pedro (Saint Peter) and Jesucristo (Jesus Christ), or similar cognate figures. Let us begin immediately with a particularly rich tale that occurs with high frequency in various forms in all of these cultures. This is the Yaqui version:

> One time San Pedro and Jesucristo were walking along, and Jesucristo sent San Pedro up to a nearby house to get a cooked chicken. On the way back Pedro ate one leg of the chicken.
>
> When Jesucristo saw what San Pedro had brought back he asked, "Why has this chicken but one leg?"
>
> "It never had another leg," answered Pedro. "All of the chickens around this part of the country have but one leg, Sir."
>
> The two proceeded and came to a big tree under which were sleeping many chickens. All of the chickens had one leg tucked up out of sight under their feathers.
>
> Pedro pointed to them and said, "You see! All of the chickens have but one leg apiece."
>
> Jesucristo took a small rock and threw it at one of the chickens. It woke up and stood on both feet.
>
> "Oh," said Pedro, "A miracle!" He then took up a large rock and threw it to awaken the rest of the chickens. "You see," he said, "I can perform miracles, too." (Giddings 1959: 46)

This tale advances the image of Peter as impulsive and deceptive. However, a number of improvements have been added that develop more fully his trickster potential. Pedro now attempts both to deceive and to steal from Jesucristo directly. Here we have both the quick brilliance of the practiced liar and the inventive ability of the *bricoleur* to capitalize on events on the spur of the moment. Jesucristo is the hungry master/ requestor and Peter the servant/messenger who illicitly eats that for which he has been sent. Jesucristo's powers are not only imitated, they are openly mimicked and parodied. There is some shape-shifting, not of Pedro himself, but of the inert chicken. Queried about the missing leg,

Pedro lies, attributing its absence to the type of chickens found in this area. He is quick to reinforce this deception when they happen upon a flock of chickens. When Jesucristo challenges and inverts this life with a well-placed pebble, Pedro rapidly crafts a new and larger lie, and a greater challenge and inversion, by deeming the act a miracle. Then he prankishly inverts the situation one more time by trumping Jesucristo's miracle with a greater one of his own. These inversions and the more fully wrought trickster characteristics result not only in a greater comic pace but also in a much more sprightly apostle.

There is a striking Italian parallel to this Yaqui tale entitled "The Hare Liver" in which Peter prepares a hare for Jesus and himself. Stopping at a local inn, Jesus orders a half-bottle of wine while Peter cooks the hare. In the process, Peter grows quite hungry and steals the liver with a crust of bread for a snack. When asked by Jesus why there is no liver, Peter attempts to argue that the hare had none and then finds that he can no longer swallow. The next day, Jesus turns the trick upon Peter by sending him to cure the daughter of the king, instructing Peter to cut off her head, soak it in a bucket of water for an hour, and replace it on her shoulders. However, when Peter follows this prescription, it fails to revive the daughter, and he is accused of murder. The Lord intervenes, raises the daughter from the dead, and they are rewarded with a large sack of gold. Jesus proceeds to divide it into three piles: "Five for me, five for you, five for the other one . . ." When Peter asks who is this other one, for there are only two of them, Jesus replies that the third pile is for the one who ate the liver. Peter admits that he is the one who ate the liver so he can gain the third pile of gold, and thus Jesus catches Peter (Calvino 1957: 123–24).

As might be expected, Peter often fails in his endeavors to imitate or improve upon Jesus' powers. In another Yaqui tale, Peter tries to imitate a shamanistic cure previously performed by Jesus. He carries out a mock operation on a sick person, all the while contemplating charging a fee at the end. When the patient fails to recover, Jesus must be sought to correct Peter's botched work. The tale concludes with the moral that Peter subsequently repented his "capricious ways" and was thereafter allowed to cure but "always with the help of Jesucristo" (Giddings 1959: 47).

In the folk-Catholicism of New Mexico, Peter is associated not only with healing but also with psychopompic activities. In particular one prays to him as the "patron of a happy death and admission into heaven" (Steele 1974: 190). In the chapter house of the Penitentes of lower Arroyo Hondo there hung for many years a large painting of San Pedro, which bore on its reverse side a list of all the members of the chapter who had died between 1916 and 1943. (This retablo [#1676] currently hangs in the Taylor Museum, Colorado Springs Fine Arts Center, Colorado.)

There are other close cognates of these San Pedro tales from the same region, particularly those recounting the antics of Pedro di Urdemales or Pedro de Ordimales, that is, Peter of the holy water font. In both Spanish and New Mexican Spanish folklore, the figure of Pedro di Urdemales/ Pedro de Ordimales is viewed as a trickster, one who is perpetually dissatisfied, "ever wishing more," and "a genius who is not subject to ordinary rules." The term itself dated at least to Cervantes' play entitled *Pedro de Urdimales* (A. M. Espinosa 1914: 220).

In both Yaqui and Spanish tales this Pedro is generally a psychopomp closely tied with holy water fonts and the gates of heaven. Here we find distinct evidences of shape-shifting occurring on Peter's part. Thus, he often turns into a holy water font or a herm-like pillar at the gate of heaven, as can be illustrated by the following tale as translated and summarized by José Manuel Espinosa:

> Pedro and Juan are brothers. Pedro goes to herd the goats, fills them with air, and they appear well fed. When he remains at home he feeds his mother cornmeal until she chokes. He dresses her up and places her at the door spinning. When Juan opens the door she falls and he thinks he has killed her. Pedro puts the corpse on a horse and lets the horse loose in a rich neighbor's wheat field. The latter throws a stone at the woman and she falls to the ground. He is sorry, pays for her funeral, and gives the boys money. Twice death comes for Pedro and is caught with pitch. The third time Pedro is taken to Purgatory. He whips the souls there and is sent to Limbo. There he throws the children that cry for water into a river and being baptized they go to heaven. Pedro is taken to hell, puts a cross at every exit, the devils complain, and Pedro is called to task. He asks for a look into heaven and when the door is opened he jumps in. Pedro is turned to stone and remains at the gate of heaven with eyes to watch all those who enter. (J. M. Espinosa 1937: 207. A number of Pedro di Urdemales stories in their original colloquial Spanish can be found in A. M. Espinosa 1914: 119–34.)

This brief summary could easily provide grist for a much larger mill than this present small chapter. In these tales death is continuously manipulated and even captured with pitch, reminiscent of the tar or gum babies of some trickster tales. The trickster *bricoleur* inverts and transforms into profit even the negativity of death. Furthermore, he breaks and resets the very borders and defined limits of Purgatory, Limbo, Hell, and Heaven. In the last situation, Pedro succeeds in sneaking into heaven to assume his post as doorkeeper. In another version of this same tale, Pedro's form is shifted to that of a stone holy water font, which retains some human animation so as better to guard the door of heaven. Even where this turning-to-stone is viewed as a punishment from Jesucristo, Pedro manages to get in the last word. Jesucristo might say something like: "Okay then, Pedro, for your shrewdness, remain here in heaven but you will have to be turned into stone," only to have Pedro reply: "Okay, Lord, but with eyes to watch everything which goes on there" (Rael 1977: 2:237, 246, and 281).[1]

The same Spanish and New Mexican tales of Pedro di Urdemales recount lewd behavior linked with Pedro. One example of scatological humor can be found in the Yaqui tale in which Jesucristo and his ever-present sidekick Pedro are again walking down a road. As they walk, Pedro picks up figs and places them in his small bag. Later on he takes them out one at a time and begins to eat. When Jesucristo asks what it is that Pedro is eating, he responds that it is just burro dung. Of course, the next time Pedro reaches into his bag what he pulls out is dung (Giddings: 47).

In another Pedro and Juan story, we have a noteworthy coincidence of curing, transforming, the breaking of the blood taboo, and infanticide. In this tale Pedro and Juan are not brothers but friends who have been given the honorific title "Don." Don Pedro is married and has a newborn child. When Don Juan falls mortally ill, Don Pedro learns through a revelation that his friend will live only if anointed with the blood of Don Pedro's own child, so he slays his child and anoints his friend, who is then cured. When Don Pedro tells his wife what he has done, they go to examine the dead child only to find it alive and unharmed (J. M. Espinosa: 205). Here the gift of health/life is conveyed only through the breaking of important taboos. Yet not only is the breaker immune from the punishment attached to the breaking of such taboos, but the child is restored as well.

TRICKSTER POTENTIAL IN CHRISTIANITY

From these tales it seems clear that the trickster elements of the New Testament portrait of Peter, both implicit and explicit, are expanded, embellished, and recast by the popular imagination into a figure who more closely resembles a classic trickster. It would be very interesting to pursue a far more comprehensive study of the extent to which this phenomenon is replicated in other Christian folklores. (For an interesting account of how Saint Peter came to be substituted in Louisiana for such West African tricksters as Legba, see Reed 1974: 137.) For the moment, however, let us conclude by commenting on the possible wider significance of this transformation of the picture of Peter within Christianity.

As noted several times in this volume, the trickster has most often been understood as a social steam valve that can vent the pent-up emotions and suppressed feelings resulting from the constrictions of any system of belief and behavior. Laughter at the profanations of the trickster provides a temporary ritual opportunity for a group to remove itself vicariously, as well as to distance itself psychologically, from its own beliefs.

Yet by the same token these negative examples can serve actually to reaffirm the social order (Gluckman 1964: 109). The trickster "affirms by denying" (Zucker 1967: 317). As Vecsey argues in another chapter, in breaking the rules the trickster confirms the rules. That which is "being broken is always implicit there, for the very act of deconstructing reconstructs" (Babcock-Abrahams 1978: 99).

However, this process does not simply repeat a pattern of affirmation/release/reaffirmation. Something more is gained in these transactions and reconstructions. So it is that beyond the surface reaffirmation of a given belief system there is a deeper, broader meta-affirmation that life is more than its socially constructed representations. Thus the trickster redramatizes and reacquaints us with the "more than this" dimension of existence. He evokes the polysemous quality of life (Lorenz and Vecsey 1988 [1979]: 1–11). Its unbordered multivocality is affirmed over and against all univocality. In short, the trickster makes the cyclopean eye of monoculturality swivel in its socket; he roils the tribal waters of life lest they go stagnant.

Accordingly the apparent return to order following the trickster's antics can be deceptive. In fact, humans have now moved "beyond order and disorder to transformed order" (Pelton 1979: 8). At the very least, in this process tricksters offer opportunities for ritual rebellion in place of actual rebellion, inasmuch as a belief system can become more bearable by its brief reexposure to its own relativity. At the maximum, on the other hand, tricksters certainly can prepare the way for adaptation, change, or even total replacement of the belief system. They are in this manner potential preludes to social change. Complaints are registered in remote places and opportunities given for subsequent amendment.

Some view the trickster as the prototypical human symbolizing "that aspect of our own nature which is always nearby, ready to bring us down when we get inflated, or to humanize us when we become pompous . . . to make it possible for us to gain a sense of proportion about ourselves" (Singer 1972: 289–90). Carl Jung views the trickster as a "shadow," which at a first level brings to the surface the underside of dominant values, playing out human forbiddens in a dreamlike fashion. At a metaphorical level, the trickster might be said to be a creative mediator toward that which is differentiated, unordered, spontaneous, and whole. Playing in and with the inchoate other, the trickster puts us in contact with the yet-to-be-focused energies of the psyche.

Peter's ambiguity can serve as a convenient index to two very different worlds of experience within Christianity. The first is that of mainstream, official Christianity, wherein Peter serves as the prototypical Christian and apostle. Peter can be said to stand for the proclaimed order and orthodox beliefs of the overworld, a mediator among principles that are differentiated, predictable, and distinct. The second world of experience is that of popular Christianity, wherein Peter stands for the underworld of rampant disorder and Christian forbiddens, all that is undifferentiated, spontaneous, and whole.

If the first world possesses a dependable and socially reinforcing Peter, it also lacks the distinctive ritual vent which Peter as trickster offers, through which Christians can periodically air frustrations and tensions resulting from the constrictions of the belief system. By contrast the less sober popular Christianity created for itself not just a steam-valve trickster through whom potentially disruptive feelings are released, but one who, ironically, by breaking the rules actually confirms them again.

Like so many other tricksters, the Peter of popular Christianity drama-tizes the contingency and fickleness of existence. Life in general and Christianity in particular are seen as larger than their social or religious construct. At the same time, while Christianity occasionally accentuates the "more than this" dimension, for example in mysticism, there is also the less than subtle implication that for all their limitations we must have social and religious constructs. For the most part unsuccessfully, main-stream Christianity attempts to capture the dynamics of this contingency in the notion of the arbitrary will of God, which lies above all rationality. (We are indebted to Conrad Hyers for recalling our attention to this often forgotten doctrine.) Ultimately, however, the Stoic rationality surround-ing the God of mainstream Christianity proves too deeply rooted to be dislodged entirely.

Without disrupting the enfranchised traditions, there can be neither the exhilaration of exception nor the fecund power of intermingled categories. In short, the creative production of new possibilities resulting from the playful transgressions of borders by tricksters is foreclosed to those who view only the one side of Peter, attending neither to his more disruptive side in the New Testament nor to his more expanded trick-sterish personality in popular Christian folklore.

Tricksters and their foolishness lie somewhat fallow within main-stream Christianity after the close of the New Testament canon, and they are often subject to suppression when they develop within popular Christianity. This suppression is profoundly deepened by the mono-culturalism occasioned by the post-Renaissance rationalism and scien-tism of Western Europe. When Erasmus penned his *In Praise of Folly,* foolishness was still seen, at least residually, as a sign of God's presence. Within a century, religious and political authorities deemed such activity a disease of sufficient cultural embarrassment and social danger to require that such mental innocents be placed in the conveniently vacant leper hospitals (Foucault 1965: 65–67). Official assemblies of main-stream Christianity, both ascetic Protestant and reactionary Catholic, roundly criticized and suppressed the Feast of Fools and various other forms of saturnalia (Davis 1971: 41–48). By the seventeenth century, even court jesters were hard to find. This intolerance of foolishness was paralleled in the discovery and subsequent suppression of the diversions and inversions associated with wildmen and witches (White 1972: 3–38; Szasz 1970: 293–322).

In the end, the existence of Saint Peter as a trickster within popular Christian folklore stands as a poignant witness to the disparate Petrine images found within Christianity, to the creative process whereby the popular imagination perceives Peter as a trickster and sets about clothing his person accordingly, and finally, to the inherent difficulties within mainstream Christianity that foreclosed integration into its belief system of the playfully chaotic dynamics and fertile inventiveness of the trickster.

ELEVEN

THE MORAL IMAGINATION OF THE KAGURU: SOME THOUGHTS ON TRICKSTERS, TRANSLATION AND COMPARATIVE ANALYSIS

T. O. Beidelman

If comparison is the characteristic method of social anthropology, it does not follow that we shall be very effective with it.
—Needham 1978: 32

Any claim to universality demands in the nature of things an historical or psychological, rather than a sociological, explanation, and thereby defeats the sociological purpose, which is to explain differences rather than similarities . . .
—Evans-Pritchard 1963: 16

Recently I was asked to participate in a seminar on the concept of the trickster in African societies. As I surveyed the literature I became increasingly unsure as to whether this was a meaningful exercise, mainly because I doubted the usefulness of such a general analytical category as *trickster*. As I pondered why this should seem so, I began to question some of the ways anthropologists employ the comparative method to understand the meaning of collective representations in other societies. I found no satisfactory solution to my questions, but I have now recognized some of the misleading assumptions that impede our understanding. In this chapter I indicate what these seem to be. While I begin this essay as a consideration of tricksters, I end by addressing critical but insoluble issues at the heart of what anthropology is about.

TRICKSTERS

The theme of the trickster has prompted a wide range of explanations for what seem to be, to quote Evans-Pritchard (1967: 29), "unedifying incidents." Anthropologists leave us with confusing arguments as to what this figure means. For example, at one pole we find Evans-Pritchard (1967: 29) writing: ". . . there is nothing buried. All is on the surface and there are no repressed symbols to interpret." At the other pole, his student Street (1972: 101) reanalyzes the same Zande material and concludes that the trickster is at the very heart of Zande metaphysics, presenting "a model of the 'meaningful' to the audience and show[ing] how it developed and is continually being developed out of the meaningless, the amorphous." Recently, Babcock-Abrahams (1975: 182–85) surveyed the writings on tricksters, coming up with six functional explanations, although favoring a Turnerian interpretation of a trickster as a liminal figure expressing "anti-structure," a phrase that Turner has employed to characterize situations in which the hierarchical and authoritative aspects of societies are purported to be temporarily dissolved. While I am not in full agreement with Babcock-Abrahams' views (see Beidelman 1978b), she does provide useful coverage of the basic literature. There is little to be gained by covering the same ground, from Radin to Lévi-Strauss, especially when I believe that few new insights on the topic will be gained from such a general, global approach rather than from more intensive studies, single or comparative, of particular societies.

It may be that *trickster* is too general a category and that those such as Babcock-Abrahams who consider characters as culturally disparate as Ture the Spider and Easy Rider may have begun backwards. Unless we know particular tricksters and their contexts well, we cannot assume that they represent a valid analytical grouping. In an argument similar to mine attacking the global concept of *trickster,* Kirk (1974: 18–21) criticizes the tendency to place a wide and disparate range of texts under the rubric of *myth.* This is not to reject such terms out of hand, but rather to urge analysts not to begin their analyses by assuming the obviousness of categories they are about to examine. The category of *trickster* may be merely the product of a series of false translations, much as terms such as *family* and *witchcraft* seem incomparable cross-culturally when taken out of context. Certainly, all six functions cited by Babcock-Abrahams seem plausible[1] and may well apply to any such material, even that not related to such figures. What this suggests is that perhaps broad questions of function are unprofitable; instead, we may ask what texts suggest about a particular society's mode of thought and form of organization, rather than raise questions about tricksters in general.

Not surprisingly, I propose as my particular case the oral literature of the Kaguru, an East African people with whom I am familiar. In so doing, I include a group of characters that everyone may not agree to call *tricksters*, but which exemplify certain forms of supposed disorder and mischief, sometimes even malevolence, though ultimately commenting on morality and order by their play with boundaries and ambiguities of these key concepts. In presenting material in order to criticize a global definition, one is drawn into using the very terms and references which one is subjecting to question. In this paper I use the term *trickster* for characters in Kaguru oral literature, even though my aim is to advocate abandoning the term as applied on a global basis. I use *trickster* in a shorthand manner to refer to a category of figures only in part resembling what are conventionally termed *tricksters* by those making universal categorizations. Yet no term corresponding to our term *trickster* is used by Kaguru themselves to subsume these various characters under one category, even though certain symbols are shared by many (though never all) of these figures, and even though the actions and plots in which these figures appear seem, at least to an outsider, to be considered similar by Kaguru—if one can judge from their responses as listeners when certain tales are recounted. Yet when queried, no Kaguru would agree to place all such characters (as I list below) together in any formal manner such as might please the anthropologists.

KAGURU TRICKSTERS

While liminality or blurring of categorical attributes and roles is, according to Babcock-Abrahams, the essence of the *trickster*, a reader or listener could not discern this liminality if he were not already familiar with the symbolic categories peculiar to a particular society. Turner and others sometimes write as though liminality were somehow a manifest aspect of content rather than a relational category derived from prolonged and intensive consideration of a particular symbolic idiom.

Kaguru often recognize the ambiguity of certain characters, even before the plot develops, because Kaguru already are attuned to the qualities assigned. There are seven prominent ambiguous (trickster) figures in Kaguru oral literature, four from the animal world (hares, hyenas, birds and snakes) and three from the human (scabious youths, certain senior and junior kin, and old women). Several other animals and humans may also qualify, but they do not appear frequently in the extensive texts so far collected. (My conclusions about Kaguru oral literature are based on my own collection of 167 tales, along with some riddles and oral history; I also rely on the five tales collected by Busse 1936.)

HARES AND HYENAS

Among Kaguru certain animals are most likely to be considered tricksters by those, such as Babcock-Abrahams, who discuss tricksters on a global basis. The two that appear most frequently are hare (see Beidelman 1961; 1962: 227–29; 1963a; 1963c: 138–41; 1965: 24–27; 1967a: 79 [two tales]; 1967b: 170; 1974b; 1975a; 1975b: 567–70; 1976a: 50–53, 53–55, 55–57; 1978a: 84–85; Busse 1936: 63–64 also records two tales that feature the hare) and hyena (Beidelman 1961; 1963a; 1963c: 138–41; 1974b: 252–53; 1975a; 1976a: 53–55, 55–57, 57–71, 72–75, 75–79, 79–81, 81–84, 84–89), often in opposition to one another (Beidelman 1961; 1963a; 1963c: 138–41; 1974b: 252–53; 1975a; 1976a: 53–55, 55–57, 57–71, 84–89). I have published elsewhere on the significance of hare and hyena in Kaguru thought (Beidelman 1961, 1963a, 1974b, 1975a: in the first three I comment in detail upon various texts; in the last I try to summarize what Kaguru believe about hares and hyenas). These two figures have been reported as tricksters for many African societies and would undoubtedly qualify for inclusion in any global survey. Tales featuring their exploits are especially common in East and Central Africa.

The discussion of such tales may interest folklorists, but what interests me as a cultural anthropologist is the particular notions which Kaguru hold about these animals and their exploits. Hare and hyena oppose and complement one another: the hyena occupies an essentially negative, sometimes menacing, more often grotesquely comic role, the hare, a positive role. The hyena is closely associated with witchcraft, with deviancy from morality. It is the inverse of what proper animals should be. It is active at night, devours carrion (including human flesh), has a wild (almost human) laugh, stinks, is supposedly hermaphroditic; it is thought to be greedy and indiscriminate in its diet (uncultured), untrustworthy, scheming and calculating, yet ultimately doomed to failure because of its clumsiness and shortsightedness.

By contrast with the hyena, the hare is thought to be the swiftest, most agile, cleverest and shrewdest of the animals in the bush. In various tales, nevertheless, the hyena and hare are often portrayed as kinsmen or friends. In such cases, the hyena is usually a harsh and exploitative mother's brother or elder, and the hare an unjustly persecuted nephew or junior who eventually gets his own back through guile. In large part, the good hare and the bad hyena are distinguished not just by their acts but by their physical attributes. In the course of their machinations and struggles, each protagonist commits cruel and hurtful deeds: lying, maiming, stealing, cheating and killing. The actions of the hare are almost always presented as justified, self-defensive retaliations against the abusive hyena. Where he appears less favorably is when he is paired with and opposed to innocuous creatures such as guinea fowl and bushbucks. By contrast, even when other animals are paired with the hyena, the latter always appears in a bad light.

While the hare is usually justified, this is not always so; and while the hyena is selfish and harmful, he cannot really help being so, for that is his inherent nature. There is a poorly defined line between the exploitative villain (hyena-witch) and the shrewd, roguish manipulator of others (hare = opportunist and leader). One of the topics of all such hyena and hare tales is the exploration of the various possibilities and difficulties involved, however perilous they often are, in steering a course of judicious social behavior while not confusing reasonable survival with heartless self-interest; there is a bit of hyena in hare and vice versa. These tales are told almost exclusively to young people and may be their first lessons in the more difficult realities of social relations where the protagonists embody that vague and somewhat troubling social ambiguity that Weber recognized as occurring between rightful authority and abused power, between pursued duty and mere opportunism. This interpretation, while probably valid, takes us little beyond Babcock-Abrahams' third, fourth and fifth functions.

BIRDS AND SNAKES

Two other creatures, birds (Beidelman 1963b; 1963d: 743–51; 1964a: 16–24, 24–25, 34; 1964b: 113–14; 1965: 21–22, 37–40; 1967a: 75–76 [two tales]; 1967b: 174–75; 1967c: 11–16, 34–35; 1970: 335–41; 1973: 92–93; 1974a; 1974b: 239–50, 252–53; 1975b: 550–55, 563–64; 1977: 68–69, 70–71) and snakes (Beidelman 1964a: 1–9; 1965: 27–37; 1970: 335–41; 1971a: 21–23 all refer to a supernatural, malevolent, seven-headed serpent; other tales feature less spectacular though still supernaturally endowed snakes: Beidelman 1965; 1967c: 3–8; 1970: 341–48; 1971a: 23–24; 1975b: 558–61, 563–64; 1977: 57–63, 71–73, 79–80) also occupy highly ambiguous roles in Kaguru tales. These seem close to being animated embodiments of abstract forces, which we might term *fortune* or *misfortune*. Both birds and snakes turn the tables on others in a sense similar to our classic notions of handmaidens of fate.

To Kaguru, the word *ndege* means both "omen" and "bird," and many birds are associated with omens (Beidelman 1974a). In all texts where they appear, birds possess supernatural qualities, rarely malevolent, but usually directed toward turning events in some amazing way back toward order and morality. There is no question that the association of birds with the sky relates to their supernatural significance, inasmuch as both God and sometimes the ghosts of the dead are thought to reside somewhere above. The notion of quick and unrestricted movement associated with birds is, for Kaguru, also associated with supernatural powers, whether good or bad, as with the hare and hyena or with heroes and witches.

Conversely, Kaguru repeatedly associate snakes with the earth and water, problematical elements that must be constantly controlled through rituals of purification and supplication. About half of the tales present snakes as benevolent, half as malevolent; but in all these tales, snakes have supernatural powers. They are never described as the ordinary snakes found in Kaguruland, which Kaguru show no hesitation in killing. Snakes in Kaguru oral literature are portrayed as immense, nearly invulnerable serpents. Like birds, they sometimes "speak," and they may turn into creatures resembling humans and mate with them. Many Kaguru believe that deserted mountain areas (especially those that are heavily wooded and that have water holes or deep crevices) are guarded by fabulous serpents. Some reputed sorcerers and rainmakers are said to have special, sympathetic relations with these creatures.

Birds and snakes in Kaguru oral literature seem to represent those forces in nature—in the wilderness—that, when social life is out of joint, may appear either to help set matters in order or as the very product of such disorder. The chameleon and hyrax may also resemble these forces, but they rarely appear. To an outsider, these last two appear so anomalous that it seems odd that they have not appealed more to Kaguru imagination, though Kaguru do view the former with revulsion and associate the latter with certain aspects of female fertility.

SCABIOUS YOUTHS

In several tales the hero is a youth named Chauhele, a name indicating that one is suffering from scabies and is considered repugnant by one's fellows (Beidelman 1964a: 33–35; 1973: 90–92; 1976a: 72–75; 1978a: 86–87, 108–10). Kaguru view severe physical distortion as potentially conveying supernatural qualities, for good or ill. The more negative parallel to the scabious youth, with his skin covered with infected, itching sores, would be a leper with blotched skin and disfigured features. Whereas lepers were slain or driven into the bush (a sphere of danger and disorder), the scabious youth retreats temporarily into the bush and gains added powers, becoming a hero. Although he acquires abilities, the point is that this was possible only because of his special character revealed through disfiguration.

SENIORS AND JUNIORS

Kaguru tales often stress the tensions between seniors and juniors. Where such tensions involve deception (trickster-like behavior), it is either an unjust elder abusing a junior who eventually vanquishes him or the youngest of several brothers who has greater qualities of leadership (including deception, wiliness, and magical skills) than his seniors (who should, but do not, master difficult situations). The images of both the unjust or incompetent elder and the precociously gifted but long-suffering youth confound traditional principles of Kaguru authority (Beidelman 1961; 1964a: 18; 1964b: 113–14; 1966a: 76–78, 78–82; 1967a: 77; 1967d: 377–79; 1973: 90–92, 93–96; 1975b: 558–61; 1976a: 47–50; 1977: 66–68, 91–93; 1978a: 77–81).

OLD WOMEN

In some Kaguru texts, old women possess supernatural powers and animal familiars, often predators such as hyenas and lions. Sometimes these powers are used to help people, usually by conveying skills or knowledge to facilitate some journey or quest, but often old women are portrayed as greedy, evil and dangerous, and sometimes sharp-toothed. They reside alone in the bush. Kaguru men hold ambivalent attitudes about old women (Beidelman 1961), especially widows. They are not considered fully women if they are beyond menopause. An old woman dwelling alone in the bush stands for a subversion of male authority. Such women are often described as devouring others, especially children whom they ensnare through deception. Such plots associate old women not only with witches but also with dangerous ghosts of the dead residing in the bush and linked with birth and the dangers of infancy. (In several tales, old women provide supernatural help after a younger person licks mucus from an old woman's eyes so that she can see. Kaguru ordinarily associate such a gesture with the expression of affection by adults toward children. Kaguru mothers are said to do this to their infants as a way of showing solicitous care. Such licking of old women by a younger person symbolically equates old women with children, with whom they are already structurally [alternate generations] and supernaturally [two persons nearest to ghost-land] equivalent.)

Infertile and near death on account of their age, old women, like the dead, bestow and withhold life. The ambivalence of Kaguru men toward old women may, perhaps, be understandable in a society where men monopolize authority, but where the crucial spheres of affect are dominated by women. In their roles as sisters and mothers, women become the objects of highly charged, positive emotions. Elder women retain the powers of affect but elude the constraints of men on account of their age and possible widowhood.

KAGURU PLOTS, SETTINGS AND MODES
OF NARRATIVE

"Good" and "bad" acts are often juxtaposed and are described in a manner that leads them to resemble one another superficially. Murder, theft and deceit are committed by both good and bad protagonists, but how these acts are judged depends on the details of character and motivation provided by the storyteller. The difference hinges on the contrast and interplay between rules and responsibilities, on the one hand, and personal loyalties and common sense, on the other—the interplay of what Durkheim terms *justice* (maintenance of rules and propriety) and *charity* (affectual and altruistic generosity). Actions are judged as much by motives as by outcomes. In this, the prevailing Kaguru tricksters are nearly always moral in that their victims are judged selfish, greedy, deceitful, cruel or stupid. (For Kaguru, stupidity and foolishness merit mistreatment because they may lead to misconduct and harm.) The initiator of trickery or bad conduct is devalued, desocialized as it were, so that he may be defeated by being paid back in kind without confounding morality. This represents an inversion of Mauss' notion of initial prestation: the initiators of positive exchange (benefactors) hold permanent superiority over those who subsequently respond. Inversely, in the present case, the initiator of trickery through bad faith can never entirely regain moral standing over those who respond in kind. One wrong does not necessarily cancel out another. In this attitude, Kaguru tricksters ultimately affirm order, for only very rarely do the unsociable and unjust prevail, because they are discredited as the sources of all such subsequent actions. If the bad had not been bad, the supposedly good would have no justification for being harsh (bad). What these Kaguru figures express is ambiguous and complex, much like the individual's relation, as a person, to society: but social constraint, for better or for worse, seems to gain the final verdict for Kaguru.

The settings of such tales sometimes make use of the morally contrasting spaces of the settlement (society) and the bush (nature); a variant contrasts the good protagonist's settlement with that of outsiders or strangers, where proper customs either do not exist at all or exist in inverted form. Trickery occurs where social beings enter the morally problematical space of the bush, where creatures nominally of the bush enter settlements. Sometimes a hero, deviant owing to some misfortune, is forced into the bush where he secures positively valued trickery.

Trickery is often expressed through deviant speech patterns. For example, a narrator will portray a hyena's speech as slurred and bumbling, an old woman's as hoarse and grotesque, and a hare's or youngest sibling's as high and lilting. In discerning relations between words and meanings, there are profound ambiguities and difficulties involving misunderstanding and deceit and varying degrees of eloquence and guile.

CONCLUSIONS AND KAGURU TRICKSTERS

For figures that I term *tricksters*, Kaguru often employ wild animals epitomizing extreme and distorted forms of attributes valued in humans. In contrasting protagonists, tact is distorted into guile, the quest for security and esteem is distorted into greed and envy, and single-minded dedication is distorted into ruthlessness. With human protagonists, good or bad, a physical defect or taste may dehumanize them; they become discolored, distorted, cannibalizing, diseased or deathlike (female barrenness).

Such Kaguru figures also call to mind others appearing in Kaguru society—witches, sorcerers (Beidelman 1963e), rainmakers and certain elders, all thought of in some way as presenting difficult and challenging problems in social life and involving dangerous ties between the world of humans and that of animals and nature. Yet even here evaluation is problematical, for many suspected of witchcraft are so considered because in social matters they are the least easily controlled, a quality that may be as much caused by their being rich and powerful as to the fact that they may have little to lose since they are "down and out." Sorcerers, rainmakers and others may appear less problematical inasmuch as they, like witches, possess ties with the world outside society, with animals, plants and weather. Besides, supernatural powers of sorcery may be employed for evil as well as good. Rains may be withheld spitefully by those who should bring them, and elders are often thought to misuse their powers, which in part relate to their ritual and mystical access to the capricious and dangerous dead.

While these Kaguru figures manifest what some would term "liminal attributes," they are not truly marginal to society or culture. Kaguru beliefs often emphasize maintenance of boundaries and order, yet some powerful Kaguru notions involve bridging categories, as manifest by rituals. Through ancestral propitiation, marriage, joking relations and other ceremonies, these rituals unite the living and the dead, cognates and affines, men and women, kin and outsiders. Similarly, rules of proper behavior may be recited by Kaguru adults to recalcitrant children and enquiring anthropologists, yet at other times these same Kaguru express admiration and envy toward the successful man, the "sharp operator" who is adroit at playing hard and fast with these same norms. Such figures are not odd in that they cannot be fitted into Kaguru categories, but are odd in that they represent recognized characteristics, feelings, motives and roles that cannot all be met by the same person or in one situation. In this representation, then, they are far from being liminal, for they exemplify key dilemmas involved in combining Kaguru belief with successful social action, something at the heart of social life.

Hence, we should not be surprised that many such trickster stories involve issues of elders' authority and knowledge and their relations to power. While by definition authority implies moral assent from the ruled, power and knowledge imply something more problematical morally, for these sometimes involve coercion, misuse of authority or exclusion from information needed for decisions. The very nature of age may involve moral ambiguity. One accumulates wisdom and descendants as one rises toward the apex of a lineage, yet this ascent also creates social distance between those who rule and those beneath, proportionately as a lineage it increases in size. As Bohannan (1958) points out, suspicions of sorcery and witchcraft may be inevitable reflections of such social distances within aging lineages. Similar tensions and ambiguities are often reflected in Kaguru elders portrayed as tricksters. In such roles as those discussed above, the Kaguru repeatedly exercise and challenge their ability to discern the proper from the wrong aspects of certain crucial social roles. Anomalies serve didactically to stimulate Kaguru moral imagination so as to understand existential dilemmas that involve choice in conduct and ends, rather than categorical puzzles in the strict sense of that phrase (e.g., as employed in the works of E. R. Leach and Mary Douglas). To some extent, this purpose is also true for all Kaguru tales, and to consider dilemmas is to consider affectual, moral commitment. Nothing less would drive the Kaguru to embrace the embodiments of their confusions and conflicts in stories, in ritual and in the etiquette of their everyday life.

At this point, it would be useful to consider what I mean by the term *imagination,*[2] at least as I apply it to Kaguru stories. I use the term in a restricted sense to mean the picturing of characters and events in the mind's eye in a manner or form resembling, but significantly different and removed from, reality. The Kaguru storyteller presents extremely simplified groups and situations. For example, two protagonists—such as mother's brother and sister's son—contend for wealth, but other kin and neighbors do not figure in the plot. Or, two such protagonists struggle with reference to only one common relative; or two characters contend over rights toward one set of jural rights and obligations. In reality, issues such as settlement of bride wealth could not be made without reference to numerous past and future unions by others, not to mention myriad other social factors. Characters are also presented in extreme form—as exceedingly greedy, crafty, wily, patient, generous or gullible—whereas few such clear-cut and enduring stereotypes are formed in real life.

Instead of considering situations and persons as inextricably linked to a totality of phenomena over a long, even enduring, period of time, as in real life, the Kaguru storyteller presents an extreme and limited case. The full complexities of overlapping group affiliations, the long history of past relations, the moral vagaries and ambiguities of personalities, are simplified or ignored. No more than one or two principles or problems are explored within a limited social framework and in terms of accentuated moral facets and short-lived situations. While stories avoid the complexities of possibilities in these daily problems, they do point out implications and difficulties posed as one tries to succeed where conflicting and competing loyalties perplex people and where yesterday's enemies may be tomorrow's friends. Their very simplicity gives stories their attraction, just as the simplicity of sociological models both reduces yet helps explain a social reality (Beidelman 1963a). These stories are odd, not in the sense that they do not represent recognized characteristics, feelings, motives and roles, but in the sense that, whereas in real life these cannot all be properly judged and met by the same person or in one situation, here they are clearly defined and resolved. Indisputable, unambiguous moral judgments and permanent resolutions must remain imaginary so long as a person lives.

There is also a sense of the imaginary in finding animals portrayed as Kaguru villagers. Elsewhere (Beidelman 1971b), I try to explain this sense in terms of allowing social distance for contemplating what otherwise might appear as intolerably disturbing acts, such as matricide and fratricide, theft, cannibalism, and cruelty between kin and neighbors. It may be that theriomorphism not only involves distance from the social world, so that it may be toyed with reflectively, but also involves the reverse—subjection of the broader world of creatures into a universe common to Kaguru experience. Perhaps, like Lévi-Strauss, Kaguru sometimes seek to efface the gap between culture and nature (Lévi-Strauss 1966: 246–47; see Crick 1976: 43–44).

The occasions of storytelling also contribute to a sense of the imaginary. Stories are told at evening leisure, when kin and neighbors are gathered around a fire after a meal, during periods which Kaguru value for their sociability (in Simmel's sense) and their aura of satiety and comfort. The supposed triviality of stories, their playful and anecdotal tone, may allow Kaguru to mask their speculative freedom regarding what is otherwise too subversive to be treated so daringly. Furthermore the storytelling space itself, the home sequestered from public contention, display and decorum suggests a temporary relaxation of the wider communal norms. Finally, the most important of all, the quintessential storytelling situation for Kaguru involves the young and the old, ideally grandchildren and grandparents. While parents may tell children stories, it is agreed that it would be more proper for tellers and listeners to be of alternate generations. The reasons relate to the fact that, whereas parents are seen as those holding immediate authority over oneself, one's grandparents are removed from this relation. Because grandparents hold authority over one's parents, they have interest in mitigating parental authority. One can be friendly and free with those persons who try to restrict the persons who try to repress oneself. Kaguru repeatedly describe relations between alternate generations as open, joking and at times sexually uninhibited, as contrasted to the restrictive behavior between parents and children, or between older and younger siblings in general, and brothers and sisters in particular. What better storytellers and audience than those kin least constrained by authority and rules of inhibiting etiquette?

SOME CONCLUSIONS ABOUT TRANSLATION AND MEANING

Hypothetical constructs expand and liberate, if only ephemerally, our sense of choice, as they also profoundly intensify and enlarge the import and drama of social characters making these choices. In this process, imagination and sympathy are inextricably linked when applied to social life, albeit sympathy may lead to repulsion as well as attraction. Thus, imagination becomes a feature of moral awareness. Yet this awareness is not to produce some vague and formless *anti-structure*, to use Turner's idiom, but rather to draw attention to the tensions and interdependence between the individual and his role as a social person, to the conflicting demands and interests that contrasting social roles involve, and to the incongruity inherent in the relations between language, thought, and motivation (a cursory examination of the origins of English words such as *trick* and *prank* suggests notions of antisocial greed [*trick, cheat*] and egoistic self-glorification [*prank* implying both play and display]—see *trick, prank,* in Partridge 1961). Language serves as a midwife to thought, but feelings extend beyond it; motivation is expressed through language and reflects thoughts and feelings, but in a manner that makes it not the sum of these factors but rather a product of their interplay, supportive and yet contradictory, and in some ways impoverishing. One way to characterize this relationship is to contrast the ideal and orderly with the "real" (disorderly, ephemeral, ambiguous). Social ideals are formulated as to what should be, but social life is lived within "reality." We cannot know the ideal in the sense that we can realize it in our daily actions, but we can palliate and subdue what seems real or familiar by subjecting it to the constraints of ratiocination, of wit, of imagination, and of rhetoric, as Kaguru do in their oral literature. In so doing, Kaguru speculate about the nature of their morality and experience, and strike a connection between their vision of the ideal and their experience of the "real."

The title of this essay refers to Kaguru imagination; there I apply the adjective *moral*, suggesting that, for Kaguru (and probably for many others), imagination is not so much involved with epistemological as moral problems. The epistemological is embedded within the moral, but not vice versa. Of course, common thoughts and practices tend to assume the reverse, and I here include anthropological analysis as well as Kaguru belief. In fact, however, what we know is embedded in what we believe, the latter being a base of assumptions and assertions from which we derive our decisions about what is possible and real. What we set up as meaningful is informed with goodness and propriety. The polysemic complexity of such terms as *cosmology* (cosmos, cosmetics—the whole, the ordered, the attractive), or of the French word *conscience* (consciousness, conscience), informs us of this meaning. Morality, with its constraints and affectual implications, is more basic to what symbols are and do than is epistemology, a point that Turner often makes. Leach (1964) seems to make the same point in his criticisms of some of Lévi-Strauss' many deficiencies, but he later seems to neglect this (Leach 1976: 5).

Contrasts and conflicts similar to those described above characterize every society; what we may ask, however, is how these vary cross-culturally, from society to society. If these Kaguru tales examine basic social questions within that society, then a consideration of tales resembling these in other societies would seem likely to take on many of the basic questions raised by cultural anthropology: the nature of words and meaning, the forms of social categorizations, and the relation between beliefs and social action. This is, of course, a kind of functionalist assertion, but at a more suggestive level than examination of material entirely within the purview of one society or rashly at a pancultural, global level, unsustained by intensive comparative analysis. The great problem is how we may discern what constitutes a genuine correspondence between two institutions or two societies.

Societies place different values on deviance, disorder and insubordination. Two well-documented examples nicely illustrate this: ancient Egyptians and the Yoruba of West Africa deify the embodiments of tricksters and disorder and place them centrally in their pantheons (Te Velde 1967; Pemberton 1975). In other societies, such as the American Indians of the Pacific Northwest and of the Southwest, tricksters are described in tales but also incorporated into various ceremonies and rituals. Kaguru have no such institutions, although their joking relations have some parallels (see Beidelman 1966b). Considering the Kaguru, further questions may be asked, although I am not able to answer them. Is there a connection between the situations portrayed in Kaguru trickster tales and those ritual and formalized occasions where deviance and disruption are recognized, such as joking relations and ritual abuse? Is there any way we may characterize the relation of the individual to a society, such as Kaguru, that would lead to better understanding of the form and quality of Kaguru trickery?

Three useful points seem clear. First, not all societies regard apparently deviant, ambiguous or disorderly characters in the same way. In some, figures of disorder and deviance stand at the center of the belief system, being gods activating key cosmological events. The Kaguru material clearly does not resemble this belief, for ambiguous and disorderly figures are not cosmological or mythic in scope. Instead, they appear in a kind of anecdotal oral literature reserved for children that comments upon the complex interplay between roles, norms, and individualistic aims and qualities, as exhibited in social actions. Disparate figures have all frequently been termed *tricksters,* yet this term is clearly the product of the analysts' ethnocentric evaluations of deviance and disorder and does not always derive squarely from the evaluations held by the members of the cultures in which they appear. Disorder and ambiguity serve different functions in different societies and are manifest at different levels of the formal order of beliefs and behavior. They may characterize central moral concern rather than deviancy or subversion. For example, Bulmer (1967) informs us that the Karam of New Guinea regard the cassowary as peculiar, as a kind of cross cousin, fitting various social relations, animals, plants and spatial areas into a broad structural mold. This key figure, while problematical, is anything but peripheral or liminal to Karam concern or social structure. Bulmer also makes gentle criticism of Douglas' explanations about problematical categories, but fails to get at the ideological root of Douglas' difficulties—her apparent assumption of some kind of epistemological "reality."

Second, when considering tricksters—at least as reported here—the concept of *communitas,* as advanced by Turner and taken up by his followers such as Babcock-Abrahams (e.g., 1978), distorts and confuses the issues. The evaluation and comprehension of apparent cohesion and disorder depend entirely upon the perspective from which one regards such phenomena, not only in terms of the concepts involved within a society but also from the perspective of the protagonists within its various units. What may represent disorder and conflict for a lineage may represent order for a household; what represents disorder and conflict at one level may represent inclusive and instrumentally powerful and valued categories at another. Order and disorder, even when culturally defined, are evaluations to be considered as refracted through various levels and segments of a society, intraculturally as well as cross-culturally problematical. Disorder itself represents a further form of order in that it has no meaning outside a broader yet still restricted system of symbolic reference, grounded in both social forms and psycho-physiologically determined perceptions, the latter themselves culturally rooted. This is a contradiction that Turner may be trying to contain when he cites Sutton-Smith's use of the term *proto-culture* to describe "the latent system of potential alternatives from which novelty will arise when contingencies in the normative system require it" (Turner 1978: 294). Turner expands on this with the term *metastructural* to describe the means by which "a system develop[s] a language for talking about normative structures" (Turner 1978: 294). Nominalistic exercises do not solve the difficulty. It may be useful to differentiate between how persons in a society see themselves and how they imagine other conditions or possible societies. Yet some difficulty still seems to be reflected in Turner's concern about deviance and conflict as signs of innovation, change and breakdown in some literal sense, whereas these rest entirely upon and within the existential symbolic systems by which they are perceived and evaluated.

Third, in much of my previous work—as in that by many other American, British and French students of beliefs, symbols and society— there was an implicit assumption that somehow reality involves a myriad of continuously related phenomena, whereas culture is a more limited, discretely constructed assemblage, and that the application of culture to reality creates problems of ambiguity and dissonance. Such a view can be of some limited use, but I now believe that this perspective may blind one to other, more important issues.

[In several pages excised here, Beidelman discusses further the concept of "the real world" and universalist perspectives that pose serious problems for the comparative method; in a sense, however, all is translation,[3] and that is almost impossible to bring off satisfactorily.]

CONCLUSIONS

I began with tricksters, a narrow topic, but end by grappling with questions of epistemology and the comparative method. I provide no direct solution to the problems posed by the concept of *trickster* but suggest we abandon the term and renew analysis from the concerns manifest within each particular society considered. If we later construct broader analytical categories, these would relate to the more complicated systems produced by such particular reportage and analysis. Resulting terms may well divide material previously grouped under the term *trickster.* I also urge that we avoid global explanatory terms, such as Turner's *communitas* and *liminality* or Leach's and Lévi-Strauss's forms of reductive structuralism. Instead, we should try to relate attributes and actions of tricksters and similar figures to different and shifting roles and values within particular societies, especially avoiding judgments about these being good or bad, integrative or disruptive, central or liminal, rational or irrational, in any holistic sense. We should remain suspicious of approaches that allocate ambiguity, contradiction and conflict to the peripheries of society. Contrary to being indications of change, dysfunction, or "cognitive dissonance," these phenomena under scrutiny represent the essence of social life. Rodney Needham (1970: xxviii) observes that long ago Hocart (1970 [1936]) wisely noted "the prime value of social life is not society but life"; at about the same time, Wittgenstein observed that language holds no meaning except in terms of the totality of the lives of those who employ it. Some of the difficulties exhibited by those I have criticized derive from the implicit constructions of some meaning for societies or cultures beyond the very lives, actions, feelings and ideas of those within them.

Yet good translation remains worth attempting even if it may be unrealizable. Paraphrasing Wittgenstein, Winch observes: "Whether a man sees point in what he is doing will then depend on whether he is able to see any unity in his multifarious interests, activities, and relations with other men; what sort of sense he sees in his life will depend on the nature of this unity . . . [and this is important for] . . . we may learn different possibilities of making sense of human life" (1970: 106). The possible bases for translation and common understanding, however vague and precarious, may lie in what Winch (1970: 107) terms "limiting notions," imbedded in such irrefutable experiences as birth, sensation, sexuality and death, what Needham (1978) has recently termed "primordial characters," and to which I implicitly allude in earlier works (see especially Beidelman 1964c, 1966b, 1966c).

In search of common ground, I am not advocating physiological reductionism, nor Jungian archetypes, nor Lévi-Straussian fundamental structures; yet, such notions do touch upon the problem. No suitable terms have yet clarified exactly how we may clearly discern any common bases. If I am right in my arguments, these cannot be firmly and lastingly achieved. Common understanding can only occur in a faltering manner, through an altered focus, at those times that translators (and I include literary critics, art critics, historians and others besides anthropologists) remain at least partially and haltingly convinced that—for the moment at least—they have caught a glimpse of what they seek to understand. That they entertain such a belief rests ultimately on no absolute methodology, no encompassing philosophy—as Wittgenstein observes—but instead is encapsulated in the nature of their own lives. To be sure, such a view veers dangerously close to solipsism. But, if well done in terms of thorough scholarship and sympathy, it will reflect, paradoxically, both how well such persons understand themselves within their culture and how well they recognize that the limits of that understanding domain remain problematical and in need of constant comparative revision.

ACKNOWLEDGMENTS

A preliminary draft of this paper was presented at a session of the African Studies Association Meetings held in Baltimore on November 1, 1978. I am grateful to Dr. Marion Kilson for forming this session and inviting me to contribute. I am grateful to Dr. Jon Anderson, Ms. Sandra Cohn, Dr. Dale Eickelman, Ms. Michelle Gilbert, Dr. Ivan Karp, Prof. John Middleton and Prof. Rodney Needham for reading various drafts of this paper.

TWELVE

INHABITING THE SPACE BETWEEN DISCOURSE AND STORY IN TRICKSTER NARRATIVES

Anne Doueihi

. . . Trickster has been an embarrassment to Western scholars, particularly scholars of religion. Trickster's inner contradictions and complexity of character are again and again referred to, but are usually treated in terms that show the hidden problem to be the problem of Trickster's sacredness: how can a figure apparently so profane constitute part of a sacred tradition? This problem gains some new dimensions when approached through certain distinctions fundamental to contemporary literary criticism. . . . Despite their quarrels and disagreements, critics universally agree on a basic distinction between "discourse" and "story." "Story" may be defined as "a sequence of actions or events, independent of their manifestation in discourse," and "discourse" as "the discursive presentation or narration of events" (Culler 1981: 169–70).[1]

In trickster narratives [as Section II of the original version of this essay demonstrated in a detailed literary analysis of the incident in which the Winnebago trickster finds an elk's skull with flies buzzing in and out, where he thinks he has heard many people drumming and shouting (Radin 1955)], there is a flagrant juxtaposition of the discursive, signifying aspect of the narrative and the referential, signified aspect of the text as story. Yet scholarly study and analysis of the trickster have tended to focus on the trickster as a character *in* stories, thus taking trickster narratives only at their referential (face) value. This approach, which treats language conventionally, as a transparent medium for the communication of some meaning or another, consequently leads to the search for some univocal meaning to which the trickster and his stories might be reduced.

A DISCOURSE OF DOMINATION

By taking narrative and meaning referentially—as story and as signified—scholarship on the trickster has opened the way for a parallel conception of trickster stories as themselves meaningful in that (and only in that) they figure in the great story of human civilization, or in the great story which is the history of religion. Thus at the end of the nineteenth century, Daniel Brinton, in his study of the Algonquian Manabozho or Great Hare, determined that this trickster figure was a degenerate form of an original figure that Brinton hypothetically posited and called the Great God of Light (Brinton 1896: 194, cf. Ricketts 1966: 328). For Brinton, Trickster, the Great Hare, was a figure whose fall was away from the sacred reality into history, or rather, a fall that *is* history. Franz Boas, who identified the trickster as an original, primitive form of the culture hero, disagreed with Brinton (Ricketts 1966: 329). He believed that religion developed from amorphous and amoral figures such as the trickster toward increasingly good and noble figures.

What Brinton and Boas' approaches have in common is that they seek to establish the trickster's meaning in terms of a story of human religious and cultural history, and particularly in relation to the origin. The origin is conceived as the reality, the moment of meaning and presence, to which history refers. History, whether it is seen as an increasing revelation of (sacred) meaning, as a progress from primitive darkness and ignorance toward clarity and meaning, or as a gradual devolution, a loss of meaning and of being, is in any case judged and measured with reference to a moment of presence that lies outside history, a moment that is conceived as the ultimate origin of the world that exists in history and as the origin of history itself. History is the story told by that presence: that is to say, history is always a fall from presence (even if it is ultimately, teleologically, a return to that presence) just as story (language) is seen as once removed from the utterer who is represented in this metaphor as the origin of the utterance. This conception of history thus entails a judgment on language; or rather it is the conception of language as utterance that both is tied to its origin *and* represents a loss of presence, which allows history to be conceived as a fall from presence.[2]

Following Boas and Brinton, most analyses of trickster narratives and of the trickster figure remain within this discourse and the ideology of presence, seeking to argue, develop, or reconcile various aspects of the trickster's meaning, which is now generally understood to reside in the question of the trickster's origin, the origin of the concept of God (or of a purely good deity), and finally the origin·of literature and culture. [In a passage omitted here the author develops an extended discussion and critique of interpretations by Paul Radin, Mac Linscott Ricketts, Raffaele Pettazzoni, and Åke Hultkrantz, many of which are elaborated elsewhere in this book.] . . . Although this is not the place for pursuing the question, it is worth reflecting whether the interpretation by scholars of religion of the trickster's profanity as a function of his literariness may not be linked to the fact that these scholars speak from the perspectives of "religions of the Book" for which the distinction between the sacred and "mere" literature has perhaps been crucial.

In their approaches to the trickster, Western scholars, both in anthropology and in the history of religions, have tended to impose their own terms on the trickster narratives instead of attending to the terms set by the narratives themselves. In this respect the discourse of Western scholarship on the trickster, as on so many other aspects of Native American culture, has been a discourse of domination, in two senses of the phrase. First, it is a discourse that analyzes the conquered civilization in terms of the conquerors, and it is therefore, secondly, a discourse *of* conquest, a discourse that continues to express and accept an ideology sanctioning the domination of one culture over another. In this discourse, Western conceptions of the sacred and profane, of myth and literature, and of origin, evolution, and degeneration, are used to frame the trickster particularly, and Native American culture generally, so that Western civilization can see the primitivity or degeneracy of the Other— and so justify its own domination and its own discourse.

While analyzing the mythologies of primitive peoples such as the Native Americans, Western scholarship has been to a large extent guided by the myths of origins, which is implied by conceptions of the sacred, of literature, etc. In this "myth" the origin is conceived as an ahistorical moment of being or presence, an archetypal source, the primordial "time" that is outside time but "inside" being and sacrality, while what is not original, not the origin, is devalued because [it is] removed from the pole of sacrality, goodness, being, and truth. As we have seen, in this ideology the origin is often confused with the beginning. In this case the beginning is valorized as being close to or identical with the origin, the moment of presence. From another perspective, however, the beginning is seen as a fall away from the origin, a fall into history, and is represented as a primitive, chaotic, and undeveloped period, which gradually leads to order and civilization, knowledge and truth, as it moves toward an ideal and eternally deferred future, or toward its realization in the present by a privileged individual or group.

Within the terms set by this ideological framework, the trickster, the liar, deceiver, and cheat, cannot be "at the origin." If he is represented as a figure "of the beginning," it is usually as a figure of the primitive, chaotic beginning. Ricketts and Pettazzoni, it is true, would have him at the sacred origin (considered to be the same as the beginning), but in giving him this privilege, they both must transform him immediately into a morally superior being and discard everything about him that is obscene, profane, stupid, and so on. In other words, they make of him a hypothetical figure invented to fit a theory and having little relation to the trickster of the stories. In all these theories, the trickster is bounced back and forth, stretched and twisted, so as to fit within the framework staked out by the discourse of domination by means of which the Western world, scholars included, distorts and suppresses its Other.[3]

Within this frame the trickster's literary existence is used to set up evidence of his cultural and moral (i.e., religious) inferiority. While the sacred myth is defined as the true, living, and orally recounted story, the profane, literary story of the trickster is considered false, dead, and "literarily reworked." It is not, like the true myth, the spontaneous word that is close to the origin because it is close to a moment of presence. Trickster stories are seen as fairy-tales, fables—false, inexact, and empty "signs" without intrinsic relation to presence and to origin. Finally, the profanity of trickster stories is read as a function of their literariness. Remarkably, the ideology derived from the metaphysics of presence, in which the spoken word is valued as better than the written word, has managed to be used by a literary civilization in its own favor against an oral civilization. Thus the Western tradition finally describes oral speech itself as "literary" in the sense of static and fixed, of something fashioned and refashioned. By thus reinscribing writing within its concept of oral tradition, Western scholarship undermines the very distinction that is the basis of its discourse.

[A section omitted here presents a discussion of materials by Dennis Tedlock, Laura Makarius, and Karl Kroeber that treat North American literature—both appropriately and inappropriately—as myth.] Past scholarly studies of the trickster, using a comparative or historical approach, tend to be reductive of trickster narratives. By taking them simply at their face value as stories referring to a figure and his actions, these approaches to the trickster reveal a literary naiveté and an ideological posture responsible for repressing a distinction between discourse and story that is manifested in Native American literary tradition, particularly in the trickster narratives, as shown in the earlier version of this essay. Thus the scholarly discourse about the trickster is a discourse that reflects a cultural bias; by imposing on Native American culture its own frame of concern, Western culture turns the discourse about the trickster into a discourse by Western culture about Western culture, with the trickster serving only in a nominal function so that the discussion may begin. This is a form of domination and repression of which any discourse about any "Other" must be guilty unless that discourse is self-questioning, that is, unless it involves a questioning of the very language it itself uses and a questioning of the discourse of which that language is a part.

. . . .

Thus traditional Western approaches, while trying to frame the trickster in a context of Western metaphysics and ontology, ultimately end up being the victim of a not untricksterlike joke. This joke is itself set up by the undecidable coexistence of story and discourse in every trickster narrative. Although this coexistence is ultimately true of any narrative at all, the trickster tale seems particularly designed to highlight and play upon this undecidability. Past scholarly approaches to the trickster are already victims of one of the trickster's pranks when they take the myths, right from the start, as *stories* referring to unequivocal events. For what is the story but a trick played by the discourse of the trickster? The illusion of a clear, unique, referential meaning given by the rhetorical body of the discourse is precisely what the trickster, as discourse, is able to conjure forth, with our unprotesting and willing occlusion. As Radin remarked about the trickster, "if we laugh at him, he grins at us. What happens to him happens to us" (Radin 1955: 169).

The trickster story opens us to the way our minds function to construct an apparently solid but ultimately illusory reality out of what is on another level a play of signs. And on yet a deeper level, there is still another meaning to trickster stories. The playfulness of language in the trickster tales reveals a different order of reality, one that makes possible both an ordinary, conventional meaning (the face-value, referential meaning of the discourse as story) and a level of meaning that is extraordinary, unconventional, and sacred.

The trickster thus fulfills a role that is fundamentally the same as that of the shaman. Ricketts, who wants to contrast the trickster figure with the figure of the priest or shaman, sees the episode discussed in the original version of this essay as an example of a "large class of anti-shaman stories" (1955: 337), for after getting his head stuck in an elk's skull, the trickster claims to be a supernatural being so that the Indians who find him will help get the skull off his head. But the trickster cannot really be said to trick the Indians, as Ricketts claims, because in fact he does give them the sacred "medicine" he promised them, and thus he fulfills the role of a supernatural being or shaman. This episode, then, cannot be interpreted as anti-shamanic. On the contrary, it reveals that the trickster's role is closely linked to, if not identical with, that of the shaman. Both the trickster and shamans utilize the power of signs to produce effects. They seem to use tricks, sleight of hand, but at the same time they *are* able to heal, to bring the rain, and so forth.

This episode gives a key to the sacred power of trickster stories in general. By playing in the space between discourse and story, trickster stories point to the way ordinary, conventional reality is an illusory construction produced out of a particular univocal interpretation of phenomena appearing as signs. This deeper wisdom about the linguisticality of our constructed world and the illusoriness of that construction is where trickster stories open onto the sacred.

THE PLAY OF TRICKSTER NARRATIVES

The value and validity of a critical reading are positive to the extent that the reading can account for the whole of the material it analyzes.

Past scholarly studies of the trickster are not exhaustive of all the features present in trickster narratives, for, by treating them only as stories, details visible on the level of discourse are entirely disregarded. A closer look at the language and wording of a specific trickster narrative will show that the referential value of language so important to previous analyses is undermined in these narratives. Instead of having one meaning, the text opens onto a plurality of meanings, none of which is exclusively "correct," because as the narrative develops in the trickster stories, the conventional level of meaning ceases to be appropriate. A "signified"—a local unit functioning in a specific field where it makes meaning possible—turns out to be only a "signifier" and functions as a signifier. Language loses its referential value and becomes profound. On the other hand, the story loses its solidity and breaks down into an open-ended play of signifiers. Language becomes a semiotic activity. In this game played with and through signifiers, meaning is made possible by the space opened between signifiers. It is in the reversals and discontinuities in language, in the narrative, that meaning is produced—not one meaning, but the possibility of meaningfulness.

. . . .

The story itself [of the Winnebago trickster finding the flies buzzing in and out of an elk skull] thus deconstructs into a semiotic activity, a free play. It invites the reader to recognize in this play of signifiers a "seeming as if" they signified a particular story, a clear and univocal meaning. For the entire episode of the narrative capitulates under the terms of the "it seemed as if." In this expression, "it seemed" combines with "as if" to render fiction itself unreadable; the "as if" of fiction becomes an undecidable "seeming to be." It both seems to be a fiction and is a fiction that seems to be.

[Three voices in the Winnebago incident are complexly interwoven, two of them belonging to the trickster—what he thinks, and what he says out loud in the story.] Throughout the text of the Winnebago trickster cycle there are reversals and contradictions that reconstruct the text from within itself, breaking down the referential, conventional value of the narrative, undermining its viability as a story. And throughout the narrative the perspective of the narrator shifts almost imperceptibly between telling "facts" and telling the trickster's interpretation of events. Because of this shifting perspective, which works together with the reversals in the story, the narrative allows itself to be read as a story at the same time that it reveals itself to be a semiotic play.

. . . The narrative tells us what the trickster and other characters do and say and what the trickster thinks; it repeats interpretations and responses to interpretations. Whether these interpretations are true or false, appropriate or inappropriate, ultimately cannot be decided, for the narrator's perspective can never be completely distinguished from that of the characters who interpret events.

CONCLUSION: THE POWER TO SIGNIFY

The features commonly ascribed to the trickster—contradictoriness, complexity, deceptiveness, trickery—are the features of the language of the story itself. If the trickster breaks all the rules, so does the story's language; it breaks the rules of storytelling in the very telling of the story. If the trickster is a practical joker and a deceiver, so is the language of the story. While the story is usually read as showing the absurdity and inappropriateness of trickster behavior, the joke is not just on the trickster, but is in fact also on the reader who finds the trickster amusing. For the joke is on us if we do not realize that the trickster gives us an insight into the way language is used to construct an ultimately incomplete kind of reality.

The trickster shows us a way to see the world by opening our minds to the spontaneous transformations of a reality that is always open and creative. It is only to the closed, ordinary mind that trickster stories seem absurd or profane. It is in the language out of which they are constructed that trickster stories make accessible this deeper wisdom about the nature of reality. By dividing himself, so to speak, into narrator and character, he both tells the story and is "in" the story. Just as one cannot grasp or define this trickster, but only say *how* he seems to be, so the story can only be approached by seeing how the language of the discourse "seems to be" a story.

If trickster stories tell us about anything, it is about the difference between, and the undecidability of, discourse and story, referential and rhetorical values, signifier and signified, a conventional mind and one that is open to the sacred. It is only by missing such differences, by taking trickster narratives solely as stories, that scholarly readings have regarded them as "obscene," "immoral," and "profane." While on one level they may indeed correspond to what is meant by those terms, on another they are, as the Native American traditions often claim, sacred and powerful. The sacredness and power of this trickster, who is in the space between discourse and story, lie in his making meaning possible. The reversals and breaks in the narrative perspective produce openings in the story that allow a number of meanings to be read in it.

Western scholarship on the trickster has traditionally tended to be reductive, treating the narratives as stories and ignoring the breaks and contradictions that tip off the language of the story into a free play of signifiers, a play of discourse with its own possibilities of being meaningful. While traditional studies have sought to establish what the trickster's meaning is, the stories show that the trickster is meaning(s). The problem of the trickster's sacredness that has preoccupied past scholarship turns out to be based on a conventional reading of trickster stories that ignores the discursive features of those stories. Those features reveal that trickster stories embody the power that makes meaning possible, the power that allows sounds, noises, signs, to be significant. It is the power of signification, the possibility to mean, that the trickster celebrates. Not without reason is it said that the trickster speaks the language of all living things; for in the trickster's universe, everything is already a sign *of* something. It is a sign because it is part of a sacred world; it is a sign of the sacred. The universe is essentially linguistic and ultimately, infinitely interpretable. The trickster is thus not *a* sacred being, but the way the whole universe may become meaningful, sacred, and filled with "power."

THIRTEEN

INCONCLUSIVE CONCLUSIONS: TRICKSTERS—METAPLAYERS AND REVEALERS

William J. Hynes

Something about the antics of the trickster causes this figure to be enjoyed worldwide. The heartiest laughter within belief systems seems to be reserved for those mythic and ritual occasions when tricksters profane the most sacred beliefs and practices—be they occasioned by Hermes in Greece, Maui in Hawaii, Loki in Scandinavia, or Agu Tomba in Tibet. Systems normally busy generating firm adherence to their constitutive values are discovered to be simultaneously and contradictorily maintaining a raft of tricksters who perpetually counter, upend, and loosen adherence to these same values.

The preceding chapters witness the variety, frequency, and pervasiveness of tricksters. What significance may be attributed to the trickster phenomenon, sighted in such various contexts? Many of the authors of the preceding chapters have proposed insights into this question. Although the phenomena of tricksters are so rich as to put us on guard against definitive conclusions, this last chapter offers a range of interpretative theses ranging from the most apparent to the less obvious. In conformity with trickster logic, they can be considered to be inclusive of one another or not.

1. *Trickster myths are deeply satisfying entertainment.* These myths are entertaining at a variety of levels, both to those who tell them within their respective belief systems and to those who study them formally

from without. That it is necessary to begin here with such an apparently obvious observation again reveals the attempts in this book to offset a dominant Western cultural bias. Is there a bifurcation between matters serious and matters humorous? Between matters educational and matters entertaining? Contributors here have argued otherwise. Most of our authors would support the insight of the Catholic novelist, Flannery O'Connor that "the maximum amount of seriousness admits the maximum amount of comedy" (O'Connor 1980: 167).

Confronted with the inherent humor, dramatic timing, and narrative tension of the trickster myths, more than one scholar has remarked, perhaps a trifle sheepishly, that a central personal if somewhat unconscious motivation in studying the structure of these myths is the entertainment they provide. Witness Katharine Luomala of the Bishop's Museum in Hawaii: "Their basic human appeal, independent of cultural differences, is their initial attractive quality and their most enduring, for I find that rereading them and once more enjoying their humor soon dissipates any weariness from my endless dissection and attempts at synthesizing information about them and about the cultures in which they are popular" (Luomala 1966: 157).

Within Western cultures during the last century, a clear delight in and fascination with the trickster and tricksterish characteristics have gone a great distance toward establishing the trickster narrative as a literary genre. One volume of studies, *The Fool and the Trickster* (Williams 1979), cites tricksters across a range of Northern European mythology, medieval European fools, *Dr. Faustus*, and Shakespeare. Confidence men have been the central characters of Herman Melville's *The Confidence Man: His Masquerade* (1875) and Thomas Mann's *Confessions of Felix Krull: Confidence Man* (1954). Susan Kuhlmann's *Knave, Fool, and Genius* (1973) concentrates on the literary uses of the confidence man in nineteenth-century American fiction.

Within the more specific American literary scene, Gary Snyder has exhibited an intense fascination with the modalities of the Coyote tricksters in his poetry and fiction (1977). Playwright Murray Medick has recently completed a cycle of seven plays based upon the trickster myth cycle (see Kroll 1985; cf. Gelber 1981 on the work of playwright Sam Shephard). Gerald Vizenor's *Earthdivers: Tribal Narratives on Mixed Descent* (1981) is one of the most successful sets of short accounts of contemporary trickster figures. Vizenor prefaces his book with a version of the "whites have headaches, skins have anthropologists" saying: "The creation myth that anthropologists never seem to tell is the one where *naanabozho*, the cultural trickster, made the first anthropologist from fecal matter. Once made, more were cloned in graduate schools from the first fecal creation" (xv). The stories in *Earthdivers* parody a wide range of academic sanctities, particularly those about how to treat "minority cultures" (trickster themes reappear in Vizenor 1987 and 1988).

Although there are various real-life, twentieth-century tricksters, more often than not the tenor of their character tends not to be as rich, multivocal, or polychromic as that of mythic tricksters. Hugh Trevor-Roper wrote one study of a famous English scholar-trickster in his *Hermit of Peking: The Hidden Life of Sir Edmund Backhouse* (1977). One of the leading sinologists of his time (1873–1944), Backhouse "discovered" and brokered rare Chinese literary texts to Oxford University and merchandized strategic military information to the British Foreign Office. He was professor of Chinese studies at the University of London and very nearly appointed to a similar chair at Oxford. By the time of his death, many of the texts he had passed along, such as the Empress Dowager's diaries, were discovered to be clever forgeries and the information sold to the Foreign Office equally bogus. Given Trevor-Roper's close familiarity with the guises and forgeries of tricksters, as well as his own earlier scholarly reputation as a scholar of the Hitler regime, it was doubly ironic that several years ago he was one of the first scholars to confirm the authenticity of the Hitler Diaries only days before they were revealed as forgeries.

More recently Bernard Wasserstein has traced the European career of a figure similar to Backhouse, Trebitsch Lincoln, who was variously a Jew, a Christian, and a Buddhist abbot, a member of the British House of Commons, and a German spy (Wasserstein 1988). Neither education nor social class forms dependable protections against the deceptions of the trickster; rather, they offer attractive occasions for his predictable deflations.

Carlos Castañeda, a contemporary American scholar whose several volumes documented a twelve-year encounter in the Sonoran desert with a Yaqui sorcerer, Don Juan Matus, might be cited as a case of the category "scholar-trickster." The initial volume earned Castañeda a doctorate in anthropology at UCLA, fame as a countercultural writer in the 1960s, and significant financial gain, but there are those who argue that Castañeda's writings are entirely fictive. Richard De Mille in *Castañeda's*

Journey (1976) suggests persuasively that Castañeda's meetings with Don Juan were completely fabricated. Within this fiction, De Mille suggests that there are other tricksterish elements, particularly those in which the sorcerer trains the budding anthropologist, Carlos, by using continual deceptions to open his more ordinary and linear perceptions to the realms of the extraordinary and nonlinear. The search for such realms by the counterculture of the 1970s resulted in near cultic status for Castañeda's works.

Conrad Hyers has explored the film persona of Charlie Chaplin as a trickster figure (1981). Howard Movshovitz, film critic for National Public Radio, treated both Chaplin and Chaucer in a dissertation at the University of Colorado entitled "The Trickster Myth and Chaucer's Partners" (1977). Real-life contemporary American tricksters have been celebrated both in book form and film: for example *The Flim Flam Man* (1967), the tale of a famous southern trickster in the Great Depression, as chronicled by Guy Owens, and *The Great Imposter* (1961), which told the story of Fred C. DeMerra and his complex imposterings as prison warden, navy surgeon, and Trappist abbot in the 1950s. The trickster theme could be traced readily in a wide range of popular films, as well as in other forms of popular culture. An example of the former might be the role played by Burt Reynolds in such films as *W. W. and the Dixie Dance Kings* and *Smoky and the Bandit*. With regard to popular culture, Abrahams (1968: 176) suggests that the trickster reappears in American white urban joke cycles in the form of Moron, Hophead, Drunkard, Moby Pickle, or Kilroy, as well as in the Traveling Salesman and in Elephant jokes. The recent collection, *American Indian Myths and Legends* by Erdoes and Ortiz (1984), demonstrates repeatedly that the trickster is very much alive in contemporary Native American culture, even as the figure spills over into mass media transformations.

Both within specific cultures and worldwide, the humor and laughter evoked by trickster myths are never exhausted in a single telling. Obviously something is being communicated that bears repeating. As Pelton argues, beyond the surface humor, there is a deeper type of insight, irony, and transformation at work in the trickster myths. So too Anthony Yu, in his translation of the Chinese classic, *The Journey to the West*, makes a parallel judgment about the monkey trickster, in which he sees him as both the occasion for humor and the bearer of enlightenment (Yu 1977).

Thus, the trickster's humor melds entertainment and education. We may laugh, but a deeper unfolding is at work. At one level, the trickster bears the gift of laughter, but it is tied to another level, linked to another gift, one that evokes insight and enlightenment.

2. *Trickster myths are ritual vents for social frustrations.* Historically, the single most common significance overtly attached to tricksters and their antics by Western cultures has been their ability to function as a vent through which pressures engendered by a system of beliefs and behaviors can be dissipated. A good example of this position can be found in the fifteenth-century debates within the theological faculty of Paris I referred to at the end of chapter 3. Note the social utility argument implicit in this recounting of a defense of the Feast of Fools by a member of that faculty:

> But they [the defenders of the Feast of Fools] say, we act in jest and not seriously, as has been the custom of old, so that the foolishness innate in us can flow out once a year and evaporate. Do not wineskins and barrels burst if their bungs are not loosened once in a while? Even so, we are old wineskins and worn barrels; the wine of wisdom fermenting within us, which we hold tightly all year in the service of God, might flow out uselessly, if we did not discharge it ourselves now and then with games and foolishness. Emptied through play, we may become stronger afterwards to retain wisdom. (Davis 1971: 48)

Fools and tricksters seem to have an affinity for linking foolishness and play with wisdom and work. Both "the foolishness innate in us" and "the wine of wisdom fermenting within us" need to be discharged through games.

Another example of this social venting explanation can be seen in the far more utilitarian and calculating view voiced at the end of the sixteenth century by the French lawyer Claude de Rubys: "It is sometimes expedient to allow the people to play the fool and make merry lest by holding them in with too great a rigor, we put them in despair. . . . These gay sports abolished, the people go instead to taverns, drink up and begin to cackle, their feet dancing under the table, to decipher King, princes . . . the State and Justice, and draft scandalous defamatory leaflets" (Davis 1971: 41).

Such a calculating view illustrates a darker use of tricksters, humor, sports, and diversions. Separating the entertaining humor from any inherent link with enlightenment results in mere diversions that distract people from deeper social complaints, awareness, or action. Without this deeper element, sports, circuses, and other spectacles simply divert people from the more serious matters in need of attention and reformation.

Some time after the invention of steam power, the metaphor chosen to describe this social venting shifted away from the agrarian model of wine barrels and bungholes toward steam engines and safety valves. Babcock-Abrahams notes one of the first mentions of such rituals acting as social steam valves in Heinrich Schurtz's *Alterklassen und Männer-bunde*, published in 1902 (Babcock-Abrahams 1984: 22).

Trickster myths and parallel ritualizations can offer an officially sanctioned escape clause whereby people can elude momentarily the rigidity or demands of their belief system and "blow off" the repressed vapors of frustration. That these myths can act as escape mechanisms while being both entertaining and educational, and also graph out the societal ethics, is remarkable. Perhaps, contemporary Western societies that sometimes separate humor and enlightenment, replacing this link with a heavy dose of moralism, might learn from trickster materials and emulate this lighter sort of temper so that "emptied through play, we may become stronger afterwards to retain wisdom" (Davis 1971: 48).

3. *Tricksters reaffirm the belief system.* In belief systems where entertainment is not separated from education, trickster myths can be a powerful teaching device utilizing deeply humorous negative examples that reveal and reinforce the societal values that are being broken (Gluckman 1965: 109). Breaching less visible but deeply held societal values serves not only to reveal these values but to reaffirm them (Garfinkel 1967: 35ff). Indeed, Garfinkel suggests this process can become a formal method whereby the sociologist or anthropologist can bring to the surface hidden values: only when one breaches supposed overt or possibly covert rules will one know if they really exist; only when there is a societal response will one know how seriously this rule is taken. Of course, the inventor of the method is not himself immune: Garfinkel was the professor at UCLA who signed off on Carlos Castañeda's anthropology dissertation that was supposedly based upon the *sine qua non* for anthropologists, that is, extensive fieldwork.

As Vescey argues in this collection, in breaking the rules, the trickster confirms the rules. Thus, the process is both disruptive and confirmatory. What is mocked is maintained. The trickster "affirms by denying"

(Zucker 1967: 317). For Babcock-Abrahams that which is "being broken is always implicit . . . for the very act of deconstructing reconstructs" (Babcock-Abrahams 1978: 99).

The trickster profanes yet affirms the sacred. Each time he causes laughter by his imitation of the powers and prerogatives of another being, the relative wisdom of the locus and boundaries of these rights and privileges is reconfirmed. Every time the trickster breaks a taboo or boundary, the same taboo or boundary is underlined for non-tricksters. Thus examples of the trickster's negative activity, such as the profaning of sacred beliefs, being seduced by pride, or engaging in antisocial behavior, can be understood as an adroit reverse stressing of the need for reverence, humility, or dedication to the common good.

Because tricksters are so often the official ritual profaners of the central beliefs of a given system, they can act as a camera obscura in which the reversed mirror image serves as a valuable index to the sacred beliefs of that same system. As the seventeenth-century Jesuit, Balthasar Gracian, notes in his novel *El Criticon* (1651), "The things of this world can be truly perceived only by looking at them backwards" (Babcock-Abrahams 1978: 13). Flannery O'Connor has remarked that the best way for her to understand and critique her own writing is to read it backwards: "Try rearranging it backwards and see what you see" (O'Connor 1980: 67). She also saw the value of distortion: "I am interested in making up a good case for distortion, as I am coming to believe it is the only way to make people see" (O'Connor 1980: 79).

Poised to explore and understand a new culture or belief system, the traveler might wish to inquire about indigenous trickster myths. If such myths exist and are shared without censorship, their profanations might serve to reveal the sacred beliefs at the heart of this system. Even as these sacred beliefs are ritually profaned by the trickster, they are simultaneously being reconfirmed, particularly for those who are not themselves tricksters.

4. *Tricksters are psychic explorers and adventurers.* The trickster has also been understood, particularly from psychological points of view, as representing a *speculum mentis* within which the central unresolvable human struggles are played out (Radin 1955: xxiv). As a prototypical human, the trickster "symbolizes that aspect of our own nature which is always nearby, ready to bring us down when we get inflated, or to humanize us when we become pompous. . . . The major psychological

function of the trickster figure is to make it possible for us to gain a sense of proportion about ourselves" (Singer 1972: 289–90). Thus, we can see the trickster as a jester holding forth in both the macrocosmic court of human society and the microcosmic court of the self.

In Freudian terms the trickster could be said to embody in dramatic form the ongoing battle between the id and the superego. The trickster constantly oscillates back and forth between self-gratification and cultural heroism (Piper 1978: 15). In neo-Freudian terms, the trickster is caught in a struggle between the pleasure principle and the reality principle (Bettelheim 1975: 33–34). Abrahams sees the trickster as the embodiment of a "regressive infantilism," and yet the pattern of a small animal outwitting a larger animal or human can also provide a model of hope to children or adults who find themselves suppressed (1968: 173–75). Pelton makes the same point more poetically when he observes: "The purpose of the stories is to put an adult mind in a child's heart and a child's eye in an adult head" (Pelton 1980: 279).

The contemporary and controversial psychologist of schizophrenia, R. D. Laing, has himself been described as a trickster advocating tricksterish logic by the social anthropologist Joan Wescott:

> [R. D. Laing has] a tremendous talent for turning things upside down in order to free you from old modes of perception. He's like the Trickster, whose name means *the guide to travelers*. Among the Yoruba the Trickster is regarded as both father and child of all the other gods. He's responsible for change, an essential force in any culture. . . . Basically, I think [Laing] sees his task as mediating between man's present and potential states. The Trickster is also a mediator. He's usually pictured standing at a crossoads. He's very cunning. In one myth he walks along the boundary line between two farms wearing a hat that's white on one side and black on the other. Needless to say, this provokes a dispute between the two farmers as to the identity of the trespasser. You see, the Trickster is absolutely against any authority and without any allegiances. He's capable of transformations, a shape shifter. Ronnie [Laing], too, wears many hats—to show people that they see what they want to see. (Mezan 1972: 94–95)

The most familiar psychological interpretation of the trickster is that of Carl Jung and some of his disciples. Here the trickster is viewed as "a primitive 'cosmic' being of *divine-animal* nature, on the one hand superior to man because of his superhuman qualities, and on the other hand inferior to him because of his unreason and unconsciousness" (Jung 1955: 203–4). Jung considers the trickster to be a "shadow" that brings to the surface the underside or reverse of dominant values. Breaking through into the world of normalcy and order, the trickster plays out subterranean forbiddens in dreamlike fashion. For Jung this process represents both the ongoing fugue between the personal consciousness and the more trans-personal unconsciousness, as well as the dynamic byplay between the civilized and the primitive. As a civilization rises to consciousness, it may attempt to clean up or repress the trickster altogether (Jung 1955: 202–9), yet even as civilization constructs a shared, conscious order of beliefs, the pesky trickster disrupts all such orderings with reminders of a shared disorder or collective unconsciousness (Neumann 1954: 8).

In Jungian interpretation, the trickster, as shadow, can therefore serve as the breakthrough point for the surfacing of repressed values. At a deeper level he remains a creative mediator between that which is differentiated, ordered, predictable, and distinct, on the one hand, and that which is undifferentiated, unordered, spontaneous, and whole, on the other. In this way the trickster may be understood as the embodiment of such productive chaos as creativity, play, spontaneity, inventiveness, ingenuity, and adventure. The trickster not only helps us encounter these yet-to-be-focused energies but also ventures forth in an ongoing exploration and charting of the inchoate, the "otherness" that always resurges to challenge our neat and organized sense of personal control. Even when he charts an aspect of the inchoate, however, the trickster would be the first to disassemble rapidly any chart. Even if maps are only pointings, they are essentially inadequate guides to the typography of the inchoate because the inchoate will always exceed their grasp.

When the Jungian trickster begins to resemble an archetypal or universal entity, it opens itself to strong criticism from the particularists. For example, T. O. Beidelman's critique is pertinent here: "Disparate figures have all too frequently been termed *trickster*, yet this term is clearly the product of the analysts' ethnocentric evaluations of deviance and disorder, and does not always derive squarely from the evaluations held by the members of the cultures in which they appear" (1980: 35). Even Beidelman, however, cannot resist using the "*trickster* in a shorthand manner to refer to a category of figures only in part resembling what are conventionally termed *trickster* by those using universal categorizations" (1980: 28).

Implicit in both this discussion and the earlier treatment of universals and particulars in chapter 1 is the confrontation of a continuum: at one extreme a universal, so obvious to some so as not to need to be demonstrated, and at the other extreme, the particular aspects of a single trickster figure within a single culture, viewed as so distinctive so as to be virtually *sui generis*. In between are such terms as Beidelman's "shorthand" and my own "heuristic guide or typology." These middle terms imply that it is not necessary for the term "trickster" to have a set number of characteristics in all existing belief systems for the term to have meaning. As long as a number of shared characteristics are found in a large number of instances, it is possible to speak, albeit carefully, of "a trickster figure." Whatever one says generally still remains subject to revision by the specific aspects of individual belief systems.

As mentioned in chapter 3, in the process of bringing this volume to fruition, Laura Makarius suggested that only if a comprehensive grid of characteristics could be applied to all cultural instances of supposed trickster figures might we finally lay this issue to rest. For my part, I see the problem more at the level of the nature of knowledge, having less to do with the design and application of an empirical grid and more to do with the long-standing battle between universals and particulars. At times this battle has been played out as the issue of "analogy of proper proportionality," or the difference between the *Naturwissenschaften* and the *Geisteswissenschaften,* or the nature of metaphor.

If never adequately captured by a formula, as psychic adventurer the trickster continues to go where others wish to venture yet fear to tread. He is guide both to actual travelers who live by their wits and to armchair explorers who live by their hopes. A stalking horse of the improbable, the trickster occasions discoveries of the possible while he proffers an exemplar for subsequent imitation. What makes the trickster's journeys those of a psychopomp is not simply his moving back and forth across the borders of life and death, but his passage and return across the stages and states of life itself as well. If we are the myths we myth, the trickster myth beckons us toward innovation; he is a psychic guide or hermeneut leading us on through the thickets of personal and social signifiers toward invention of the self and society.

5. *Tricksters are agents of creativity who transcend the constrictions of*

monoculturality. Perhaps the greatest empowerment that the trickster brings is the excitement and hope occasioned by "the suggestion that any particular ordering of experience may be arbitrary and subjective" (Douglas 1968: 365). Beyond mere venting of frustrations, beneath the clever reverse reaffirmation of a given belief system, there is a more subtle, deeper, and broader meta-affirmation that life is much more than the sum of its social or religious constructs. Beyond all mere "scouting out" of possible alternate personal or social constructs, the trickster reminds us that every construct is constructed. Not only is someone not confined to a single construct or system of order, she is not confined to a choice among alternative constructs. The hermeneut puts us in contact with the sources of creativity from which we can be empowered to construct our own construct. The trickster's constant chatterings and antics remind us that life is endlessly narrative, prolific and open-ended.

No narrative, category, or construct is ever fully watertight. Each one leaks, some more than others. The trickster redramatizes and reacquaints us with the "more than this" dimensionality of existence; he evokes the polysemous quality of life (Lorenz and Vecsey 1988 [1979]: 1–11). Unbordered multivocality triumphs over bordered univocality. As Tom Steele and I argued in chapter 10: "The trickster swivels in its socket the cyclopean eye of monoculturality; he roils the tribal waters of life lest they go stagnant." Just as the presence of a child reminds adults how rigidly they have taken on a certain kind of order, the trickster reminds us there is no single way to play. "Thus the trickster incarnates in every culture the oxymoronic imagination at play, literally 'fooling around' to discover new paradigms and even new logics. As such, he reveals man's freedom to shape the world just because it actively offers itself to him— even if he must trick it to make it come across" (Pelton 1980: 272).

The apparent return to order following the trickster's antics can be misleading because now the imagination has been stimulated toward envisioning "a wholly different kind of world" (Cox 1969: 3). At the one end of a scale of social consequences, the trickster offers ritual rebellion in lieu of actual rebellion—briefly reminding adherents of a belief system of its own inherent relativity may make it more bearable. But at the other end of this scale of social consequences, however, the trickster may prepare the way for adaptation, change, or even total replacement of the belief system—the very process of registering and sharing social complaints can initiate movement toward a new consensus. In fact, the system is reopened to its own inward resources of power where imaginative alternatives are glimpsed. Victor Turner reminds us that the liminal figure of the trickster breaks "the cake of custom and enfranchises speculation" so that there is a "promiscuous intermingling and juxtaposing of the categories" (Turner 1969: 106). Furthermore, this promiscuous intermingling may engender new progeny, never of a type previously envisioned: "Such 'creative negations' remind us of the need to reinvest the clean with the filthy, the rational with the animalistic, the ceremonial with the carnivalesque in order to maintain cultural vitality. And they confirm the endless potentiality of dirt and the pure possibility of liminality. The *mundus inversus* [inverted world] does more than simply mock our desire to live according to our usual orders and norms; it reinvests life with a vigor and a *Spielraum* [an arena of playful inventiveness] attainable (it would seem) in no other way" (Babcock-Abrahams 1978: 32). Thus the trickster's breaking and reaffirming the rules represent a move "beyond order and disorder to transformed order significantly revitalized and repopulated with a wider breadth of options" (Pelton 1979: 8).

As an agent of creativity, the trickster is often associated with activities that center upon human creativity: the bringing of culture, laughter, business transactions, as well as opening of the doors of perception. As was noted in chapter 1, the trickster's association with creativity parallels his common linkage with creation and innovation; the creative process mimics the creation process itself. Tricksters in their own way counter the Stoic argument that the trait that we have in common with God and the universe is *logos*: word, logic, and order. Tricksters argue that the common trait is creativity: imagination, invention, and experimentation.[1]

As Makarius notes in chapter 5, innovations and creativity have a price. The cost of obtaining inventions, innovations or aspects of creation, is the breaking of taboos, which then unleashes punishments. However, the trickster has the knack of operating as a "pass-through-mechanism." He manages to break a given taboo, pass on the related cultural gift, and deflect the respective punishment from the recipients of the cultural benefit onto himself. This is nearly a paradigmatic truism of the pattern for many inventors: they create an innovation, whose benefits are utilized by others, while the creators are the recipients of the punishment and scorn bestowed directly upon them because they broke the set patterns of order and their reciprocal taboos.

As the agent of imposturing and ingenuity, the trickster often circles around the sources of creativity and transformation. For example, in reviewing a recent novel by Maxine Hong Kingston, *Tripmaster Monkey: His Fake Book* (1989), Gerald Vizenor, himself the author of the highly acclaimed *Griever: An American Monkey King in China* (1987), notes that ultimately the central trickster's "simian moves are comic transformations rather than mere imposture" (Vizenor 1989: 10). When we look beyond the trickster's surface antics, border-breaking, and profanities, in addition to the bas relief profile of the central beliefs of a dominant belief system, there is the path of vicarious explorations, potential new inventions, and behind all these the profile of human inventiveness.

6. *Tricksterish metaplay dissolves the order of things in the depth of the open-ended metaplay of life.* Clifford Geertz notes in his essay, "Deep Play: Notes on the Balinese Cockfight" (Geertz 1972), one of the essential characteristics and attractions of "deep play" is that those involved in it are "in over their heads" because of the size of the stakes or because of the probability of disaster. Hence, Jeremy Bentham's *The Theory of Legislation* (1789), in which Geertz believes the concept of deep play is found for the first time, attempted legally to prevent such nonsensical opportunities. Those who engage in deep play are clearly "irrational—addicts, fetishists, children, fools, savages, who need only to be protected from themselves." (Geertz 1972: 433ff).

In *Man at Play*, Hugo Rahner captures precisely this distinctive transrational aspect of play: "To play is to yield oneself to a kind of magic, to enact to oneself the absolutely other, to pre-empt the future, to give the lie to the inconvenient world of fact" (Rahner 1967: 65); in short, there is an "otherness" to play that we might call metaplay. To be sure, such otherness can often be viewed as irrational and threatening by the orderly and established that may seek to control or suppress it. Perhaps, because metaplay is fundamentally closer to the inchoate powers of creativity from which ordered social constructs have themselves originated and from which *new* constructs will arise, such metaplay can easily be perceived as a menace to those who represent the existing social constructs. Isn't this Adolph von Harnack's point about how religions evolve? Religions of heart, spirit, and substance all too soon pass into religions of law, form, and custom; expressions that were once fresh and lucid become outmoded, obscuring and encrustating the intangible creative forces they once so ably communicated (Harnack 1900/1957: 197). Is it not predictable that the old order should fear metaplay, dancing as it does at the source of creativity, fecund with new orderings itching to replace the old?

Almost in programmatic fashion, metaplay ruptures the shared consciousness, the societal ethos, and consensual validation—in short, the very order of order itself. Thus when the trickster engages in metaplay he places the normal order of things under question. From the advent of metaplay, all previous orders and orderings are clearly labeled contingent.

Most chapters in this book argue that precisely this otherness of the trickster, often manifested in a blizzard of polyvalent activity, has confounded most serious scholarly studies. As Doueihi in particular argues, all too often this scholarship has attempted to sort through this ambiguous and contradictory activity in order to reduce it to a single key; for example, determining earliest features to use them as the key by which to interpret later additions and redactions. Such an approach results not only in a failure to understand the polysemous diversity and endless semiotic activity of the trickster, but it collapses the extraordinary into the ordinary; it trivializes the trickster's otherness, suppressing the underlying fecundity that is the source of the depth and breadth of his metaplay.

Just such a refusal to accept such polyvalent activity on its own terms, insisting that such activity be reduced down to a more manageable monochromic minimum is illustrated most vividly in a historical example given by Jean Dalby Clift in her study of Shakespeare's *Measure for Measure* (1972). Over the years, directors of this play have often been confused when confronted by the range of tricksterish activities in the key character Lucio. How could it be that the same character can utter some of the most profound, positive things about matrimony in one breath and then say some of the most scurrilous, demeaning things in another? Directors and scholars often speculated that two disparate characters must have been combined, perhaps because of the limited number of players in the original company of performers. Accordingly, when staging the play with a modern cast, some directors often separated Lucio's lines into two parts and assigned one set to another character; or worse yet, occasionally a director simply casts away one set of lines altogether (Clift 1972).

Because so much of what is said about the trickster comes from the perspective of order, it is not too surprising that the trickster is often seen as the disrupter, the spoiler, and the thief. From the inverse perspective of the trickster, however, that which is ordered and set is viewed as pre-determined and closed. The inchoate, on the other hand, is the creative wellspring of the yet-to-be. What is undifferentiated and spontaneous can be understood as life-giving and generative. Nietzsche used this inversionary logic when he declared: "objections, digressions, gay mis-trust, the delight in mockery are signs of health: everything uncondi-tional belongs to pathology" (Nietzsche 1966: 90). The logic of order and convergence, that is, logos-centrism, or logocentrism, is challenged by another path, the random and divergent trail taken by that profane metaplayer, the trickster.

On this trail, all creative inventions are ultimately excreta. Like the mystic who constantly reminds us that no words or doctrinal construct can express adequately the ineffable nature of God, the trickster reminds us that no one creative ordering can capture life. Insofar as an ordering continues to express life, it continues to be viable. If not viable, such orderings will drop away, be replaced by new productions, or these orderings will work to repel their potential replacements. As demigod the trickster constantly reminds us that there are no realms that are excepted from this process, be they sacred or profane. As Robert Pelton has put it so elegantly: "How amazingly large that order is, how charged with both danger and delight, how opposed to the mindless tinkerings with mystery so fashionable in the secularized West, the trickster reveals, ironically: as he grasps for the ungraspable and spells out the unsayable, he shows forth divination's power to redraw in the plain earth of daily life the icon of all that truly is" (Pelton 1980: 289). The trickster brings us face to face with such richness of life, but none so rich as the continual rediscovery of the unquenchable fecundity of all that truly is and can be. So say we.

There is a special joy that comes from both studying and then putting aside the trickster for a while. It is exhilarating to watch this character reveal so much of the creativity at the heart of the source of order, while busily profaning and confirming all specific orderings, especially gram-mar and syntax. Yet, however far one attempts to trace the trickster's tracks, the trickster is ever so much more than what we can find and understand—be he a demigod, a mythic figure, a genre, a symbolic embodiment of the human imagination, or a postmodernist hermeneut momentarily reflecting back to us our relative place in a nearly infinite chain of signifiers. Thus, when we put our studies to rest for a moment, there is both a distinct sensation of relief as well as a lucid realization that whatever acumen we may have gained, future students of the trickster will still find much to study and ponder in this intriguing and perplexing phenomenon.

NOTES

1. INTRODUCING THE TRICKSTER FIGURE
Hynes and Doty

1. Only recently have we begun to appreciate the significance of the Uncle Remus stories; at an earlier date they seemed to be trivializing of African Americans, but they are now recognized as fairly accurate studies of African-American folklore and dialect. Brer Rabbit is one of the characters Harris uses to portray a version of the traditional trickster figure, a figure who survives by using his well-developed wit and cleverness ("I don't keer w'at you do wid me, Brer Fox, so you don't fling me in dat brier-patch," and Fox does, and Rabbit gets off scot-free). The Uncle Remus trickster has counterparts in contemporary urban society: Levine (1974), Genovese (1974), and Edwards (1978: 67–79 and 1984: 92) demonstrate ways tricksters refract the social settings in which they appear, in instances where African Americans were confronting the dominant white society. Gates treats "as a repeated theme or topos" (1988: 4) a range of trickster figures in Africa, North and South America, and the Caribbean. He sees "these individual tricksters as related parts of a larger, unified figure," so well represented in one of them that he refers to them collectively "as Esu, or as Esu-Elegbara" (5–6).

2. Because this work will be cited frequently in this volume, an extended bibliographic notation for Radin 1955 is appropriate here. The National Union Catalogue gives both 1955 and 1956 as original publication dates for *The Trickster;* the essays by Kerényi and Jung were translated by R. F. C. Hull. New York:

Philosophical Library, 1955; New York: Bell Publishing Company, 1956; London: Routledge and Kegan Paul, 1955 and 1956; New York: Greenwood, repr. 1969; New York: Schocken, repr. 1972 and 1976—this paperback edition includes Stanley Diamond's "Introductory Essay: Job and the Trickster" (other versions of which appeared in *Alcheringa: Ethnopoetics* 4[1972]: 74–82, and in Diamond's *In Search of the Primitive: A Critique of Civilization* [New Brunswick, N.J.: Transaction, 1974], 281–91).

Jung's essay is standardized to the conventions of his Collected Works in vol. 9/1, pars. 456–88 (Princeton: Princeton University Press, 1959); reprinted in *Four Archetypes: Mother, Rebirth, Spirit, Trickster* (Princeton: Princeton University Press, 1969). It was originally part 5 of Radin, Jung, and Kerényi, *Der Gottliche Schelm: Ein Indianischer Mythen-Zyklus* (Zürich: Rhein Verlag, 1954; Blowsnake's narrative was translated into German; titles were Jung, "Zur Psychologie der Schelmenfigur," Kerényi, "Mythologische Epilegomena"). The French translation by Arthur Reiss carried the title *Le fripon divin: une mythe indien* (Genève: Georg, 1958; Analyse et synthèse, 3; sequence of authors cited is: Jung, Kerényi, Radin). Outside this essay, the figure was not of much importance to Jung—there is only one other reference to the trickster in the General Index (Collected Works 20: 680) in addition to four references to Mercurius (Hermes) as trickster. See Pelton 1980: 228–34 for a careful negative critique of Jung's approach, and Basso 1987: 363 for a judgment that the collaboration by the three scholars was a failure.

3. MAPPING MYTHIC TRICKSTERS
Hynes

1. There are interesting vestiges of the activity of these societies in the twentieth century. The full and proper name of the English humor magazine, *Punch*, is *Punch, or the London Charivari*. The American word "shivaree" is derived from the French "charivari" and refers to a mock serenade by blowing horns and beating on pans beneath the window of a newly wed couple, particularly if there is a significant age difference between the husband and wife.

2. The Musical Heritage Society has issued a phonographic recording of the Mass of the Ass by the Guillaume Dufay Ensemble (*The Feast of Fools: Officium Fest Faturorum and Missa Asini*, 1980, MHS 4292). Based upon the Sens Codex (ca. 1222), Henri Villetard attributes the text to Pierre de Corbeil, Doctor of Theology and Archbishop of Sens. This version represents a notable attempt partially to sanitize this profane parody of the mass so that both it and its aherents could be brought back into the church. The ass is cast as "the lord of asses and bishop" (Asinorium dominus noster et episcopus). Participants and

celebrants answer responsorial prayer with brays: "ter respondebit: hin han, hin han, hin han."

3. It appears that most tricksters are male, but there are some very interesting studies of female tricksters; see *Reasoning with the Foxes: Female Wit in a World of Male Power*, vol. 42 of *Semeia: An Experimental Journal for Biblical Criticism*, ed. J. Cheryl Exum and Johanna W. H. Bos, 1988. In particular, see Naomi Steinberg, "Israelite Tricksters: Their Analogues and Cross-cultural Study," pp. 1–13; Claudia V. Camp, "Wise and Strange: An Interpretation of the Female Imagery in Proverbs in Light of Trickster Mythology," pp. 14–36.

4. HERMES AS TRICKSTER
Doty

1. Some background materials: Doty 1978a is primarily a review essay of Kerényi 1976, but also sketches the broad contours of the figure of Hermes. Doty 1978b provides a comprehensive survey of several hundred epithets applied to Hermes, as a way of approaching a deity from native (emic) characterizations rather than modern (etic) handbooks; that piece displays linguistic bases for many elements discussed in this essay.

The present essay presumes some familiarity with the wider contours of the trickster mythologem and myths; attempts to refine technical approaches to trickster materials continue to be made: Grottanelli 1983; Pope 1967; Carroll 1981; Doueihi 1984. My citation of the Jungian analyst Singer should not be taken to indicate a particular "Jungian" slant to what I am doing here; those who wish to see such a perspective in operation should consult some of the works in which it is truly influential: Lopez-Pedraza 1977; Monick 1987; Stein 1983: Ch. 1; Schechter 1980; Bolen 1989.

2. See Brown 1947; Eitrem 1912; Kerényi 1976; Otto 1954: 104–24; and Scherer 1886–90, on the Hermes figura, and Babcock-Abrahams 1975; Campbell 1959: 267–81; Evans-Pritchard 1967; Pelton 1980; Radin 1955; and Ricketts n.d. and 1966, on the trickster.

When stories and characteristics of Hermes are compared with traits of tricksters in other culture-areas, the convention of applying the epithet trickster to the Greek god makes immediate sense. Brown 1947 apparently originated the convention on the basis of the usage of Greek cross-formations from *kleptein* and *phêlêtês*, for which lexica usually give as first meanings "to thieve" and "thief," but whose contextual usages clearly support the expanded sense.

The English "trickster" apparently derives from the French *triche*, but the *Oxford English Dictionary* notes that the connotations of *trick, trickster*, are much broader in English. (Note also the cognate *treacher,* which we now use primarily in the adjective *treacherous.*)

Uses of the English "trickster" in translations of classical literature are found in Brown 1953, Hesiod's *Theogony,* referring to Prometheus; in Rouse 1940, Nonnos 47: 274/65, referring to Dionysos *(doliên);* and Green 1957, Sophokles' satyr-play *Ichneutai,* referring to Hermes: The Seilenos hopes "To catch this trickster in the very act" (366). Antedating Brown's practice, Farnell used the phrase "the celestial trickster" in his comprehensive history of Greek religious praxis (1909: 5/23).

That tricksterish elements can be identified for both Hermes and Prometheus within the same mythological tradition (Bianchi 1961b) should alert us to the fluidity and multiplicity of trickster-traits. Babcock-Abrahams notes the problem of differentiating between the trickster, the picaro, and the rogue, and lists some sixteen differentiae for identifying tricksterish behavior, all representing "different kinds of anomalousness" (1975: 159–60).

3. Farnell 1909: 5/30–31. Ovid, *Metamorphoses* 11, says that Hermes' son Autolykos "made white look like black and black like white," and with reference to the *moly* that Hermes took to Odysseus (Ulysses), that it was "a fabulous white plant / Sprung from black roots." Babcock-Abrahams 1975 notes that the black-white contrast is common in trickster stories.

4. Grant 1960, translation of Hyginus 2: 7. In Orphic tradition, the snakes represented Zeus coupling with Rhea. Liddell-Scott-Jones 1940: 949 refers to a proverb identified by Photius, *to kêrykeion ê tên machairan,* "peace or the sword," in which the staff functions metonymically as the agent of peace-making.

5. Athanassakis 1976, translation of Homeric Hymn 5: 574–75. On this passage see Lopez-Pedraza 1977: 50; but note against his interpretation that Hermes "loved" *(ephilêse)* Apollon already in line 508 of the Greek text (Allen, Halliday, and Sykes 1936), and that he "loves" Zeus in line 382.

6. As *leno:* Eitrem 1912: 775, 778; and illustrated in vase paintings. The sandal episode: Hyginus 2: 16. Hermes is closely involved in many ways, not just erotic, with a long list of figures, in a network of relationships: Apemosyne, Aphrodite, Apollon, Athene, Dionysos, Gaia, The Goddesses/Graces, Hekate, Helena, Herakles, Hestia, Kairos, the Nymphs, the Muses, Orestes, Persephone/Kore, Perseus, Pluton/Hades, Theseus and the Winds.

7. Kerényi's point about Prometheus could as well apply to Hermes: "The invention and first offering of the characteristic sacrifice of a religion may well be regarded as an act of world creation or at least as an act establishing the prevailing world order" (1963: 43). Bianchi's two essays cited here (1961a, b) attempt to distinguish the *culture-hero* type of trickster from the *demiurge* trickster. He argues that Prometheus is *more* "tricksterish" than Hermes (1961b: 428–

31). Carroll's 1981 essay attempts both to correct Lévi-Strauss's ethnographic error (North American coyote is *not* a carrion-eater), and to reconcile Lévi-Strauss and Freud, in terms of the establishing of civilization by sexual repression in the widest sense.

8. Graves 1968: ch. 13, develops the complex, consisting of Hermes, crane tracks, the alphabet, and the crane-skin purse.

9. Diodorus Siculus describes Hermes appropriately as being "endowed with unusual ingenuity for devising things capable of improving the social life of man" (1: 15.9). In some of his many activities concerned with new social orderings and interrelations, Hermes recovers the sinews of Zeus' arms and legs, after Typhon had cut them off, thereby immobilizing the god; joins the gods in overcoming the Titans and the Giants; proves Phrixius innocent of Demodice's false accusations, then helps him escape with Helle on the back of a flying ram (one of Hermes' motif-animals) decked with a golden fleece the god had provided—she falls off and establishes the Hellespont (Hyginus 2: 20); rescues Ares from the brass pot where the Giants Otus and Ephialtes had kept him out of action for thirteen months, until he was almost dead from suffocation (*Iliad* 5: 390); changes the daughters of Minyas, whom Dionysos made insane after they refused to join his revels, into birds, which escape by flying away; with Athene, purifies the Danaids after they killed their husbands; helps Ion discover a father and recover his true mother; helps Theseus discover the weapons of his father, then battle the Minotaur; helps Perseus to overcome the menacing Gorgon, and then to carry the weighty head, in order to free his mother, and save face; and he accompanies Orestes as Apollon's suppliant to Athene.

10. Stories involve Aineias, Aristaios, Arkas, Artemis, Asklepios, Athene, Dionysos, Erichthonios, Helena and the Dios Kouroi, Herakles, Ion, Oidipous, Pan, Pegasos and Chrysaor, Phaethon, and, in Egypt, Osiris. This mythologem deserves separate treatment.

11. Lethargy is literally "forgetfulness." Hermes has important lines of contact with Memory, which he conveyed to the *Argonaut's* herald Aithalides so successfully that it was still functioning in the underworld.

12. Compare the Aesopic tradition, Perry 1965: 178: A traveler, having vowed to offer Hermes half of everything he might find, came across a wallet in which there was no money, but there were dates and almonds. Having eaten the food, the traveler put the wallet and the almond shells and date pits on an altar, stating to Hermes that he was thereby sharing "both the outsides and the insides" of what he had found by chance. The "excluded middle" is brought into focus here in a way that shows us some of the further contours of that paradoxicality discussed in the first section of this essay.

13. I see some connection in the trickery by which Prometheus obtains for

humans the best part of the sacrifice. In that myth also, Zeus is said to laugh—but then he withholds fire from human use (Hesiod, *Works and Days*). Vernant's arguments seem convincing to me, although they reverse the traditional interpretations: Prometheus gains for mortals only the insignificant, *mortal* part of the sacrifice, while the Immortals gain the truly significant immortal aspects (1981: 43–56, 57–79; 1979). Similar: Bianchi's argument that Hesiod saw Hope in the Epimetheus-Pandora episode as a mortal surrogate for immortality (1961b: 427), Wirshbo's contention that the sacrifice scene marks "a violation of a norm of the golden age, the equality of gods and men" (1982: 109), and Nagy 1981 on "the deceptive gift."

The theme of Zeus' laughter recurs: In Lucian 7: 3, "Zeus was doubled up with laughter" at the swiftness—implying deceit?—with which Hermes overcame Eros in a wrestling match; his laughter was somewhat mitigated when he discovered that Hermes had stolen his scepter, Aphrodite's girdle *(cestus)*, Poseidon's trident, and Hephaistos' tongs.

14. But wishing a boon from Hermes demands caution and foresight: Phaedrus (transmitting Aesop; Perotti's Appendix 4, in Perry 1965) reports the story of Hermes rewarding two ungenerous hostesses. The wish of the first that her baby son might speedily wear a beard (i.e., metaphorically, to mature early) was readily and literally granted: the infant sprouted whiskers while still in the cradle. The wish of the second woman, that she might draw after her whatever she touched (evidently meaning customers) leads to chaos: she laughs at the results of her friend's wish, but then trying to blow her own nose, draws it out to a prodigious length.

15. Hermes Trismegistos, supposed author of all the Hermetic literature, "was believed to have prophesised [sic] the coming of Christianity through his allusions to a "Son of God" (Yates 1966: 153). Young serving-boys called Hermai assisted at the famous oracle of Trophonios (Pausanias 9.39.1–14); and Cicero (*De natura deorum* 3.25.56) refers to a Mercury identified with Trophonios. Note also the association between the Yoruba trickster Eshu-Elegba, and Ifa divining: Wescott 1962: 342 and plate 4, and with elaboration, Pelton 1979.

16. *Ichneutai* 402–03. On the hermeneutics of lying, and the polarity of strangeness and familiarity (in H.-G. Gadamer's hermeneutics), see Sheehan 1978.

17. One tradition makes Hermes the father, and Hekate the mother, of the Charities. In addition to Hermes' musical skill in Homeric Hymn #4, we learn in the Hymn *To Apollon* 3: 200 that he, Ares, and Apollon made music together. Dempsey 1968 traces Botticelli's treatment of the motif of Hermes leading the Graces as an emblem of the season of early summer. From my own iconographic studies, I would wager that this scene is represented more frequently, over a longer span of European art history, than almost any other.

5. BREAKER OF TABOOS
Makarius

1. Trickster signifies "player of tricks" (French: *jouer de tours*), but with a malignant nuance that the French expression does not convey. One of the first authors to have made a close study of the problem has written, concerning Napi, the trickster of the Blackfoot Indians: "In the serious tales, where it is a question of the creation, one speaks of him respectfully and there is no allusion to the malicious qualities that characterize him in other stories, in which he is powerful, but sometimes crippled; full of wisdom, but sometimes so destitute of mind that he must ask for help from the animals. At times he appears full of sympathy for humans, while at other times out of pure spitefulness he plays abominable, truly diabolical, tricks on them. He represents a combination of strength, weakness, wisdom, puerility and malice" (Grinnell 1893: 257; see also Brinton 1868: 161–62).

2. Brelich observes that "in order to create, preserve, and remodel a mythic figure like that of the trickster, a society must have had its own reasons, needs, and aims. . . . It is difficult to see what could be the reason for creating and preserving . . . a figure such as that which emerges from Radin's reconstruction . . . [a figure] that . . . is not composed originally of important realities" (1951: 134–35).

3. Of course blood is not always considered malignant, its use does not always inspire fear, and it does not inevitably clash with prohibitions. For example, it is used to establish pacts of brotherhood; or again, the blood of certain people is ingested in order to become imbued with their qualities. Australians even use blood to make the down of their ritual disguises adhere to their bodies. The most common form of ritual use of blood is the "bloody ransom," a voluntary shedding of human or animal blood, supposed to take the place of the uncontrollable blood-letting that one fears when the blood taboo has been broken, or when one anticipates possible effusions of blood.

Such a coexistence of the blood taboo and the free use of blood, of an extreme fear of blood and the absence of this fear, becomes comprehensible if we refer to the observations of Hubert and Mauss on the phenomena of exclusive attention and of direction of intention (1964). These authors have shown that the magical mentality has the ability to disregard the aspects of a phenomenon that are foreign and even contradictory to the aspect on which attention is exclusively concentrated in order to attain a sought-after result. When blood is used for purposes of sympathetic magic or redemption it is abstracted from its dangerous character. When it is a question of a rite of transgressing magic, the dangerous aspect is emphasized. It is precisely the extensive use of blood not accompanied by manifestations of fear that has not permitted us to discern the determinative role of the fear of blood in the establishment of taboos. However the most diffuse of the uses of non-dangerous blood, the "bloody ransom," gives evidence of the fear that blood inspires and of the strength of the taboo that surrounds it. For when the blood taboo is broken, or is in danger of being broken, the bloody ransom is seen as a remedy or a precaution against the danger that this breach involves. The fact that men scarify, slash, or mutilate themselves, or sacrifice animals and even humans (although every sacrifice ought not to be compared automatically to a redeeming sacrifice), shows that these sufferings and these losses appear preferable to the menaces carried by an "unredeemed" shedding of blood.

4. This obscene behavior likewise represents an allusion to incest. Cf. Makarius and Makarius 1968: 225 n. 17, and 226 n. 23. Brinton observes about Joskeha, the Iroquois twin trickster who lived with his grandmother, that he served her as a husband, and invokes on this subject the theme of pharaonic incest (1882: 58–59). Cf. likewise Makarius and Makarius 1968: 225 for the constant relationship between the taboo violator and the grandmother or sometimes the grandfather. Manabozo also cohabits with his grandmother.

5. In the Winnebago cycle of the Hare, the hare (a double of the trickster) throws some blood on the thighs of his grandmother, while pretending that she is having her period and, thereupon, lies with her (Radin 1955: 109). Coyote, animal personification of the trickster, takes a bit of blood and throws it on his daughter. She begins to menstruate and goes to the menstrual lodge (Shoshoni; Lowie 1908: 248–50).

6. To spend the night with a woman in the menstrual hut is one of the gravest violations that a man can commit. But it is exceeded by a man spending the night in the same conditions with his sister. In a narrative of the Sanpoil Indians such a crime is related to the beginnings of harmful magic and the appearance of death in the world (Ray 1948: 129–87).

7. This version is given by D. Moulding Brown with respect to Manabozo (n.d.: 6). See also Hoffman 1892–93: 118–19 and 206. Cf. the Fox narratives on the same theme: Jones 1911: 209–11; Jones 1907: 333–37. Among the Assineboine, the man who asks for eternal life is changed into stone by the trickster Sitonski (Lowie 1910: 123).

8. A Pawnee tale speaks of a woman called "Bear Woman" who had received from bears the power to heal wounds and to render men invulnerable and who nursed them with menstrual blood (Dorsey 1906: I.346–55). This narrative shows the equivalance between the power given by bears and menstrual blood.

9. For the significance of the *Cyprae moneta*, cf. Smith 1919: 150 ff. The author also points out the association of the shells with blood (150 n. 3). Concerning the *Cyprae*, cf. also Junod 1936: 11, 495. Frazer underlines the ambiguity of the shell among the Ojibwa. For Kohl it represents "the sickness, the evil inherent in each one of us," while for Hoffman it represents the life-force that it infuses in the

candidate (III, 488). The association between female sexual organs and shells is encountered frequently in poetry. Cf. Verlaine, "Les coquillages" *(Les fêtes galantes)* and Mallarmé, "Une Négresse par le démon secoueé."

10. Another example of trickster as founder of the great tribal ceremony is encountered among the Arapahos. Nihaca has the characteristics of the trickster: he is deceitful, incestuous, and phallic. But he directs the building of the cere-monial lodges, the execution of which he has entrusted to a murderer, whom he has enabled to go on a miraculous buffalo hunt. This man has promised to construct the first lodge and works according to the directions contained on a painted hide that the trickster has given him. Nihaca inspects the ritual orna-ments and the progress of the construction of the lodges. "All that was given to the people, the lodges were erected in order to teach them" (Dorsey and Kroeber 1903: 17–19). We should note a relationship between the ritual medicine drunk at the time of the great ceremony of the Arapahos (the Sun-dance) and men-strual blood (Dorsey 1903: 145–46).

11. See Hickerson 1963: 76. Cf. for the establishment of the ceremony of the Midewiwin among the Menomini, borrowed from the Ojibwa, Hoffman 1892–93: 69 ff. In the ceremony that took place in 1890, the founder's role of Man-abozo was underlined by the chant of the leader of the ritual. The Narrator chanted the exploits of Manabozo and the privileges he had received from The Great Mystery (Hoffman 1892–93: 82, 86, 89, 91, 94).

12. Whoolers, cited by Luomala, notes that in Polynesian the word *Maui* signifies left or left-handed but that he is ignorant of the significance of this fact. In the context of taboo violation the significance of Maui's relatedness to the left side is clearly manifest (cf. Makarius and Makarius 1968).

13. The account of a princess who leads people into violating taboos insti-tuted by her father in order to demonstrate that they are outmoded and false is entitled "Royal Daughter as Trickster," Herskovits and Herskovits 1958: 337–78. The authors therefore draw an equivalence between trickster and taboo violator, without noticing that therein is the reason for the creation of the mythical character.

14. To lie with the daughter of the chief is one of the typical exploits of the trickster. See, for example, Nihaca of the Arapaho who deflowers the daughter of a chief (Dorsey and Kroeber 1903: 64–65); Wakdjunkaga (Radin 1955: 35–36).

15. Ellis writes that since the sacrifices had become rare, Elegba proposed to Ife (homologue of Fa) to teach him the art of divination, something that would have led the people to multiply the offerings. In exchange for this service, according to their agreement, Elegba has the first choice of all sacrifices offered (1894: 58).

16. "What Manabozo really was," writes Brinton, "we have to look for in the accounts of ancient travellers, in the invocations of prophets, and in the role assigned to him at the time of the solemn religious mysteries. In the latter we

find him described as the patron and founder of the Meda cult, the inventor of picture writing, the father and the guardian of their nation, he who governs the winds, and even as the one who has made and preserved the world and created the Moon and the Sun. . . . He was originally the greatest deity recognized by them, powerful and beneficent above all the others, creator of the heavens and the worlds. He was founder of the medicine-hunt in which, after some rites and incantations, Manabozo appears to them in a dream and tells them where they can easily find game. He is himself a formidable hunter. He invents the fishnet for catching fish. The tokens and the charms that he has discovered and transmitted to his descendants are of a great efficacy in the hunt" (1882: 176–77). This aspect of founder of the ceremonial life completely escapes Ricketts, who declares that the trickster is still more lazy (otiose) than the supreme god. That is why this author, while underlining, with Van der Leeuw, "the Titanesque insurrection" of the trickster, his challenge to divinity, his quest for mastery through knowledge, ends by seeing in him the champion of a realistic resignation to the conditions of the world such as they are (Ricketts 1966: 337–38). He thus perverts the spirit of the character in every way.

17. These authors write that in the Dahomean worldview Legba appears to be the personification of the philosophical incident as solution, permitting the individual to escape a world dominated by destiny (1958: 36 and 1933: 56). If Legba represents a possibility for self-determination, it is because he breaks the taboos that limit human freedom by forbidding them access to the magical media supposed to be able to ameliorate their condition. The trickster conquers these media, represented by medicines, charms, and forbidden acts, and he enables those who use them to ameliorate their lot and escape determinism. But Herskovits and Herskovits are mistaken in writing that Legba gives these charms because, as messenger, he is in a position to see what happens in the supernatural world (1933: 35). He gives them because it is in his mythic nature to give them and because that is the reason for his existence.

18. It may be remembered that Brinton, for example, thought that a serious and revered character had been degraded into that of "the player of tricks." Boas was of the opinion that the difficulty of uniting in one person a benevolent being and a trickster disappears if the "self-styled cultural hero" acts only in his own interest. When, in so doing, he succeeds incidentally in making himself useful to humans, he appears as a beneficent hero; but when he fails he is seen as a "stupid trickster" (1898: 7). Loeb suggested that the accounts of the "stupid" Manabozo may have been taken up by the Midewiwin society in order to exalt the hero and, with him, the society itself (1926: 473). Brelich (1951), by contrast, has expressed the opinion that "an ambivalent mythical being does not necessarily have to be composed of two figures, the one ridiculous and useless and the

other creative, of which it (the former) would be the contamination," and Ricketts makes the same point (1966: 334).

19. This secondary trait of the trickster, mediation, which springs from his role as violator, has been taken by Lévi-Strauss as the trickster's principal trait and essential mythic function. In reducing the trickster to the coyote and the crow, and in considering that these predators constitute a mediation between hunting and agriculture, he believes he has resolved what "in American mythology has long constituted an enigma" (1958: I.248). For "the trickster . . . is a mediator, and this function explains how he may retain something of the duality that it is his function to surmount—whence his ambiguous and equivocal character" (251). The trickster does not have an ambiguous and equivocal character because he is a mediator, but finds himself in the character of mediator by reason of his role of violator, which makes of him an ambiguous and equivocal individual. The ambiguity of the trickster is determined not by "a universal mode of organizing the data of sensible experience" (250), discovered by Lévi-Strauss, but by causes that are identifiable at the empirical level: the ideas, beliefs, and rituals in circulation in the societies that have produced the myth being studied.

20. This explains, for example, the role of the trickster as initiator of menstruation and also as specialist in childbirth. Gastwokwire, Californian trickster, taught women how to be delivered normally. Up to that time, one had had to open them with a pebble, entailing their deaths. The myth says that Gastwokwire met a man getting ready to open the belly of a woman in labor. He found a medicinal plant, threw it into the house, and immediately the crying child was heard. It is for that reason, concludes the text, that women being delivered invoke his name (Kroeber 1905: 96–97). The same merit is attributed to a certain blacksmith of Africa (Pettazzoni 1948: I.265, citing Frobenius). This blacksmith taught coitus to men (who believed that the vagina, bloody at the time of the menses, became ill, so they had cohabited under the armpit) and likewise taught how wives might be delivered (on the impurity of the blacksmith, cf. Makarius 1968). The merit of having taught childbirth is attributed likewise to certain oceanic violator heroes; cf. Elbert 1959: 103, citing Beckwith and Beckwith 1940. For the impurity of the trickster, cf. also material about the coyote in Makarius and Makarius 1968: 227.

21. For the punishment of the unlucky violator, cf. Makarius and Makarius 1968: 229. Ricketts draws attention to the defeats and the failures of the trickster he sees as parodying the exploits of the shaman, following Radin (Ricketts 1966: 337–38).

22. See the whole of the commentary, "The Nature and Meaning of the Myth," and above all chs. 5 and 7 (in particular pp. 142 ff.). Radin writes that the

trickster would embody "vague memories of an archaic past from the primordial ages, where the difference between that which is divine and that which is not was not yet clear. The trickster symbolizes this epoch" (145). He is followed by Jung, who writes that "it is, then, evidently a matter of a 'psychologem,' that is to say of an archetypal psychic structure springing from the remotest ages. For, in its most distinct manifestations, it represents a faithful image of a human consciousness undifferentiated in all respects, corresponding to a psyche that, in its evolution, has scarcely left the animal plane" (183).

23. The magical violation of taboo, on the other hand, is a phenomenon that appears at that moment of social evolution when the taboo, while remaining generally respected, no longer has a tyrannical and absolute power, because it is no longer absolutely necessary for maintaining the cohesion of the human group.

6. THE SHAMAN AND THE TRICKSTER
Ricketts

1. Cf. Spiro 1970 where logical contradictions within the belief system are pointed out—contradictions of which only the most sophisticated monks seem to be aware (cf. p. 125, for example). Similar "contradictions" could be found in American Christianity and American "democracy," of course, and yet most Americans have no difficulty incorporating these contradictions in a unified worldview. So also it may be assumed did the Native Americans in the case of the shamanistic and trickster viewpoints.

9. A JAPANESE MYTHIC TRICKSTER
Ellwood

1. See also Miller 1984: 35, who emphasizes the contrast between Susa-no-o as principle of disruption and Amaterasu as principle of order, setting up a table contrasting him as male, undisciplined, chaos, disorder, impure, etc., with her as female, disciplined, cosmos, order, and pure. This certainly puts him on the side of the trickster in his destructive, antisocial and anarchist aspect. The weaving being done in the hall at the time of Susa-no-o's incursions is a mythical representation of order. Yet Miller is at pains to show that Susa-no-o is not portrayed as a purely evil god, but that his deed is part of a dynamic out of which good also comes in the form of new life on earth.

2. Naumann 1982 suggests that the skinning of an animal is, mythologically, assimilated to the death and new life of the moon and so a life-giving act. The backward-flaying would therefore, however, reverse this and be a death-giving

deed. But combined with Susa-no-o's other fertility gestures, it shows that he is a bestower of both life and death. Yet he, in trickster fashion, bestows them in a way separate from the ordinary regimen of Sun and Moon, characteristically associated with First Function deities.

10. APOSTLE TRANSFIGURED INTO TRICKSTER
Hynes and Steele

1. An interesting European psychopompic tale featuring Jesus and Peter entitled "The Twelve Apostles" is recounted by the Grimm brothers. Three hundred years before the advent of Jesus, Peter's starving mother sends him out to look for food. Peter falls prostrate with hunger in the forest and is awakened by a little baby who asks him why he stays there so afflicted. Repeating his mother's hope as his own, Peter states that "I go through the world to procure bread for myself, so that I might be able to live long enough to see the promised Redeemer: it is my greatest desire." The baby says "come with me and your desire will be fulfilled." Taking Peter to a cave of gold and silver where there are twelve cradles, the baby instructs him to go to sleep in the first cradle; eleven others are similarly conducted to the cave. After a three-hundred-year-sleep, they awaken to become Jesus' disciples.

11. THE KAGURU TRICKSTER
Beidelman

1. The six types of explanations cited by Babcock-Abrahams are: (1) entertainment, (2) support of some belief or values of a culture, (3) expression of notions ordinarily repressed in a culture, (4) social criticism, (5) analytical apprehension of the existential nature of culture, and (6) creation of communitas, as that is understood by Victor Turner.

2. A useful description of the anthropologist's own use of imagination recently appeared; while I had completed this paper before reading that work, I cite it for an introductory preface and also recommend its final chapter as an account of the functions and attractions of imagination. Unfortunately, the author does not address himself specifically to the moral implications of imagination (Needham 1978: 51–76); for the moral imagination, see Geertz' excellent 1977 essay and Crick's thoughtful 1976 survey.

3. Two excellent accounts of the problem of translation have recently appeared, one anthropological (Crick 1976) and one literary (Steiner 1977).

12. BETWEEN DISCOURSE AND STORY
Doueihi

1. As "Trickster: On Inhabiting the Space Between Discourse and Story," by Anne Doueihi, the much-longer version of this essay appeared in *Soundings: An Interdisciplinary Journal* 67/3 (1984): 283–311. The revision, with bracketed summaries, is by William Doty, with Doueihi's agreement and additions, and the permission of *Soundings*.

2. For a discussion of the relation of the ideas of presence and speech, see Derrida 1981.

3. See Todorov 1982 [English translation 1984] for a study of the Indian as Other during the period of discovery and conquest of America.

13. METAPLAYERS AND REVEALERS
Hynes

1. As notorious border-breakers, tricksters move back and forth across segmented categories, intermingling seemingly disparate things from which come new progeny and invention. There are significant parallels between this approach and some current business literature that counsels the need for a return to creativity and entrepreneurship in the management of American corporations, particularly as a means of reattaining America's world stature. Rosabeth Moss Kanter, in *The Change Masters: Innovation and Entrepreneurship in the American Corporation* (1983), observes that the spirit most likely to produce innovations is an "integrative spirit," that is, "the willingness to move beyond received wisdom, to combine ideas from unconnected sources, to embrace change as an opportunity to test limits" (1983: 27). By the same token, the contrasting spirit preventing innovation and creativity is "segmentation," in which a large number of compartments are all walled off from each other: "only the minimum number of exchanges takes place at the boundaries of segments."

Kanter speaks insightfully about this creative ability to see in a fashion that integrates the apparently disparate and contradictory: "To see problems integratively is to see them as wholes, related to larger wholes, and thus challenging established practices—rather than walling off a piece of experience and preventing it from being touched or affected by any new experiences. Entrepreneurs—and entrepreneurial organizations—always operate at the edge of their competence, focusing more of their resources and attention on what they do not yet know . . . than on controlling what they already know" (1983: 28).

BIBLIOGRAPHY

In-text citations are abbreviations that follow the pattern: *Author's last name. Date. Relevant pages.* This bibliography combines references from all the essays in this volume; the works listed represent a basic and comprehensive bibliography for the field, although data-base searches will bring up additional references, especially for the descriptor "Trickster in Literature."

Items here marked [TC] are *collections* of trickster tales; those marked [TM] are judged by the editors to have significance in engaging the *methodology* of trickster studies.

Christopher Vecsey helped with the earliest version of this biliography; Angela Bramlett prepared the initial electronic files of the manuscript, on a subsidy provided by the College of Arts and Sciences, University of Alabama, and Betty Dickey, Secretary to Dr. Doty, produced the final version.

Abrahams, Roger D. 1968. "Trickster, the Outrageous Hero." In Tristram P. Coffin, ed. *Our Living Traditions: An Introduction to American Folklore*, 170–78. New York: Basic Books.

Abrams, David M., and Brian Sutton-Smith. 1977. "The Development of the Trickster in Children's Narrative." *Journal of American Folklore* 90:29–47. [TM]

Adamson, Thelma. 1934. *Folk Tales of the Coast Salish*. Memoirs, 27. New York: American Folk-Lore Society.

Addae, T. 1970. "Some Aspects of Ashanti Religious Beliefs." *Africa* 25:162–65.

Akesson, S. K. 1950. "The Secret of Akom." *African Affairs* 49:237–40.

Allen, T. W., W. R. Halliday, and E. E. Sykes, eds. 1936. *The Homeric Hymns.* 2nd ed. of Greek text. Oxford: Clarendon.

Appiah, Peggy. 1966. *Ananse the Spider: Tales from an Ashanti Village.* New York: Pantheon. [TC]

———. 1967. *Tales of an Ashanti Father.* London: Deutsch.

———. 1969. *The Pineapple Child and Other Tales from Ashanti.* London: Deutsch.

Apte, Mahadev L. 1985. *Humor and Laughter: An Anthropological Approach.* Ithaca: Cornell U P.

Arewa, Ojo, and G. M. Shreve. 1975. *The Genesis of Structures in African Narrative,* vol. 1: *Zande Trickster Tales.* Studies in African Semiotics. New Paltz: Conch. [TC]

Ashley, Kathleen M. 1988. "Interrogating Biblical Deception and Trickster Theories: Narratives of Patriarchy or Possibility." In Exum and Bos 1988:103–16.

Athanassakis, Apostolos N. 1976. *The Homeric Hymns: Translation, Introduction, and Notes.* Baltimore: Johns Hopkins U P.

———. 1977. *The Orphic Hymns.* SBL Texts and Translations, 12; Graeco-Roman Religion, 4. Missoula: Scholars.

Auerbach, Erich. 1953. *Mimesis: The Representation of Reality in Western Literature.* Trans. Willard R. Trask. Princeton: Princeton U P.

Aycock, D. Alan. 1983. "The Mark of Cain." In Edmund Leach and Aycock. *Structuralist Interpretations of Biblical Myth.* New York: Cambridge U P and Royal Anthropological Institute.

Babcock-Abrahams, Barbara. 1975. "'A Tolerated Margin of Mess': The Trickster and His Tales Reconsidered." *Journal of the Folklore Institute* 11/3:147–86. [TM]

———, ed. 1978. *The Reversible World: Symbolic Inversion in Art and Society.* Ithaca: Cornell U P.

———. 1984. "Arrange Me into Disorder: Fragments and Reflections on Ritual Clowning." In John J. MacAloon, ed. *Rite, Drama, Festival, Spectacle: Rehearsals toward a Theory of Cultural Performance,* 102–28. Philadelphia: Institute for the Study of Human Issues.

Bakhtin, Mikail. 1968. *Rabelais and His World.* Trans. Helene Iswolsky. Cambridge: MIT P.

———. 1984. *Problems of Dostoevsky's Poetics.* Ed. and trans. Caryl Emerson. Theory and History of Literature, 8. Minneapolis: U Minnesota P.

Bal, Mieke. 1988. "Tricky Thematics." In Exum and Bos 1988:133–55.

Ballard, Arthur C. 1929. *Mythology of the Southern Puget Sound.* Publications in Anthropology, 3/2. Seattle: U Washington.

Bandelier, Adolf F. 1954. *The Delight Makers.* New York: Dodd.

Barker, W. H. 1919. "Nyamkopon and Ananse in Gold Coast Folklore." *Folk-Lore* 30.

————, and C. Sinclair. 1972. *West African Folk-tales*. Northbrook: Metro [reprint from 1917].

Barnaby, Karin, and Pellegrino d'Acierno, eds. 1990. *C. G. Jung and the Humanities: Toward a Hermeneutics of Culture*. Princeton: Princeton U P.

Barnouw, Victor. 1977. *Wisconsin Chippewa Myths and Tales and Their Relation to Chippewa Life*. Madison: U Wisconsin P.

Bascom, William. 1969. *The Yoruba of Southwestern Nigeria*. New York: Holt, Rinehart and Winston.

Basso, Ellen B. 1987. *In Favor of Deceit: A Study of Tricksters in an Amazonian Society*. Tucson: U Arizona P. [TC, TM]

Beattie, H. 1921. "Mama." *Journal of the Polynesian Society* 30.

Beck, Peggy V., and A. L. Walters. 1977. *The Sacred: Ways of Knowledge, Sources of Life*. Chapter 13, "Sacred Fools and Clowns." Tsaile: Navajo Community College P.

Beckwith, Warren, and Martha Beckwith. 1940. *Hawaiian Mythology*. New Haven: Yale U P.

————. 1951. *The Kumulipo: A Hawaiian Creation Chant*. Reprint. Honolulu: U P Hawaii, 1972.

Beecher, D. A. 1987. "Intriguers and Trickster: The Manifestations of an Archetype in the Comedy of the Renaissance." *Revue de Littérature Comparée* 61/1:5–29.

Beidelman, T. O. 1961. "Hyena and Rabbit." *Africa* 31:61–74.

————. 1962. "Three Kaguru Tales." *Africa und Uebersee* 46:218–29.

————. 1963a. "Further Adventures of Hyena and Rabbit." *Africa* 33:54–69.

————. 1963b. "The Blood Covenant and the Concept of Blood in Ukaguru." *Africa* 33:321–42.

————. 1963c. "Four Kaguru Tales." *Tanganyika Notes and Records* 61:135–46.

————. 1963d. "Five Kaguru Texts." *Anthropos* 58:737–72.

————. 1963e. "Witchcraft and Sorcery in Ukaguru." In John Middleton and E. H. Winter, eds. *Witchcraft and Sorcery in East Africa*, 57–98. London: Routledge and Kegan Paul.

————. 1964a. "Ten Kaguru Texts." *Journal of African Languages* 3:1–37.

————. 1964b. "Three Kaguru Tales of the Living and the Dead." *Journal of the Royal Anthropological Institute* 94:109–37.

————. 1964c. "Pig *(Guluwe)*: An Essay on Ngulu Sexual Symbolism and Ceremony." *Southwestern Journal of Anthropology* 20:359–92.

————. 1965. "Six Kaguru Tales." *Zeitschrift für Ethnologie* 110:17–41.

————. 1966a. "Further Kaguru Tales." *Journal of African Languages* 5:74–102.

————. 1966b. "*Utani*: Some Kaguru Notions of Death, Sexuality and Affinity." *Southwestern Journal of Anthropology* 22:354–80.

————. 1966c. "Swazi Royal Ritual." *Africa* 36:373–405.

——. 1967a. "Kaguru Folklore and the Concept of Reciprocity." *Zeitschrift für Ethnologie* 92:74–88.

——. 1967b. "More Kaguru Tales." *Baessler-Archiv* 15:169–82.

——. 1967c. "Eleven Kaguru Tales." *African Studies* 26:3–36.

——. 1967d. "Eight Kaguru Texts." *Anthropos* 62:369–93.

——. 1970. "Kaguru Texts." *Baessler-Archiv* 18:335–61.

——. 1971a. "Nine Kaguru Tales." *Zeitschrift für Ethnologie* 96:14–29.

——. 1971b. "Foreword." In Marion Kilson. *Kpele Lala*, xi–xvi. Cambridge: Harvard U P.

——. 1973. "Three Kaguru Texts." *Zeitschrift für Ethnologie* 98:90–101.

——. 1974a. "The Bird Motif in Kaguru Folklore." *Anthropos* 69:162–90.

——. 1974b. "Kaguru Texts." *Baessler-Archiv* 22:247–63.

——. 1975a. "Ambiguous Animals." *Africa* 45:183–200.

——. 1975b. "Kaguru Oral Literature. Texts 1." *Anthropos* 70:737–74.

——. 1976a. "Kaguru Oral Literature. Texts 2." *Anthropos* 71:46–89.

——. 1976b. Review of E. R. Leach, *Culture and Communication. Man* (n.s.) 11:605–6.

——. 1977. "Kaguru Oral Literature. Texts 3." *Anthropos* 72:56–96.

——. 1978a. "Kaguru Oral Literature. Texts 4." *Anthropos* 73:69–112.

——. 1978b. Review of Barbara Babcock-Abrahams, ed., *The Reversible World. Anthropos* 73:934–36.

——. 1980. "The Moral Imagination of the Kaguru: Some Thoughts on Tricksters, Translation and Comparative Analysis." *American Ethnologist* 7:27–42. [See chapter 11 in this volume.] [TM]

——. 1981. Review of Pelton 1980. *Times Literary Supplement*, 23 January:78.

Bellows, Henry Adams, trans. 1923. *The Poetic Edda.* New York: American-Scandinavian Foundation.

Belmonte, Thomas. 1990. "The Trickster and the Sacred Clown: Revealing the Logic of the Unspeakable." In Barnaby and d'Acierno 1990:45–66.

Berger, Peter. 1969. *A Rumor of Angels: Modern Society and the Rediscovery of the Supernatural.* New York: Doubleday.

Berry, J. 1961. *Spoken Art in West Africa.* London: School of Oriental and African Studies.

Best, Elsdon. 1924. *The Maori.* 2 vols. Wellington, N.Z.: Dominion Museum.

Bettelheim, Bruno. 1975. *The Uses of Enchantment: The Meaning and Importance of Fairy Tales.* New York: Vintage.

Bianchi, Ugo. 1961a. "Der demiurgische Trickster und die Religionsethnologie." *Paideuma—Mitteilungen zür Kulturkunde* 7:335–41. [TM]

——. 1961b. "Prometheus, der Titanische Trickster." *Paideuma—Mitteilungen zür Kulturkunde* 7:414–37. [TM]

Bierhorst, John. 1985. *The Mythology of North America.* New York: Morrow.

——. 1987. *Doctor Coyote: A Native American Aesop's Fables.* New York: Macmillan.

Blue Cloud, Peter. 1982. *Elderberry Flute Song: Contemporary Coyote Tales.* Trumansburg: Crossing P.

Boas, Franz. 1894. *Chinook Texts.* Bulletin of the Bureau of Ethnology 20. Washington: Smithsonian Institution.

———. 1895. "The Social Organization and Secret Societies of the Kwakiutl Indians." *Reports of the U.S. National Museum,* 331–738.

———. 1898. "Introduction." In J. Teit. *Traditions of the Thompson River Indians of British Columbia.* Boston: Houghton Mifflin.

———. 1905. *Kwakiutl Texts,* Second Series. Jessup North Pacific Expedition, 10/1. Leiden: Brill.

Bock, Felicia G. 1972. *Engi-shiki: Procedures of the Engi Era.* Tokyo: Sophia U.

Bohannan, Paul J. 1958. "Extra-Processual Events in Tiv Political Institutions." *American Anthropologist* 60:1–12.

Bolen, Jean Shinoda. 1989. *Gods in Everyman: A New Psychology of Men's Lives and Loves.* San Francisco: HarperCollins.

Brelich, Angelo. 1958. "Il Trickster." *Studi e Materiali di Storia delle Religioni* 29:129–37 [review of Radin 1955]. [TM]

Bright, William. 1987. "The Natural History of Old Man Coyote." In Swann and Krupat 1987:339–87.

———, ed. 1978. *Coyote Stories. International Journal of American Linguistics*— Native American Texts Series, 1. Chicago: U Chicago P.

Brinton, Daniel G. 1882. *American Hero Myths.* Philadelphia.

———. 1896. *Myths of the New World.* 3rd ed. Philadelphia: David McKay.

Brown, E. J. P. 1929. *Gold Coast and Ashanti Reader.* Book 2. London: Crown Agents.

Brown, Norman O. 1947. *Hermes the Thief: The Evolution of a Myth.* New York: Random House.

———. 1959. *Life Against Death: The Psycho-Analytical Meaning of History.* Middletown: Wesleyan U P.

———. 1966. *Love's Body.* New York: Vintage.

———, trans. 1953. *Hesiod, Theogony.* Library of Liberal Arts, 36. Indianapolis: Bobbs-Merrill.

Brown, Raymond E., Karl P. Donfried, and John Reumann, eds. 1973. *Peter in the New Testament.* New York: Paulist P.

Brun, Victor. 1976. *Sug, The Trickster Who Fooled the Monk: A Northern Thai Tale with Vocabulary.* London: Curzon P.

Budge, E. A. Wallis. 1904. *The Gods of the Egyptians, or Studies in Egyptian Mythology.* 2 vols. Reprint. New York: Dover, 1969.

Bulmer, Ralph. 1967. "Why is the Cassowary Not a Bird?" *Man* (n.s.) 2:5–25.

Busia, K. A. 1954. "The Ashanti of the Gold Coast." In Daryll Forde, ed. *African Worlds: Studies in the Cosmological Ideas and Social Values of African Peoples,* 190–209. London: Oxford U P.

Busse, J. 1936. "Kaguru-Texte." *Zeitschrift für Eingeborenen-Sprachen* 27:61–75.

Buttrick, George A. 1951. "Exposition of the Gospel According to St. Matthew." *Interpreter's Bible* 7. New York: Abingdon P.

Calame-Griaule, Geneviève. 1966. *Ethnologie et langage*. Paris: Gallimard.

Calvino, Italo. 1980 [1956]. *Italian Folktales*. Trans. George Martin. New York: Pantheon. [TC]

Cameron, Anne. 1986. *Dzelarhons: Myths of the Northwest Coast*. British Columbia: Madeira Park Harbour Publishing Co.

Camp, Claudia V. 1988. "Wise and Strange: An Interpretation of the Female Imagery in Proverbs in Light of Trickster Mythology." In Exum and Bos 1988:14–36.

Campbell, Joseph. 1959. *The Masks of God: Primitive Mythology*. New York: Viking.

———. 1988. *An Open Life: Joseph Campbell in Conversation with Michael Toms*. Ed. John M. Maher and Dennie Briggs. Burdett: Larson Publications.

Canda, Edward R. 1979. "The Tiger and the Shaman: Mastery of Sacred Power in Korea." M.A. Thesis. U Denver.

———. 1981. "The Korean Tiger: Trickster and Servant of the Sacred." *Korea Journal* 21/11:22–38.

Carroll, Michael P. 1981. "Lévi-Strauss, Freud and the Trickster: A New Perspective upon an Old Problem." *American Ethnologist* 8/2:301–13. [TM]

———. 1984. "The Trickster as Selfish-Buffoon and Culture Hero." *Ethos* 12/2:105–31.

Casson, Lionel, ed. and trans. 1962. *Selected Satires of Lucian*. New York: Norton.

Charles, Lucille Hoerr. 1945. "The Clown's Function." *Journal of American Folklore* 58/227:25–34.

Chatterji, S. K. 1960. *Africanism. The African Personality*. Calcutta: Bengal Publishers.

Christensen, James Boyd. 1973. "The Role of Proverbs in Fante Culture." In E. P. Skinner, ed. *Peoples and Cultures of Africa: An Anthropological Reader*, 509–24. Garden City: Doubleday.

Cirlot, J. E. 1971. *A Dictionary of Symbols*. 2nd ed. London: Routledge.

Clarke, K. W. 1958. "A Motif-Index of the Folktales of Culture-Area V West Africa." Diss. Indiana U.

Clifford, James, and George E. Marcus. 1986. *Writing Culture: The Poetics and Politics of Ethnography*. Berkeley: U California P.

Clift, Jean Dalby. 1972. "Shakespeare's Lucio in *Measure for Measure*." M.A. Thesis. U Denver.

———. 1979. "The Trickster as Light-Bringer: Lucio in *Measure for Measure*." Unpublished ms., 29 pp.

Coeur, Ch. le. 1932. *Le culte de la génération et l'evolution religieuse et sociale en Guinée*. Paris: Leroux.

Coffin, S. 1945. "Stool Worship in Ashanti." *Canadian Geographical Journal* 30.

Coffin, Tristram P., ed. 1961. *Indian Tales of North America: An Anthology for the Adult Reader.* Philadelphia: American Folklore Society. [TC]

Courlander, Harold. 1957. *The Hat-shaking Dance and Other Tales from the Gold Coast.* New York: Harcourt Brace Jovanovich.

———. 1963. *The King's Drum and Other African Stories.* New York: Harcourt.

Cox, Harvey. 1969. *The Feast of Fools: A Theological Essay of Festivity and Fantasy.* New York: HarperCollins.

Crick, Malcolm. 1976. *Explorations in Language and Meaning.* London: Malaby P.

Crumrine, N. Ross. 1969. "Japakoba, the Mayo Easter Ceremonial Impersonator: Explanations of Ritual Clowning." *Journal for the Scientific Study of Religion* 8/1:1–22.

Culler, Jonathan. 1981. *The Pursuit of Signs: Semiotics, Literature, Deconstruction.* Ithaca: Cornell U P.

Danquah, J. B. 1928. *Gold Coast. Akan Laws and Customs and the Akim Abuakwa Constitution.* London: Routledge.

———. 1968. *The Akan Doctrine of God. A Fragment of Gold Coast Ethics and Religion.* Reprint. London: Cass.

Davis, Natalie Zemon. 1971. "The Reasons of Misrule: Youth Groups and Charivaris in Sixteenth-century France." *Past and Present* 50:41–75.

Davy, G., and E. Moret. 1923. *Des Clans aux Empires.* Paris.

Debrunner, H. 1961. *Witchcraft in Ghana.* Accra: Presbyterian Book Depot.

De Mille, Richard. 1976. *Castañeda's Journey: The Power and the Allegory.* Santa Barbara: Capra Press.

Dempsey, Charles. 1968. "*Mercurius ver:* The Sources of Botticelli's *Primavera.*" *Journal of the Warburg and Courtauld Institutes* 31:251–73.

Derrida, Jacques. 1981. *Dissemination.* Translation, introduction, and notes by Barbara Johnson. Chicago: U Chicago P.

de Vries, Jan. 1933. *The Problem of Loki.* Folklore Fellows Communication 43/1, No. 1. Helsinki: Suomalainen Tiedekatemia.

Diamond, Stanley. 1974. *In Search of the Primitive: A Critique of Civilization.* New Brunswick: Transaction.

———. 1990. "Jung Contra Freud: What It Means To Be Funny." In Barnaby and d'Acierno 1990:67–75.

Diarrassouba, M. 1970. *Le lièvere et l'araignée. Deux animaux des contes de l'Ouest Africain.* Abidjan: U Abidjan.

Dobe, M. 1923. "Social Control Among the Lambas." *Bantu Studies* 2.

Dobie, James. 1938. *Coyote Wisdom.* Dallas: Southern Methodist U P.

Doran, John. 1966 (1858). *The History of Court Fools.* Reprint. New York: Haskell House.

Dorje, Rinjing. 1975. *Tales of Uncle Tompa: The Legendary Rascal of Tibet.* San Rafael: Dorje Ling. [TC]

Dorsey, George A. 1903. *The Arapaho Sun Dance*. Chicago.

———. 1905. *Traditions of the Caddo*. Washington: Carnegie Institute.

———. 1906. *The Pawnee, Mythology*. Publication #59, Part I. Washington: Carnegie Institute.

———, and A. L. Kroeber. 1903. *Traditions of the Arapaho*. Field Columbian Museum Publication, Anthropology Series, 5.

Dorsey, J. Owen. 1890. *The Cegiha Language*. Contributions to North American Ethnology, 6. Washington: Government Printing Office.

Doty, William G. 1978a. "Hermes Guide of Souls." *Journal of Analytical Psychology* 23/4:358–64.

———. 1978b. "Hermes' Heteronymous Appellations." In James Hillman, ed. *Facing the Gods*, 115–33. Irving: Spring Publications.

———. 1986. *Mythography: The Study of Myths and Rituals*. Tuscaloosa: U Alabama P.

———. 1988. "The Heterogeneous Other and the Examined Life." *Soundings: An Interdisciplinary Journal* 71/1:155–69.

———. 1990. "Writing the Blurred Genres of Postmodern Ethnography." *Annals of Scholarship: Studies of the Humanities and Social Sciences* 6/2–3:267–87.

———. 1991. "The Trickster." In C. Downing, ed. *Mirrors of the Self: Archetypal Images that Shape Your Life*, 237–40. Los Angeles: Tarcher.

Doueihi, Anne. 1984. "Trickster: On Inhabiting the Space Between Discourse and Story." *Soundings: An Interdisciplinary Journal* 67/3:283–311. [See Doueihi, chapter 12 in this vol.] [TM]

Douglas, A. B. 1931. "The Anansesem in Gold Coast Schools." *Gold Coast Review* 5.

Douglas, Mary. 1966. *Purity and Danger: An Analysis of Concepts of Pollution and Taboo*. New York: Routledge.

———. 1968. "The Social Control of Cognition: Some Factors in Joke Perception." *Man* (n.s.) 3:361–76.

Du Cange, Charles. 1733–36. *Glossarium ad scriptores mediae et infirmae lantinitatis*. Paris.

Durkheim, Émile. 1897. "La prohibition de l'inceste et ses origines." *L'Année sociologique* 1.

Edmunson, Munro S. 1971. *Lore: An Introduction to the Science of Folklore and Literature*. New York: Holt, Rinehart and Winston.

Edwards, Jay. 1978. *The Afro-American Trickster Tale: A Structural Analysis*. Monograph 4. Bloomington: Indiana University Folklore Publs. Group. [TM]

———. 1984. "Structural Analysis of the Afro-American Trickster Tale." In Henry Louis Gates, Jr., ed. *Black Literature and Literary Theory*, 81–103. New York: Methuen. [TM]

Eitrem, S. 1912. "Hermes." In Pauly-Wissowa-Kroll. *Real-Encyclopädie der klassischen Altertumswisschaften* 8/1:cols. 738–92.

Elbert, S. H. 1959. "The Chief in Hawaiian Mythology." *Journal of American Folklore* 69:99–113, 341–55.

Eliade, Mircea. 1958. *Birth and Rebirth.* New York: HarperCollins.

———. 1959. *The Sacred and the Profane: The Nature of Religion.* Trans. Willard R. Trask. New York: Harcourt, Brace & World.

———. 1961. *Images and Symbols.* Trans. Philip Mariet. New York: Sheed & Ward.

———. 1963. *Patterns in Comparative Religion.* New York: Meridian.

———. 1964. *Shamanism: Archaic Techniques of Ecstasy.* Trans. Williard R. Trask. Bollingen Series, 76. New York: Pantheon Books.

———. 1969. *The Quest: History and Meaning in Religion.* Chicago: U Chicago P.

———. 1975. *Patanjali and Yoga.* New York: Schocken Books.

Ellis, A. E. 1894. *The Yoruba-Speaking Peoples of the Slave Coast of West Africa.* London.

Ellwood, Robert S. 1967. "The Saigu: Princess and Priestess." *History of Religions* 7/1:35–60.

———. 1973. *The Feast of Kingship: Accession Ceremonies in Ancient Japan.* Tokyo: Sophia U.

Elton, G. R. 1969. *The Practice of History.* Glasgow: William Collins Sons.

Erasmus. 1958. *In Praise of Folly.* Trans. John Wilson. Ann Arbor: U Michigan P.

Erdoes, Richard, and Alfonso Ortiz, eds. 1984. *American Indian Myths and Legends.* Part 7, "Coyote Laughs and Cries: Trickster Tales." New York: Pantheon. [TC]

Espinosa, A. M. 1914. "Comparative Notes on New Mexican and Mexican Spanish Folktales." *Journal of American Folk-lore* 27:105–47, 211–31.

Espinosa, José Manuel. 1937. *Spanish Folk Tales from New Mexico.* New York: American Folk-lore Society.

Evans, H. St. John T. 1950. "The Akan Doctrine of God." In E. W. Smith, ed. *African Ideas of God: A Symposium,* 241–59. London: Edinburgh House.

Evans-Pritchard, E. E. 1963. *The Comparative Method in Social Anthropology.* Hobhouse Lectures, 33. London: Athlone.

———. 1967. *The Zande Trickster.* Oxford Library of African Literature. Oxford: Clarendon P. [TC]

Exum, J. Cheryl, and Johanna W. H. Bos, eds. 1988. *Reasoning with the Foxes: Female Wit in a World of Male Power. Semeia: An Experimental Journal for Biblical Criticism* 42.

Farmer, Kathy. 1978. "The Trickster Genre in the Old Testament." Diss. Southern Methodist U.

Farnell, Lewis Richard. 1909. *The Cults of the Greek States.* Vol. 5. Oxford: Clarendon.

Feit, Kenneth P. 1975. "The Priestly Fool." *The American Theological Review,* Supplement Series, 5:97–108.

Feldmann, Susan, ed. 1963. *African Myths and Tales.* New York: Dell. [TC]

————, ed. 1965. *The Storytelling Stone: Myths and Tales of the American Indians.* New York: Dell. [TC]

Fernandez, James. 1979. "On the Notion of Religious Movement." *Social Research* 46:36–62.

Field, M. J. 1958. "Ashanti and Hebrew Shamanism." *Man* 58.

Fortes, M. 1965. "Some Reflections on Ancestor Worship in Africa." In M. Fortes and G. Dieterlen, eds. *African Systems of Thought.* London: Oxford U P.

Foucault, Michel. 1965. *Madness and Civilization: A History of Insanity in the Age of Reason.* Trans. Richard Howard. New York: Random House.

Frazer, James George, 1910. *Totemism and Exogamy.* 4 vols. London: Macmillan.

————, ed. and trans. 1929. *Publii Ovidii Nasonis. Fastorum Libri Sex. The FASTI of Ovid.* 5 vols. London: Macmillan.

Frobenius, L. 1949. *Mythologie de l'Atlantide.* Paris.

Gaillois, Roger. 1939. *L'Homme et le Sacré.* Paris.

Garfinkel, Harold. 1967. *Studies in Ethnomethodology.* Englewood Cliffs: Prentice-Hall.

Gates, Henry Louis, Jr. 1988. *The Signifying Monkey: A Theory of Afro-American Literary Criticism.* New York: Oxford U P.

Geertz, Clifford. 1972. "Deep Play: Notes on the Balinese Cockfight." *Daedalus* 101:1–37.

————. 1973. *The Interpretation of Cultures.* New York: Basic Books.

————. 1977. "Found in Translation: On the Social History of the Moral Imagination." *Georgia Review* 31:788–810.

Gelber, Jack. 1981. "Sam Shephard: The Playwright as Shaman." In *Angel City and Other Plays.* New York: Applause Theatre Book Publishers.

Genovese, Eugene D. 1974. *Roll Jordan, Roll: The World the Slaves Made.* New York: Pantheon.

Giddings, Ruth Warner. 1959. *Yaqui Myths and Legends.* Tucson: U Arizona P.

Gill, Sam D. 1983. *Native American Traditions: Sources and Interpretations.* Religious Life of Man Series. Belmont: Wadsworth. [TC]

Gluckman, Max. 1964. *Closed Systems and Open Minds: The Limits of Naivety in Social Anthropology.* Chicago: Aldine.

————. 1965. *Custom and Conflict in Africa.* New York: Free P.

Godolphin, F. R. B., ed. 1964. *Great Classical Myths.* New York: Modern Library.

Goldsmith, Robert Hillis. 1955. *Wise Fools in Shakespeare.* East Lansing: Michigan State U P.

Good, Edwin M. 1988. "Deception and Women: A Response." In Exum and Bos 1988:117–32.

Goody, Jack. 1957. "Anomie in Ashanti?" *Africa* 27:356–63.

Gossip, Arthur John. 1952. "Exposition of the Gospel According to John." *Interpreter's Bible* 8. New York: Abingdon P.

Grant, Mary, ed. and trans. 1960. *The Myths of Hyginus.* Humanistic Studies, 34. Lawrence: U Kansas P.

Graves, Robert. 1968. *The White Goddess: A Historical Grammar of Poetic Myth.* Amended and enlarged edition. New York: Farrar.

Green, Robert L., trans. 1957. *Two Satyr Plays: Euripides' CYCLOPS and Sophocles' ICHNEUTAI* [The Searching Satyrs, or Trackers]. London: Penguin.

Greenberg, Joanne. 1982. "Tales of Hershele Osterpoler: A Jewish Trickster Figure." Unpublished ms. prepared for AAR Consultation on Trickster Myths.

Greenfield, Barbara. 1985. "The Archetypal Masculine: Its Manifestation in Myth, and Its Significance for Women." In Andrew Samuels, ed. *The Father: Contemporary Jungian Perspectives,* 187–210. New York: New York U P. [TM]

Greenway, John. 1964. *Literature Among the Primitives.* Chapter 3, "Tricksters, Tar Babies, and other Heroes." Hatboro: Folklore Associates. [TC]

———, ed. 1965. *The Primitive Reader: An Anthology of Myths, Tales, Songs, Riddles, and Proverbs of Aboriginal Peoples Around the World.* Chapter 3, "The Delight Makers: Tricksters." Hatboro: Folklore Associates. [TC]

Grinnell, G. B. 1893. *Blackfoot Lodge Tales.* London.

Grotjahn, Martin. 1957. *Beyond Laughter.* New York: Blakiston.

Grottanelli, Cristiano. 1983. "Tricksters, Scapegoats, Champions, Saviors." *History of Religions* 23/2:117–39. [TM]

Gunther, Erna. 1925. *Klallam Folk Tales.* Publications in Anthropology, 1/4. Seattle: U Washington.

Haile, Berard. 1984. *Navajo Coyote Tales: The Curly To Aheedliinii Version.* Ed. and Intro. by Karl W. Luckert. American Tribal Religions, 8. Lincoln: U Nebraska P.

Hallpike, C. R. 1971. "Some Problems in Cross-Cultural Comparison." In T. O. Beidelman, ed. *The Translation of Culture,* 123–40. London: Tavistock.

Hamilton, Angus. 1904. *Korea.* New York: Charles Scribner's Sons.

Hamilton, Edith, and Huntington Cairns, eds. 1961. *The Collected Dialogues of Plato Including the Letters.* Bollingen Series, 71; various translators. Princeton: Princeton U P.

Hampton, Bill R. 1967. "On Identification and Negro Tricksters." *Southern Folklore Quarterly* 31/1:55–65.

Harnack, Adolf von. 1900/1957. *Das Wesen des Christentums.* Trans. Thomas Bailey Sanders, *What Is Christianity?* New York: Harper and Row.

Herskovits, Frances S., and Melville J. Herskovits. 1937. "Tales in Pidgin English from Ashanti." *Journal of American Folklore* 50:60–62.

Herskovits, Melville J. 1937. "The Ashanti Ntoro: A Reexamination." *Journal of the Royal Anthropological Institute* 57:287–96.

Herskovits, Melville J., and Frances S. Herskovits. 1933. *An Outline of Dahomean Religious Belief.* Menasha: Memoirs of American Anthropological Association, 41.

Herskovits, Melville J., and Frances S. Herskovits. 1958. *Dahomean Narrative.* Evanston.

Hickerson, V. H. 1963. "The Socio-Historical Significance of Two Chippewa Ceremonials." *American Anthropologist* 65.

Hieb, Louis A. 1972. "Meaning and Mismeaning: Toward an Understanding of the Ritual Clown." In Alfonso Ortiz, ed. *New Perspectives on the Pueblos,* 163–95. Albuquerque: U New Mexico P.

Hocart, A. M. 1970 [1936]. *Kings and Councillors.* Ed. and Intro. by Rodney Needham. Chicago: U Chicago P.

Hoffman, W. J. 1885–86. "The Midewewin or Grand Medicine Society of the Ojibwa." Annual Report of the Bureau of American Ethnology, 143–300. Washington: Smithsonian Institution.

———. 1892–93. *The Menomini Indians.* 14th Annual Report, American Bureau of Ethnology.

Honigmann, John H. 1942. "An Interpretation of the Social-Psychological Functions of the Ritual Clown." *Character and Personality* 10/3:220–26.

Hubert, Henri, and Marcel Mauss. 1964. *Sacrifice: Its Nature and Function.* Trans. W. D. Halls. Chicago: Chicago U P.

Huizinga, Johan. 1949. *Homo Ludens: A Study of the Play Element in Culture.* Trans. R. F. C. Hull. Boston: Beacon.

Hultkrantz, Åke. 1983. *The Study of American Indian Religions.* Ed. Christopher Vecsey. AAR Studies in Religion, 29. New York: Crossroad; Chico: Scholars.

Hyers, M. Conrad. 1981. *The Comic Vision and the Christian Faith: A Celebration of Life and Laughter.* New York: Pilgrim Press.

———. n.d. "Sun Wu-K'ung, The Monkey King: A Chinese Trickster." Unpublished ms.

Hynes, William J. 1974. "The Infidel as Trickster: Clarence Darrow." Paper at American Academy of Religion, Washington, D.C.

———. 1979. "Trickster Myths: Cosmic Counterbalance to the Sacred." Paper at American Academy of Religion, New York.

———. 1980. "Beyond Sacred and Profane: Tricksters as Cosmic Dissembling Others." Paper at American Academy of Religion, Dallas.

———. 1981. *Shirley Jackson Case and the Chicago School: The Socio-Historical Method.* Chico: Scholars Press.

————, and Thomas Steele. 1981. "St. Peter: Apostle Transformed into Folk Trickster." *Archē: Notes and Papers on Archaic Studies* 6:1–18.

Irizarry, Estelle. 1987. "The Ubiquitous Trickster Archetype in the Narrative of Francisco Ayala." *Hispania* 70/2:222–30.

Jacobs, Melville. 1934–37. *Northwest Sahaptin Texts*. Columbia University Contributions to Anthropology 19, Part I. New York: Columbia U P.

————. 1958–59. *Clackamas Chinook Texts*. Bloomington: Publications of the Indiana University Research Center in Anthropology, Folklore, and Linguistics, Parts 8 & 11.

Jensen, Adolf E. 1963. *Myth and Cult among Primitive Peoples*. Trans. M. T. Choldin and W. Weissleder. Chicago: U Chicago P.

Jones, W. 1907. *Fox Texts*. Leiden: Publ. American Ethnological Society, 1.

————. 1911. "Notes on the Fox Indians." *Journal of American Folklore* 24.

————. 1917. *Ojibwa Texts*. Leiden: Publ. American Ethnological Society, 7/1.

Jonson, Ben. 1958. *Volpone, or The Fox*. Ed. Jonas A. Barish. Northbrook: AHM Pub. Corp.

Jung, Carl G. 1955. "On the Psychology of the Trickster Figure." In Radin 1955:195–211. [TM]

Junod, H. A. 1936. *Moeurs et coutumes des Bantous*. 2 vols. Paris.

Jurich, Marilyn. 1986. "She Shall Overcome: Overtures to the Trickster Heroine." *Women's Studies International Forum* 9/3:273–79.

Kanter, Rosabeth Moss. 1983. *The Change Masters: Innovation and Entrepreneurship in the American Corporation*. New York: Simon and Schuster.

Kazuo, Higo. 1942. *Nihon shinwa kenkyu*. [Summarized in Ouwehand 1958–59.]

————. 1943. *Kodai Densho Kenkyu*. [Summarized in Ouwehand 1958–59.]

Kenji, Kurano. 1960. *Kojiki Hyokai*. Tokyo: Yseido.

Kerényi, Karl. 1955. "The Trickster in Relation to Greek Mythology." In Radin 1955:171–91. [TM]

————. 1963. *Prometheus: Archetypal Image of Human Existence*. Trans. Ralph Manheim. Bollingen Series, 65/1. New York: Pantheon.

————. 1976. *Hermes Guide of Souls: The Mythologem of the Masculine Source of Life*. Trans. Murray Stein. Zurich: Spring Publications.

Kern, Alfred. 1960. *The Clown*. New York.

Kesey, Ken. 1962. *One Flew Over the Cuckoo's Nest: A Novel*. New York: Viking.

Keuls, Eva C. 1985. *The Reign of the Phallus: Sexual Politics in Ancient Athens*. New York: Harper and Row.

Kingston, Maxine Hong. 1989. *Tripmaster Monkey: His Fake Book*. New York: Knopf.

Kirk, G. S. 1974. *The Nature of Greek Myths*. Harmondsworth, U.K.: Penguin.

Kluckhohn, C. 1944. *Navaho Witchcraft*. Cambridge: Papers of the Peabody Museum, 22/2.

Kock, Gösta. 1956. "Der Heilbringer. Ein Beitrag zur Aufklarung seiner religionsgeschichtlichen Voraussetzungen." *Ethnos* 21/1–2:118–29. [TM]

Koepping, Klaus-Peter. 1985. "Absurdity and Hidden Truth: Cunning Intelligence and Grotesque Body Images as Manifestations of the Trickster." *History of Religions* 24:191–214. [TM]

Kopp, Sheldon B. 1974. *The Hanged Man: Psychotherapy and the Forces of Darkness.* Palo Alto: Science and Behavior.

——. 1976. "Trickster-Healer." In Edward W. L. Smith, ed. *The Growing Edge of Gestalt Therapy,* 69–82. New York: Brunner/Mazel.

Kroeber, A. L. 1905. "Wishosk Myths." *Journal of American Folklore* 18.

——. 1907. *Indian Myths of South-Central California.* Berkeley: U California Publications in Anthropology and Ethnology 4/4.

Kroeber, Karl. 1977. "Deconstructionist Criticism and American Indian Literature." *Boundary 2* 7:73.

Kroll, Jack. 1985. "A Lie of the Mind." *Newsweek,* 16 December:85.

Krupat, Arnold. 1985. *For Those Whom Come After: A Study of Native American Autobiography.* Berkeley: U California P.

Kuhlmann, Susan. 1973. *Knave, Fool, and Genius: The Confidence Man as He Appears in Nineteenth-Century American Fiction.* Chapel Hill: U North Carolina P.

Kyeretwic, K. O. Bonsu. 1964. *Ashanti Heroes.* Accra: Waterville.

LaBarre, Weston. 1970. *The Ghost Dance: Origins of Religion.* New York: Doubleday.

Laing, R. D. 1967. *The Politics of Experience.* New York: Ballantine.

Lankford, George E. 1987. *Native American Legends. Southeastern Legends: Tales from the Natchez, Caddo, Biloxi, Chickasaw, and Other Nations.* Chapter 12, "Tricksters." Little Rock: August House.

Leach, E. R. 1964. "Telstar et les Aborigenes ou la Pensee Sauvage." *Annales: Economies, Sociétés, Civilizations* 6:1100–16.

——. 1976. *Culture and Communication.* Cambridge: Cambridge U P.

Ledyard, Gari. 1975. "Galloping Along With the Horseriders: Looking for the Founders of Japan." *Journal of Japanese Studies* 1:154–217.

Lenz, William E. 1985. *Fast Talk and Flush Times: The Confidence Man as a Literary Convention.* Columbia: U Missouri P.

Levine, Jacob. 1961. "Regression in Primitive Clowning." *Psychoanalytic Quarterly* 30/1:72–83.

Levine, Lawrence W. 1974. "'Some Go Up and Some Go Down': The Meaning of the Slave Trickster." In Stanley Elkins and Eric McKitrick, eds. *The Hofstadler Aegis: A Memorial,* 94–124. New York: Knopf. [TM]

Lévi-Strauss, Claude. 1958. *Anthropologie Structurale.* Paris. 1963. *Structural An-*

thropology. Trans. Claire Jacobson and Brooke Grundfest Schoepf. New York: Basic Books.

————. 1966. *The Savage Mind*. Chicago: U Chicago P.

————. 1974. *Tristes Tropiques*. Trans. John Russell and Doreen Weightman. New York: Atheneum.

Lienhardt, Godfrey. 1961. *Divinity and Experience*. Oxford: Clarendon Press.

Loeb, E. M. 1926. "The Creator Complex among the Indians of California." *American Anthropologist* 28.

Loeb, Edwin W. 1932. *The Western Kuksu Cult*. Berkeley: U California Publications in Anthropology and Ethnology 33/1–2.

Lopez, Barry Holstun. 1977. *Giving Birth to Thunder, Sleeping With His Daughter: Coyote Builds North America*. Kansas City: Sheed Andrews and McMeel. Reprint, New York: Avon, 1981. [TC]

Lopez-Pedraza, Rafael. 1977. *Hermes and His Children*. Zürich: Spring Publications.

Lorenz, Carol Ann, and Christopher Vecsey. 1988 [1979]. "Tricksters in the Plaza: Hopi Ceremonial Clowns." See Vecsey 1988.

Lowie, Robert H. 1908. *The Northern Shoshoni*. New York: Anthro. Papers of the Amer. Mus. of Nat. Hist., 2.

————. 1909. "The Hero-Trickster Discussion." *Journal of American Folklore* 22/86:431–33. [TM]

————. 1910. *The Assineboine*. New York: Anthro. Papers of the Amer. Mus. of Nat. Hist., 4/1.

————. 1924. "Shoshonean Tales." *Journal of American Folklore* 37.

————. 1954. *Indians of the Plains*. New York: McGraw-Hill.

Luckert, Karl W. 1979. *Coyoteway: A Navajo Holyway Healing Ceremonial*. Tucson: U Arizona P; Flagstaff: Museum of Northern Arizona P.

————. 1984. "Coyote in Navajo and Hopi Tales." Introductory Essay to Haile 1984:3–19.

Luomala, Katharine. 1949. "Maui of a Thousand Tricks." *Bernice P. Bishop Museum Bulletin* 198.

————. 1966. "Numbskull Clans and Tales: Their Structure and Function in Assymetrical Joking Relationships." In John Greenway, ed. *The Anthropologist Looks at Myth*, 157–98. Austin: U Texas P.

Lynch, William. 1973. *Images of Faith: An Exploration of the Ironic Imagination*. Notre Dame: Notre Dame U P.

McBay, Mary C. 1987. Review of Vidal-Naquet, *The Black Hunter*. *Religious Studies Review* 13/4:348.

Maier, Norman R. 1932. "A Gestalt Theory of Humor." *British Journal of Psychology* 23/1:69–74.

Makarius, Laura. 1967–69. "Les jumeaux: de l'ambivalence au dualisme." *L'Année Sociologique* 373–90.

———. 1968. "Les tabous du forgeron." *Diogéne* 62.

———. 1969. "Le Mythe du 'Trickster'." *Revue de l'Histoire des Religions* 175:17–46 [Translated here as chapter 5].

———. 1970. "Du roi magique au roi 'divin'." *Annales E.S.C.*, 25 c annee 2:668–98.

———. 1970. "Ritual Clowns and Symbolical Behavior." *Diogenes* 69:44–73.

———. 1972. "Il Significato del Trickster in America Settentrionale." Address to XL Congresso duternazionale Degli Americanisti, Rome.

———. 1973. "The Crime of Manabozo." *American Anthropologist* 75/3:663–75.

———. 1974. "The Magic of Transgression." *Anthropos* 69:537–52.

Makarius, Raoul, and Laura Makarius. 1961. *L'origine de l'exogamie et du totémisme*. Paris.

———. 1968. "Des jaguars et des hommes." *L'Homme et la Société* 7.

———. 1969. "La symbolisme de la main gauche." *L'Homme et la Société* 9.

Malotki, Ekkehart, and Michael Lomatuway'ma. 1984. *Hopi Coyote Tales-Istutuwatsi*. American Tribal Religions, 9. Lincoln: U Nebraska P.

Malotki, Ekkehart, and Michael Lomatuway'ma. 1987. *Stories of Maasaw, A Hopi God*. American Tribal Religions, 10. Lincoln: U Nebraska P.

Manabu, Maruyama. 1950. *Minkan densho* 14/8:15–25.

Marshall, Lorna. 1962. "King Bushmen Religious Beliefs." *Africa* 32.

Marukawa, Hitoo. 1963. "Laughter of Gods." *Tenri Journal of Religion* 5:7–16.

Mauss, Marcel. 1966. *Sociologie et anthropologie*. Paris.

Melendez, Theresa. 1982. "Coyote: Toward a Definition of a Concept." *AZTLAN* 13/1–2:295–307.

Messer, Ron. 1983. "Nanabozho: History and Mythology." *Bulletin of Bibliography* 4/4:242–51. [TM]

Metman, P. 1958. "The Trickster Figure in Schizophrenia." *Journal of Analytical Psychology* 3/1.

Meyerowitz, E. L. R. 1949. *The Sacred State of the Akan*. London: Faber.

———. 1952. *Akan Traditions of Origin*. London: Faber.

———. 1960. *The Divine Kingship in Ghana and Ancient Egypt*. London: Faber.

Mezan, Peter. 1972. "After Freud and Jung, Now Comes R. D. Laing." *Esquire* 77:92–178.

Michelson, Truman. 1911. "Menomini Tales." *American Anthropologist* 13/1:68–88.

Miller, Alan L. 1984. "*Ame No Miso-Ori Me* (The Heavenly Weaving Maiden): The Cosmic Weaver in Early Shinto Myth and Ritual." *History of Religions* 24/1:27–48.

Miller, David L. 1970. *Gods and Games: Toward a Theology of Play.* New York: World.

Minz, Jerome R. 1968. *Legends of the Hasidim: An Introduction to Hasidic Culture and Oral Tradition in the New World.* Chicago: U Chicago P. [TC]

Monick, Eugene. 1987. *Phallos: Sacred Image of the Masculine.* Studies in Jungian Psych., 27. Toronto: Inner City.

Monteser, Frederick. 1975. *The Picaresque Element in Western Literature.* Tuscaloosa: U Alabama P.

Moulding Brown, D. n.d. *Manabush Menomini Tales.*

Mourning Dove. 1990. *Coyote Stories.* Lincoln: U Nebraska P. [TC]

Movshovitz, Howard. 1977. "The Trickster Myth and Chaucer's Partners." Diss. U Colorado.

Nagy, Joseph Falaky. 1981. "The Deceptive Gift in Greek Mythology." *Arethusa* 14/2:191–204.

Naumann, Nelly. 1982. "*Sakahagi:* The 'Reverse Flaying' of the Heavenly Piebald Horse." *Asian Folklore Studies* 41/1:7–38.

Needham, Rodney. 1970. "Editor's Introduction." In Needham, ed. *Kings and Councillors,* xiii–xcix. [1936, A. M. Hocart], Chicago: U Chicago P.

———. 1978. *Primordial Characters.* Charlottesville: U P Virginia.

Neumann, Erich. 1954. *The Origins and History of Consciousness.* Trans. R. F. C. Hull. Bollingen Series, 42. Princeton: Princeton U P.

———. 1957. "Art & Time." In Joseph Campbell, ed. *Man and Time: Papers from the Eranos Yearbooks,* 3. New York: Pantheon.

Nichols, Sallie. 1974. "The Wisdom of the Fool." *Psychological Perspectives* 5/2:97–116.

Niditch, Susan. 1987. *Underdogs and Tricksters: A Prelude to Biblical Folklore.* San Francisco: HarperCollins.

Nietzsche, Friedrich. 1966. *Beyond Good and Evil.* New York: Vintage Books.

Nketia, J. H. Kwabena. 1955. *Funeral Dirges of the Akan People.* Exeter: Achimota P.

———. 1963a. *Drumming in Akan Communities in Ghana.* London: Nelson.

———. 1963b. *African Music in Ghana.* Evanston: Northwestern U P.

Nobutsuna, Saigo. 1947. *Kojiki.* Tokyo: Nihon Hyobonsha.

Noel, Daniel C. 1979. *Seeing Castañeda: Reaction to the "Don Juan" Writings of Carlos Castañeda.* New York: Putnam's.

Nomland, Gladys A. 1938–40. *Bear River Ethnography.* Anthro. Records 2. Berkeley: U California P.

Norman, Howard. 1987. "Wesucechak Becomes a Deer and Steals Language: An Anecdotal Linguistics Concerning the Swampy Cree Trickster." In Swann and Krupat 1987:402–21.

Nussbaum, Martha. 1986. *The Fragility of Goodness: Luck and Ethics in Greek Tragedy and Philosophy.* New York: Cambridge U P.

Obayashi, Taryo. 1977. "The Structure of the Pantheon and the Concept of Sin in Ancient Japan." *Diogenes* 98:117–32.

O'Connor, Flannery. 1980. *The Habit of Being: Letters of Flannery O'Connor.* Ed. Sally Fitzgerald. New York: Vintage.

Opler, Morris E. 1938a. "The Sacred Clowns of the Chiricahua and Mescalero Indians." *El Palacio* 44/10–12:75–79.

———. 1938b. *Myths and Tales of the Jicarilla Apache Indians.* Memoirs, 31. New York: American Folk-lore Society.

———. 1940. *Myths and Legends of the Lipan Apache Indians.* Memoirs, 36. New York: American Folk-lore Society.

Ortiz, Alfonso. 1972. "Ritual Drama and the Pueblo World View." In Ortiz, ed. *New Perspectives on the Pueblos,* 135–61. Albuquerque: U New Mexico P.

Ortiz, Simon. 1972. "From An Interview," "Telling About Coyote." *Alcheringa: Ethnopoetics* 4:15–17.

Ostermann, H. 1952. *The Alaskan Eskimo.* Copenhagen: Report of the Fifth Thule Expedition, 1921–24, 10/3.

Otto, Rudolf. 1950. *The Idea of the Holy.* Trans. John W. Harvey. London: Oxford U P.

Otto, Walter F. 1954. *The Homeric Gods: The Spiritual Significance of Greek Religion.* Trans. Moses Hadas. New York: Thames and Hudson.

Ouwehand, Cornelius. 1958–59. "Some Notes on the God Susa-no-o." *Monumenta Nipponica* 14/3–4:138–61.

Parrinder, E. G. 1956. "Divine Kingship in West Africa." *Numen* 3.

Parsons, Elsie Clews. 1926. *Tewa Tales.* Memoirs, 19. New York: American Folk-lore Society.

———, and Ralph L. Beals. 1934. "The Sacred Clowns of the Pueblo and Mayo-Yaqui Indians." *American Anthropologist* (n.s.) 36/4:491–514.

Partridge, Eric. 1961. *Origins.* London: Routledge and Kegan Paul.

Paulme, Denise. 1976. "Typologie des contes africains du Décepteur." *Cahiers d'études africaines* 60:569–600.

———. 1977. "The Impossible Imitation in African Trickster Tales." In Bernth Lindfors, ed. *Forms of Folklore in Africa: Narrative, Poetic, Gnomic, Dramatic,* 64–103. Austin: U Texas P. [TC]

Pearson, Hesketh. 1946. *The Life of Oscar Wilde.* New York: Methuen.

Pelton, Robert D. 1974. "The Web of Purpose, The Dance of Delight: A Study of Four West African Trickster Figures in Their Social and Mythological Settings." Diss. U Chicago. [TM]

———. 1979. "Reflections on West African Tricksters: The Web of Purpose, The

Dance of Delight." Paper at the American Academy of Religion, New York.

——. 1980. *The Trickster in West Africa: A Study of Mythic Irony and Sacred Delight*. Berkeley: U California P. [TC, TM]

——. 1987. "African Tricksters." In Mircea Eliade, ed. *The Encyclopedia of Religion*, 46–48. New York: Macmillan.

Pemberton, J. 1975. "Eshu-Elegba: The Yoruba Trickster God." *African Arts* 9:20–27, 66–70, 90–92.

Perry, Ben Edwin, ed. and trans. 1965. Babrius and Phaedrus, *Fables*. Loeb Classical Library (Aesopic traditions). Cambridge: Harvard U P.

Pettazzoni, Raffaele. 1948. *Miti e Leggende*. Torino.

Phillippi, Donald L., trans. 1968. *Kojiki*. Tokyo: U Tokyo P.

Pierson, W. D. 1971. "An African Background for American Negro Folktales?" *Journal of American Folklore* 84:204–14.

Piper, Edward. 1975. "A Dialogical Study of the North American Trickster Figure and the Phenomenon of Play." Diss. U Chicago.

——. 1978. "Outline of a Ludic Hermeneutic: The Trickster Paradigm." Paper at American Academy of Religion, New Orleans.

Plaut, A. 1959. "A Case of Tricksterism Illustrating Ego Defenses." *Journal of Analytical Psychology* 4/1.

Pope, Polly. 1967. "Toward a Structural Analysis of North American Trickster Tales." *Southern Folklore Quarterly* 31/3:274–86. [TM]

Radin, Paul. 1955. *The Trickster: A Study in American Indian Mythology*. New York: Schocken. [See bibliographic note on pp. 219–20.] [TM, TC]

Rael, Juan B. 1977. *Cuentos Españoles de Colorado y Nuevo México*. Sante Fe: Museum of New Mexico P.

Rahner, Hugo. 1967. *Man at Play*. Trans. Brian Battershaw and Edward Quinn. New York: Herder and Herder.

Rattray, R. S. 1916. *Ashanti Proverbs*. Oxford: Clarendon P.

——. 1923. *Ashanti*. Oxford: Clarendon P. Reprint, New York: Negro U P, 1969.

——. 1928. "Some Aspects of West African Folk-lore." *Journal of the African Society* 28.

——. 1929. *Ashanti Law and Constitution*. Oxford: Clarendon P. Reprint, New York: Negro U P, 1969.

——. 1930. *Akan-Ashanti Folk-tales*. Oxford: Clarendon P.

——. 1950. "The Secret of Akom." *African Affairs* 49:237–40.

Ray, Verne F. 1932. *The Sanpoil and Nespelem*. Publications in Anthropology, 5. Seattle: U Washington.

——. 1945. "The Contrary Behavior Pattern in American Indian Ceremonialism." *Southwestern Journal of Anthropology* 1/1:75–113.

————. 1948. "Sanpoil Folktales." *Journal of American Folklore* 46.

Reed, Ishmael. 1974. *The Last Days of Louisiana Red.* New York: Random House.

Reichard, Gladys. 1947. *An Analysis of Coeur d'Alene Indian Myths.* Philadelphia: American Folk-lore Society.

————. 1950. *Navaho Religion: A Study of Symbolism.* 2 vols. New York: Pantheon.

Ricketts, Mac Linscott. 1964. "The Structure and Religious Significance of the Trickster-Transformer-Culture Hero in the Mythology of the North American Indians." Diss. U Chicago. [TC, TM]

————. 1966. "The North American Indian Trickster." *History of Religions* 5/2:327–50. Reprinted in H. Baumann, et al. *Readings in Mythology.* New York: Arno, 1978. [TM]

————. 1977. "The Trickster and the Shaman." Unpublished ms.

————. 1987. "North American Tricksters." In Mircea Eliade, ed. *The Encyclopedia of Religion,* 48–51. New York: Macmillan.

————. n.d. "The Sacred Trickster of the North American Indians." Manuscript based on Ricketts 1964. [TC, TM]

Roberts, John W. 1989. *From Trickster to Badman: The Black Folk Hero in Slavery and Freedom.* Philadelphia: U Pennsylvania P.

Robinson, Gail, and Douglas Hill. 1975. *Coyote the Trickster: Legends of the North American Indians.* London: Chatto and Windus. [TC]

Róheim, Geza. 1967. "Culture Hero and Trickster in North American Mythology." In Sol Tax, ed. *Indian Tribes of Aboriginal America: Selected Papers,* 190–94. New York: Cooper Square.

Rouse, W. H. D., trans. 1940. Nonnos, *Dionysiaca.* 3 vols. Cambridge: Harvard U P.

Rustad, Richard L. 1979. *The Struggling Disciple.* New York: William Collins.

Sabbatucci, Dario. 1981. *Sui protagonisti dei miti.* Quaderni di etnologia religiosa, 2. Roma: La Goliardica Editrice.

Sapir, Edward. 1909. *Wishram Texts.* Publications of the American Ethnological Society, 2. Leiden: Brill.

Schechter, Harold. 1980. *The New Gods: Psyche and Symbol in Popular Art.* Bowling Green: Bowling Green U Popular P.

Scheinberg, Susan. 1979. "The Bee Maidens of the Homeric Hymn to Hermes." *Harvard Studies in Classical Philology* 83:1–28.

Scherer, Chr. 1886–90. "Hermes." In Roscher, *Ausführl. Lexikon der griech. und röm. Mythol.* 1/2:cols. 2342–32.

Scherer, Paul. 1952. "Exposition of the Gospel According to St. Luke." *Interpreter's Bible* 8. New York: Abingdon P.

Schmerler, Henrietta. 1931. "Trickster Marries His Daughter." *Journal of American Folklore* 44/172:196–207.

Shakespeare, William. 1956. *Measure for Measure.* Baltimore: Penguin.

Sheehan, Donald. 1978. "On Archaic Studies: Hermes and Hermeneutics." *Archê—Notes and Papers on Archaic Studies* 2:5–16.

Shinkokai, Nippon Gakujutsu. 1940. *The Manyoshu.* Tokyo: Iwanami Sihoten.

Shouchen, Zang, et al. 1983. *Traditional Comic Tales.* Trans. Gladys Yang. Beijing: Panda.

Shozo, Kono, and Sakai Atsuharu. 1940. "The Hitachi Fudoki." *Culturae Nippon* 8/2.

Singer, June. 1972. *Boundaries of the Soul: The Practice of Jung's Psychology.* New York: Anchor/Doubleday.

Skinner, A. 1923. "Observations on the Ethnology of the Sauk Indians." *Bull. Public Mus. of the City of Milwaukee* 5.

Skinner, Alanson, and John V. Satterlee. 1913–15. *The Menomini Indians.* Anthro. Papers of the Museum, 13/1, 2, 3. New York: American Museum of Natural History.

Smith, E. G. 1919. *The Evolution of the Dragon.* Manchester.

Smith, E. W. 1927. *The Golden Stool.* London: Edinburgh House P.

Smith-Rosenberg, Carroll. 1985. *Disorderly Conduct: Visions of Gender in Victorian America.* New York: Knopf.

Snyder, Gary. 1977. "The Incredible Survival of Coyote." *The Old Ways: Six Essays,* 67–93. San Francisco: City Lights (partly repr. in Jerome Rothenberg and Diane Rothenberg, eds. *Symposium of the Whole: A Range of Discourse Toward an Ethnopoetics,* 425–33. Berkeley: U California P, 1983).

Sokichi, Tsuda. n.d. *Nihon Koten no Kenkyu* 1:615–26.

Sokyo, Ono. 1956. *Nihon shinwa to niiname no matsuri* 8:31–41.

Speck, Frank G. 1949. *Midwinter Rites of the Cayuga Long House.* Philadelphia: U Pennsylvania P.

Sperber, Dan. 1975. *Rethinking Symbolism.* Cambridge: Cambridge U P.

Spicer, Edward H. 1983. "Yaqui." *Handbook of North American Indians* 10:250–63.

Spiro, Melford E. 1970. *Buddhism and Society.* New York: Harper and Row.

Steele, Thomas J., S.J. 1974. *Santos and Saints: The Religious Folk Art of Hispanic New Mexico.* Albuquerque: Calvin Horn.

Stein, Murray. 1983. *In Midlife: A Jungian Perspective.* Seminar Series, 15. Dallas: Spring Publications.

Steiner, George. 1977. *After Babel: Aspects of Language and Translation.* London: Oxford U P.

Stevens, Phillips. 1979. "The Bachama Trickster as Model for Clowning Behavior." In Christine M. S. Drake, ed. *Festschrift for Edward Norbeck.* Rice University Studies.

Steward, Julian H. 1931a. "The Ceremonial Buffoon of the American Indians." Ann Arbor: *Papers of the Michigan Academy of Science, Arts and Letters, 1930* 14:187–207.

————. 1931b. "The Clown in Native North America." Diss. U California.

Stewart, Susan. 1979. *Nonsense: Aspects of Intertextuality in Folklore and Literature.* Baltimore: Johns Hopkins U P.

Stimson, J. F. 1934. "The Legends of Maui and Tahaki." *Bernice Bishop Museum Bulletin* 127.

Stocking, George W., Jr. 1987. *Victorian Anthropology.* New York: Macmillan.

Strathern, Marilyn. 1987. "Out of Context: The Persuasive Fiction of Anthropology." The Frazer Lecture, 1986. *Current Anthropology* 28/3:251–81.

Street, Brian V. 1972. "The Trickster Theme: Winnebago and Azande." In Andre Singer and Street, eds. *Zande Themes: Essays Presented to Sir Edward Evans Pritchard,* 82–104. Totowa: Rowman and Littlefield. [TM]

Sturluson, Snorri, ed. 1960. *The Prose Edda.* New York: American Scandinavian Foundation.

Sullivan, Lawrence E. 1982. "The Irony of Incarnation: The Comedy of *Kenosis.*" *Journal of Religion* 62/4:412–17 [review of Pelton 1980].

————. 1987. "Tricksters. An Overview." "Mesoamerican and South American Tricksters." In Mircea Eliade, ed. *The Encyclopedia of Religion,* 45–46, 51–53. New York: Macmillan.

Sutton-Smith, Brian. 1972. "Games of Order and Disorder." Paper at Symposium on Forms of Symbolic Inversion, American Anthropological Association, Toronto.

Swann, Brian, and Arnold Krupat, eds. 1987. *Recovering the Word: Essays on Native American Literature.* Berkeley: U California P.

Swanton, John R. 1909. *Tlingit Myths and Texts.* Washington: Bureau of American Ethnology Bulletins 39.

Szasz, Thomas S. 1970. *The Manufacture of Madness.* New York: HarperCollins.

Takeo, Matsumura. 1951. "Dohojin no minzoku-bunkashiteki kosatsu." *Minzokugoku kenkyu* 16/2:1–28.

Tedlock, Barbara. 1975. "The Clown's Way." In Dennis Tedlock and Barbara Tedlock, eds. *Teachings from the American Earth,* 105–18. New York: Liveright.

Tedlock, Dennis. 1983. *The Spoken Word and the Work of Interpretation.* Philadelphia: U Pennsylvania P.

Tegnaeus, H. 1950. *Le Héros Civilisateur. Contribution à l'étude ethnologique de la religion et de la sociologie africanes. Studia Ethnographica Upsaliensia,* 2. Stockholm: Pettersons.

Teit, James. 1927. *Folk Tales of the Salishan and Sahaptin Tribes.* Memoirs, 11. New York: American Folk-lore Society.

Testart, Alain. n.d. "Don Juan le joueur de tours." Unpublished ms.

Te Velde, H. 1967. *Seth, God of Confusion.* Leiden: Brill.

Thompson, Stith. 1929. *Tales of the North American Indians.* Chapter 3, "Trickster Tales." Bloomington: Indiana U P. [TC]

————. 1946. *The Folktale*. Part 3, Chapter 4, "The Trickster Cycle." New York: Holt, Rinehart and Winston. [TC]

————. 1955. *Motif-Index of Folk-Literature: A Classification of Narrative Elements in Folktale . . .* Rev. and enlarged ed., 6 vols. Bloomington: Indiana U P.

Titiev, Mischa. 1971. "Some Aspects of Clowning Among the Hopi Indians." In Mario D. Zamora, J. Michael Mahar, and Henry Orenstein, eds. *Themes in Culture (Essays in Honor of Morris E. Opler)*, 326–36. Quezon City.

————. 1976. "The Concept of Opposites in Primitive Religion." Unpublished ms.

Todorov, Tzvetan. 1982. *La Conquête de l'Amerique: la question de l'autre*. Paris: Editions du Seuil. (*The Conquest of America*. New York: HarperCollins, 1984.)

Toelken, J. Barre. 1969. "The 'Pretty Language' of Yellowman: Genre, Mode, and Texture in Navaho Coyote Narratives." *Genre* 2/3:211–35. [TM]

————. 1987. "Life and Death in the Navajo Coyote Tales." In Swann and Krupat 1987:388–401.

Toelken, J. Barre, and Tacheeni Scott. 1981. "Poetic Retranslation and the 'Pretty Languages' of Yellowman." In Karl Kroeber, ed. *Traditional American Indian Literatures: Texts and Interpretations*, 65–116. Lincoln: U Nebraska P.

Townsen, John H. 1976. *Clowns*. New York: Hawthorn Books.

Trevor-Roper, H. R. 1977. *Hermit of Peking: The Hidden Life of Sir Edmund Backhouse*. New York: Knopf.

Turner, Victor W. 1967. *The Forest of Symbols: Aspects of Ndembu Ritual*. Ithaca: Cornell U P.

————. 1969. *The Ritual Process: Structure and Anti-Structure*. Chicago: Aldine.

————. 1972. "Passages, Margins, and Poverty." *Worship* 46:390–412, 432–94.

————. 1978. "Comments and Conclusions." In Barbara Babcock-Abrahams, ed. *The Reversible World*, 276–96. Ithaca: Cornell U P.

Tyler, Hamilton A. 1964. *Pueblo Gods and Myths*. Norman: U Oklahoma P.

Udy, Stanley H., Jr. 1973. "Cross Cultural Analysis: Methods and Scope." *Annual Review of Anthropology* 2:253–70.

Ullom, Judith C. 1969. *Folklore of the North American Indians: An Annotated Bibliography*. Washington: Library of Congress.

Underwood, Horace H. 1915. "Hunting and Hunters' Lore in Korea." *Transactions of the Korea Branch of the Royal Asiatic Society* 6/2.

Van Maanen, John. 1988. *Tales of the Field: On Writing Ethnography*. Chicago: U Chicago P.

Vecsey, Christopher. 1988. *Imagine Ourselves Richly: Mythic Narratives of North American Indians*. New York: Crossroad.

Vecsey, Christopher, and Carol Ann Lorenz. 1976. "The Exception Who Proves the Rule." Paper at American Academy of Religion, St. Louis. [= Vecsey 1988. Chapter 2.]

Vecsey, Christopher, and Carol Ann Lorenz. 1978. "The Fullness of Hopi Clowning." Unpublished ms.

Vecsey, Christopher, and Robert W. Venables, eds. 1980. *American Indian Environments: Ecological Issues in Native American History.* Syracuse: Syracuse U P.

Velie, Alan R. 1985. "Indians in Indian Fiction: The Shadow of the Trickster." *American Indian Quarterly* 8:315–29.

Vernant, Jean-Pierre. 1969. "Hestia-Hermes. Sur l'expression religieuse de l'espace et du mouvement chez les Grecs." In *Myth et Pensée chez les Grecs: Études de psychologie historique,* 2nd ed., 97–181. Paris: Maspero.

———. 1979. "A la table des hommes: Mythe de fondation du sacrifice chez Hesiode." In Marcell Detienne, Vernant, et al. *La cuisine de sacrifice en pays grec,* Bibl. des Histoires, 37–132. Paris: Gallimard.

———. 1981. "The Myth of Prometheus in Hesiod," and "Sacrificial and Alimentary Codes in Hesiod's Myth of Prometheus." In R. L. Gordon, ed. *Myth, Religion, Society: Structuralist Essays,* 53–79. New York: Cambridge U P; Paris: Maisons des Sciences de l'Homme.

Vizenor, Gerald. 1981. *Earthdivers: Tribal Narratives on Mixed Descent.* Minneapolis: U Minnesota P.

———. 1987. *Griever: An American Monkey King in China.* Normal: Illinois State U; New York: Fiction Collective.

———. 1988. *The Trickster of Liberty: Tribal Heirs to a Wild Baronage.* Emergent Literatures. Minneapolis: U Minnesota P.

———. 1989. Review of Kingston 1989. *The Denver Post,* 7 May:10D.

———, ed. 1989. *Narrative Chance: Postmodern Discourse on Native American Literatures.* Albuquerque: U New Mexico P.

Wadlington, Warwick. 1975. *The Confidence Game in American Literature.* Princeton: Princeton U P.

Waida, Manabu. 1976. "Sacred Kingship in Ancient Japan: A Historical Introduction." *History of Religion* 1514:319–42.

Wang, Chi-chen, trans. 1968 [1944]. *Traditional Chinese Tales.* New York: Greenwood. [TC]

Ward, Barbara E. 1956. "Some Observations on Religious Cults in Ashanti." *Africa* 26:47–61.

Warner, L. S. 1958. *A Black Civilization: A Social Study of an Australian Tribe.* New York: HarperCollins.

Wasserstein, Bernard. 1988. "On the Trail of Trebitsch Lincoln, Triple Agent." *New York Times Book Review,* 8 May:1, 39, 41.

Welsch, Roger. 1981. *Omaha Tribal Myths and Trickster Tales.* Chicago: Swallow; Athens: Ohio U P. [TC]

Welsford, Enid. 1961. *The Fool: His Social and Literary History*. Garden City: Doubleday.

Wescott, Joan. 1962. "The Sculpture and Myths of Eshu-Elegba, The Yoruba Trickster: Definition and Interpretation in Yoruba Iconography." *Africa* 32/4:336–53.

Wescott, Joan, and P. Morton-Williams. 1962. "The Symbolism and Ritual Concept of the Yoruba Laba Shango." *Journal of the Anthropological Institute* 92.

Wesselski, Hodscha Nasreddin. 1911. *Trickster Chooses His Gift*. 2 vols. Weimar.

Weverka, Robert. 1973. *The Sting*. New York: Bantam.

White, Hayden. 1972. "The Forms of Wildness: Archaeology of an Idea." In Edward Dudley and Maxmillan E. Novak, eds. *The Wild Man Within: An Image in Western Thought from the Renaissance to Romanticism*, 3–38. Pittsburgh: U Pittsburgh P.

Willeford, William. 1969. *The Fool and His Scepter: A Study in Clowns and Jesters and Their Audience*. Evanston: Northwestern U P.

Williams, Paul V. A., ed. 1979. *The Fool and the Trickster: Studies in Honor of Enid Welsford*. Totowa: Rowman and Littlefield.

Williamson, S. G. 1965. *Akan Religion and the Christian Faith. A Comparative Study of the Impact of Two Religions*. Ed. K. A. Dickson. Accra: Ghana U P.

Wilson, Colin. 1956. *The Outsider*. Boston: Houghton Mifflin.

Wilson, Samuel M. 1991. "Trickster Treats." *Natural History* (October):4–8.

Winch, Peter. 1970. "On Understanding a Primitive Society." In Bryan Wilson, ed. *Rationality*, 78–111. New York: Harper Torchbooks.

Wirshbo, Eliot. 1982. "The Mekone Scene in the *Theogony*: Prometheus as Prankster." *Greek, Roman, and Byzantine Studies* 23/2:101–10.

Wisse, Ruth R. 1971. *The Schlemiel as Modern Hero*. Chicago: U Chicago P.

Wittgenstein, Ludwig. 1963. *Philosophical Investigations*. Oxford: Blackwell.

———. 1969. *On Certainty*. Ed. G. E. M. Anscombe and G. H. von Wright. New York: J. and J. Harper.

———. 1971. "Remarks on Frazer's Golden Bough." *The Human World* 3:28–41.

Wu, Ch'eng-en. 1943. *Monkey. Folk Novel of China*. Trans. Arthur Waley. New York: John Day Co. Reprint, New York: Grove P, 1958.

Yates, Frances A. 1966. *The Art of Memory*. Chicago: U Chicago P.

Yoshida, Atsuhiko. 1961–63. "La mythologie japonaise: essai d'interpretation structurale." *Revue de l'histoire des religions* 160:47–66; 161:25–44; 163:225–40.

———. 1977. "Japanese Mythology and the Indo-European Trifunctional System." *Diogenes* 98:93–116.

Yu, Anthony C., trans. and ed. 1977. *The Journey to the West*. 2 vols. Chicago: U Chicago P.

Zolbrod, Paul G. 1984. *Diné bahane': The Navajo Creation Story.* Albuquerque: U New Mexico P. [TC]

Zong, In-Sob. 1970. *Folk Tales from Korea.* Seoul: Hollym Publishers.

Zucker, Wolfgang. 1954. "The Image of the Clown." *Journal of Aesthetics and Art Criticism* 12/3:310–17.

———. 1967. "The Clown as the Lord of Disorder." *Theology Today* 24/3:306–17.

CONTRIBUTORS

in Order of Appearance in the Volume

DAVID AGUIRRE is a noted artist from Santa Fé, New Mexico, who specializes in ceramic works that depict the trickster's myriad forms. His work is displayed in numerous museums and galleries. The piece represented on the cover, "Trickster," 1990, was inspired by reading stories of Native American lore.

WILLIAM J. HYNES is Academic Vice President and Professor of Religious Studies at Saint Mary's College in the San Francisco Bay area. His *Shirley Jackson Case and the Chicago School* (1981) charts the socio-historical method as applied to the study of religions within their social and cultural contexts. He was the initiator of a multi-year consultation on trickster figures under the auspices of the American Academy of Religion.

WILLIAM G. DOTY is Professor of Religious Studies at the University of Alabama, Tuscaloosa. His publications in this field have included essays on Hermes and mythology and on contemporary ethnography, and edited volumes on the transformations of archaic images, on Mircea Eliade, and Clifford Geertz. His *Mythography: The Study of Myths and Rituals* (1986) graphs a variety of methodological approaches.

LAURA MAKARIUS is well known in French anthropological circles; her work on such topics as magic and taboos, as well as tricksters and symbolism, some of it written with her husband, Raoul Makarius, has been discussed both on the Continent and in America.

CHRISTOPHER NICHOLS is a classicist and translator residing in Denver, Colorado.

Professor MAC LINSCOTT RICKETTS is Chair of the department of religion and philosophy at Louisburg College in North Carolina. His dissertation at the University of Chicago (1964) was one of the first major studies of the trickster figure in the cultures of the North American Indians; his *History of Religions* reprise of that work (1966) has been supplemented recently by his article in *The Encyclopedia of Religion* (1987). His book, *Mircea Eliade, The Romanian Roots: 1907–1945*, was published in 1988.

Professor CHRISTOPHER VECSEY is Chair of the department of philosophy and religion of Colgate University. His books include *Imagine Ourselves Richly: Mythic Narratives of North American Indians* (1988) and *Handbook of American Indian Religious Freedom*. He is the editor of *Religion in Native North America*, and with Robert W. Venables, of *American Indian Environments: Ecological Issues in Native American History* (1980).

Fr. ROBERT D. PELTON is a member of the Madonna House Apostolate in Combermere, Ontario. He gained his spurs in trickster studies with the important publication entitled *The Trickster in West Africa: A Study of Mythic Irony and Sacred Delight* (1980).

ROBERT S. ELLWOOD's books have focused upon the history of religions and in particular Eastern religions. He has been Director of the School of Religion and remains Bashford Professor of Oriental Studies at the University of Southern California. He is the author of more than eleven books, on Japan, mysticism, and religions.

THOMAS J. STEELE, S.J., is author of the highly acclaimed *Santos and Saints: The Religious Folk Art of Hispanic New Mexico* (1974), and co-author of the *Guidebook to* Zen and the Art of Motorcycle Maintenance. He teaches English at Regis University in Denver, Colorado, and has been a visiting professor at Colorado College and the University of New Mexico.

Professor T. O. Beidelman teaches in the department of anthropology at New York University, where he specializes in social anthropology, religion, colonial history, oral literature, and Africa. The bibliography to this volume lists many of his wide-ranging publications, which focus upon native African texts and their interpretation.

Anne Doueihi's essay was written while she was in the doctoral program in religion at Syracuse University. She has been associated with the Population Information Program of the School of Hygiene at the Johns Hopkins University and received the AAUW American Fellowship for work on a dissertation on Hildegard of Bingen.

INDEX